GW01071758

Andrew Charnley asserts the mora
the author of this work. http://www.andrewcharnley.com

ISBN-13: 978-1495927058
ISBN-10: 1495927059

Edition: CRTSPC-1655

My deepest thanks to Danielle Carpenter, a Canadian I met on the road whom agreed to proof read this work. If later you think this book is badly written, imagine how poor it was prior to handling it over to someone that can string sentences together.

I have tried to portray all events and actualities accurately and without bias, falsehood or exaggeration. All opinions are my own, however they may reflect upon a specific point in time at which I was enduring stress or hardship. My opinions should not form yours, and in reading this book I implore you to recognise that travelling experiences always vary.

Contents

Chapter 1

Reasoning

So here it is.
I've decided to sell everything, quit the job and hit the road.

As I understand it, my role of a writer is to descriptively set the scene, introduce characters and add captive events to entice you to read all about it.

So be it.

The container was dark, packed and awash with electrical impulse. In it, entities had travelled in orderly fashion, but lately roads were congesting and friction had began. New roads were being built but poor planning was worsening the situation, and something had to be done. Two powerful voices emerged through the chaos. Neither good or evil, they sought control over the chaos. They were known as Mr. Left and Mr. Right.

This ladies and gentlemen was my brain, and in early November 2011 a civil war broke out.

Mr. Left.

Now Andrew, before you completely fuck up, lets analyse what undertaking such a decision would mean for you, pragmatically, logically, business like, leaving out the wishy-washiness. I'm talking about the benefits, the pro's and cons, risks and gains. Let's go through it.

So you're not really going anywhere with your life. Tough shit. Except the fact you're comfortable and never going to make it big. Be happy with what you have and your achievements no matter the size of them. Stop wanting more. Forget measuring yourself against those that have been more fortunate, lucky or have rich parents that set them up for life. Forget jealousy. Think like a Buddhist and be happy.

You accept all journeys have a finite lifespan, so why spend your money and end poorer? Sure, kid yourself that you may make money at the end of the day, but there's no guarantees, and if you think you'll be able to walk into another job at the end of it. You know better. 'Teacher gives up career to go travelling?' You aren't retarded enough to ignore that any employer will think; burn't out, stressed, can't take the pressure. You'll be looked upon as a liability, and you know for a fact that there's way more teachers out there than there are jobs. You remember that conversation a few year back with an intelligent man who worked and vetted staff for Oxford University's Genome research department? He said that if someone were dumb enough to promote travelling on their CV he would immediately bin it. That's going to be you. In the bin. No prospects, no money, a drifting loner. A fuck up.

Are you lonely, is that it? Well you hardly make the effort everyone tells you you should so it's your own fault. You're the one that actively chose not to do the dating websites when all your friends did. You're the one who chose to save money by buying a cheap house miles away from the town night life. You think that you'll bump into someone that'll be so willing to magically join you? Christ, you love being alone, you're selfish and easily irritated by others. Accept it.

You have no interest in seeing cities or tourist attractions and you couldn't be any further bored by religious places of worship, museums or art, and since that covers 75% of what there is to do, you're going to have nothing to do but travel.

Alright, maybe I'm being hard on you, but accept reality for what it is. You're on the wrong side of 25 and can't kid yourself into the student posse anymore, so at hostels and wherever else you'll have to sleep due to your miserable budget you'll feel like the outsider that you actually are.

Challenge yourself without taking the risk with what you've managed to build up. Do something smaller. Mould your life gracefully without the risk of one massive step, and no matter how tautological you think you can be, be sure to weigh up the truth I am telling you.

Mr. Right.

You're sad inside. You're sad because over the past few years the decisions you've took haven't turned out the way you expected and your life has flatlined. You hardly meet people and you spend most your time trying to keep yourself occupied with triviality to keep you from this inevitable truth. You avoid boredom and yet you are bored, and that in turn means you're boring. You've become what you feared most; dull.

What's life Andrew? Do you have one? You lead such a minimalistic life, fraternising over your pennies, selling crap on eBay only to buy replacement crap, occupying yourself. And the career nullified job? It's stable, sure, but it's going nowhere; teaching the same crap year in year out. You know your abilities are wasted, so why put up with it?

Is it the risk? Well, what is it you'd risk? You've a small house with a paltry mortgage, no other debt and you've a bit of money saved. You could sell the house and have a great time. You could rent the house out and not have to worry about the mortgage, just don't go crazy with the money you have in the bank. Use your monetary tightness to your advantage.

Don't think about what's out there and whether you'll enjoy it, because there's nothing here and you're not enjoying it. Positivity and happiness can only be greater than what you have at the moment.

You want an adventure – a really big adventure, and it's no more obvious then looking at all the motorcycles you've owned over the years. Those adventure bikes and your silly excursions to Morocco, why not make it your life instead of just a small part of it? Why remember when you can live it.

Use your I.T skills, build a good website, have an adventure and try to build up experience away from teaching. You'll start low but that'll be fine, you'll have little outgoings and have all the time you need. You're worried about risk and yet you really have so little to worry about.

Think of the benefits and possibilities. The doors aren't closed, you've merely been sitting on your arse instead of transiting through them. You're used to being alone and you're unafraid of different environments and yet you love the outdoors and the feeling of freedom. Why in the name of God didn't you do this earlier?

The Decision.

For every war there is an outcome, but Mr. Left and Mr. Right had dug trenches and were preparing for a long and harsh winter. Neither side really wanted to fight, but both were prepared to do so. A battle of attrition would go on for some time. What was needed, in this dark hour of madness, was a mediator. Both sides agreed to find one, but until a ceasefire was called, the war would go on.

Mr. Facebook was an opinionated, rash and volatile individual who frequently found himself at the pointy end of everything that wasn't his business. His line of work was summative polling, where he'd receive a question and submit it to a large group of uninformed and pugnacious workers for review. Feedback to the question would be analysed through an internal Like system, which was then largely ignored, and typically the loudest bellowing voice would be heard over the rest.

That evening, Mr. Facebook received a new question, a one with an almighty fallout for the individual asking it, but of no consequence to his workers. It read;

"Should I sell everything, quit my job and hit the road?"

He put it out for debate and awaited a response. After 24 hours there were many. "Yes!", everyone said.

Mr. Facebook couldn't remember such emphatic feedback, and the result was swiftly dispatched back to the clients, who decided unanimously to set aside their differences, and to bind the feedback into law. Within a small room, two individuals, Mr. Left and Mr Right, shook hands. The rest as they say, is history.

Chapter 2

Mini Biography

Only a plonker would say that the past doesn't shape your future. You don't need to know the innards of my live, and I wont bore you with the mundane trivialities of it, but for better or worse there are a few significant moments in my past which no doubt altered my perceptual thoughts on undertaking this journey. When I thinking about it, they all have something to do with risk.

I'd have been fortunate to have avoided a proper beating in my life, but after having one I believed such thinking is only bestowed by those that have haven't had one. As sadistic as it may sound, after I had mine I changed my philosophy entirely. Today I think it's an essential part of growing up. Those who don't receive a good hiding at least once are missing out.

I was fifteen. There was a girl, naturally, with great legs and boobs and who was called Lisa, and she lived on the same estate as I did, just around the corner in fact. Lisa was flighty and rather sought after. I usually got on well with her but one day I upset her and from then on there was a problem. Lisa must have bitched to other testosterone fuelled males who wanted to get in her pants, and these individuals saw an opportunity to make an impression. They gathered and waited on the field directly between my school and my house. It was a short walk home. Normally.

I was no fighter, of that I was sure, but I was smart and had done the maths, and the maths said, it would hurt. Given I'd never been properly punched, kicked and so forth, I took my fear and multiplied it by the amount of people who'd be dishing it out simultaneously. Hence, I was crapping myself, and to thwart the pain I devised a cunning plan to avoid detection by walking the long way home. This added another twenty minutes or so to my journey.

Meanwhile they waited each evening. Clearly they'd not worked it out yet, but then none of them had a reputation for intelligence. I continued to do my best to evade capture but it was only a matter of time before someone relented.

I can't remember the day, but one evening I decided to face the music. Maybe I was just tired of the long walk, but a part of me now believes my choice was made for the experience. In becoming an adult we must take bold decisions. This was my first step in growing up.

Unluckily the music on that day was not to my taste. I quickly found myself on the ground where I quickly crawled up into a ball in a miserable attempt to protect my head and organs. That made punching difficult, but the kicking went on for a lifetime.

When they'd exhausted all energy, they left, and I picked my sorry self out of the dirt and achingly hobbled home like a scuffed dog. In the mirror I inspected my swollen face, cursed the missing parts of my scalp, and found myself concerned with coming up with an explanation for the following day at school. And the surprise? Well the pain was minimal. It was truly a shock. Knowing I could take that pain and much more, I felt new confidence that if it were to happen again I would fight back. Ever since this incident this has affected the way I approach intimidating groups, believing that a display of weakness is likely to worsen a conflict. Better to be bold and get on with it, and if it comes to it, not to go down without a fight.

Manipulation, an underrated skill mostly viewed with negativity, is something that I began to get a handle on at University. The main driver of manipulation is sex, and all good looking people know it, but youth also works to an advantage, mainly because everyone wants it.

Those devoid of good looks or youth must utilise more subvert ways to manipulate typically through the means of emotion, acting or the power of the tongue or written word. I'm generalising of course, but largely it's true. We call good looking blonds dumb and it's not because they are dumb but because they've no need to use intelligence when sticking their chest out will do as well a job. Key to manipulation is correctly reading the scenario and picking the right response. My first lesson in this came towards the end of my compulsory schooling.

It was September, some six months after my beating, and I was sat at my desk in the beginning of yet another dull GCSE English lesson. I really didn't enjoy English, being as it was among my weakest subjects, but I found myself in top-set, and that meant we were all expecting, and expected, to come out with A or B grades in our examinations.

The lesson before that we'd undertook a mock GCSE exam and now we all eagerly awaited our results. The real deal was in only six months time and it would be a good indication on how well we'd do when that time came. The teacher, a gentle lady called Mrs. Roberts, wasted no time in reading the results out to the class.

"Paul... A."

Paul was one of my best mates, you'll hear more about him later. Several other high grades were read out. Then mine.

"Andrew... E"

The class erupted with laughter. Sneering abuse fired from the row of guys behind me, but I didn't turn around. The front row did to see what was happening, and of course to join in. Even Paul was in on it.

The dumbfounded expression on my face compounded the situation and I turned beetroot red trying to think how I'd messed up. The fact was, my English was subpar, and the exam merely proof of this. I felt hapless and bitter with myself for being a failure, mostly I'd never really failed at anything. Failing however is another good lesson of life, it teaches you to lower your expectations or to try harder to reach them. Unfortunately I was never going to become a literal intellect in six months.

Time went by and on the day of the real GCSE I walked into the large school sports hall having reconciled myself to the scrap heap. Over one hundred shanty wooden desks still sporting graffiti from the seventies aligned the room and on each table lay a name of a participant. Having sat down, the GCSE papers for the year 1999 were dispensed and the clock begun. I turned over the paper and read the largest and most important question on it.

'Describe a topic or event which has personally affected or changed your life.'

It was a gift from the almighty himself. It was undeniable proof that no matter how down and hopeless you feel, there are chances out there and occasionally one will come your way.

For whatever reason, most English teachers tend to be female and so the same goes for English examiners, who are themselves English teachers. The idea that examiners scrutinise every paper in detail didn't seem plausible, I thought they'd have a ton of papers to mark during their holiday time and marking the same repetitive work on how a student felt when their a cat died would be prosaic at best. If it were me I'd probably scan for grammar and try to skip the story. I needed it the other way around, because my grammar was shit. What I needed here was a good story, and injecting a few untruths to make it a great one.

A story that would play on the heart strings of the female examiner and which was energetic and fast paced? I chose the beating, focusing in detail on the juxtaposition of fear for being beaten up and blind love for the girl instigating it. Not that I loved her. Then I made up the rest; a kidney failing climax, my mother running from the house and over the field, while all the time having to watch her child being relentlessly beaten.

Whatever I wrote, and I wish I had a copy, it must have made an excellent read, for I was later issued with a miraculous 'B' grade for it. It was an important lesson in putting myself in another's shoes and working the emotions of that character.

There was no escaping my weak English skills and I vowed to improve it over time. Today you're reading my effort towards that goal.

When young I held a belief that I could do anything I put my mind to. Little has since changed, but I have become more realistic in what I can and can not accomplish. I've always been a problem solver and in some shape or form an engineer. I excel when trying to find a solution to make something difficult work. It was hardly surprising when at the age of 13 I and a friend named Todd attempted to mount a 20cc chainsaw engine onto a push scooter using its dry clutch. The welding of the frame we did at school and the teachers of the technology department were rightfully enthusiastic at our spirit. The engine was donated by an old man named Ray who lived a few doors down from my house. Ray loved the smell of petrol as much as we did, and was clearly bemused with our idea. As the engine didn't come with an exhaust we scoured a large region of the North East of England trying to find one, however when we did the thought of spending £25 on it was alarming. We christened the motorised scooter the *CharnaTodd 1000,* and I can still remember the day we took it from my garage and into the street for its maiden test run.

To start the two stroker we needed back pressure on the exhaust, and since we weren't prepared to buy one, our solution was a 30cm steel ruler we 'borrowed' from the technology department at school. The pull cord was missing so we acquired a powerful electric drill and a socket-set to turn the large bolt on the fly wheel until the thing spluttered and began. Once it began, we, the ruler and the drill would run for cover, for immensely loud and surprisingly powerful, neither of us wanted to be close. For comparison, I can still remember the noise Concorde made taking off from Newcastle Airport back in the day when spectators could stand on the roof and watch the planes taking off. Our engine was louder. Sadly the engine didn't have the gearing to move the scooter. It was, however, loud, and that made it worthy of our time.

In my last year of high school, aged 18, I planned to submit a radio control aircraft for my A-Level project. The main problem was I had to build one. The mothballed 20cc two stroker engine seemed perfect for the job, but it would require a relative wing span. Using no mathematics at all, I calculated a 5.5 metre span to be adequate and I located a shop selling balsa wood and another selling plastic heat shrink film and began to build what I presumed would be a good wing. At some point I had to admit the project had become as overwhelming as the wingspan, so I downsized the wings to about 1.5 metres and took apart a powerful radio controlled car for the motors and electronics. I didn't bother with flaps and a rudder, for all I wanted, for a brief few seconds, was to see my creation climb under its own power.

A pre-launch test flight was attempted with the tennis courts at the school doubling up as a runway. As it turned out the runway wasn't required, as at full throttle the plane would only taxi along the ground at about 2mph. That meant I had to find a more effective way to launch it, and for that I had yet another brilliant idea.

The following day, with the batteries fully charged. I gave my friend the plane and talked him through the methodology behind the madness. He would run as fast as he could and at the point of feeling lift, throw the plane as hard as he could into the sky. I would operate the remote control to ensure the throttle was always at full.

A few other friends had gathered at the side of a grass patch and now eagerly awaited the inevitable, and with the four motors creating a splendid high pitched drone, my friend ran forward and threw it as hard as he could. It nose dived into the ground and disintegrated.

Myself and Todd had a friend called Ellie, a good looking busty girl whom we both admired for that reason, although she was also a great character. In no such way did she ask us to build her a vibrator, so I'm not exactly sure why we decided to do just that. Named the unfathomable *CharnaTodd 2000,* the vibrator was made by chopping six inches off a broom handle, mounted one of the motors from my destroyed plane onto the end, and sticking an unbalanced weight on the end of the motor's spindle. Wires ran to a 9v battery, and being concerned with the safety of our product, we stuck an unused balloon over the pointy end. We presented it to our female friend and hoped, as fleeting engineers, for feedback. We received none.

Early on I took a keen interest in computers. It fitted with my slightly geeky nature and I saw the engineering and development merit of it more than the entertainment value. I built my first computer when I was thirteen, a 166MHz machine using parts from local computer fairs. While others were buying at PC World I was cursing my stupidity for I'd earthed the main-board to the case and part of it had caught fire.

14

As my knowledge in the Computing field grew I became further interested in programming and by the first year of University I was running a successful hardware website with a friend called Gavin. I became "advanced" in Microsoft Visual Basic and coded a program called *NVMax,* which tweaked and overclocked NVIDIA graphics cards, the things used for 3D gaming. I had an abnormally large success around the world with it. A competitor in the field, called *RivaTuner,* was produced by a Russian developer who had sharp C skills who could dabble at will in machine code. Unluckily for him he couldn't design an interface for shit, so my program was winning our little war. I think he admired that, plus he and his Russian buddies found it hilarious when a mate of mine used a PC at school I'd just been on (I hadn't logged out the browser) to humorously announce on my website that I was stopping the project because I was gay and needed to spend time with my boyfriend.

When the Russian cracked NVIDIA's overclocking algorithms my program was competitively as good as dead, however for whatever reason he decided to release the code to me, in drips and drabs, and in C and as machine code. The task of converting that over and using Visual Basics processes to talk to the NVIDIA drivers directly was no small feat for a teenager and it still ranks as one of the hardest things my brain has worked on.

Meanwhile the website running alongside the program was serving out 100,000 page views per day, but I was too young to capitalise on the advertising potential and after a few years of running it to claw freebee hardware that we'd review for free (if we could keep it afterwards), I disbanded it in search of my next venture.

While building the website I noticed that the more complex software became the more an engineers thoughts restricted the way the software could adapt. The programmer would lay down a backbone and everything would be built on top of it. Improving the backbone even slightly could necessitate a complete rewrite of the code built upon it, and so the software would be largely stuck with old methods and hence has issues with longevity and scaleability. Today we call such software 'legacy,' and we live with this daily. But I had plan. I asked myself, what if I could make one system that would allow a developer to design any website the correct way, and which would give them the power to change any part of it at any time and allow for their customers to have complete control over the content. What if it were perfect at everything, and if it was entirely adaptable? So in my final year of University I began building such a beast, with an intention of using it for my dissertation project. It took several months.

After handing in the project the University tutors responsible for marking it called a meeting. I'll always remember that meeting. One of the lecturers I knew briefly and he'd brought along a companion I'd never seen before. I acknowledge my write-up wasn't great, and in fairness I doubt he'd seen so much quantity of code for a dissertation. I can also say he wasn't at all interested in it, and he was itching to get out the room. They didn't want to look at it. They wanted an excuse not to.

"Why not just use Dreamweaver?", he asked.

"It's not professional and any developer knows it. Give me one large, complex website designed with it? It doesn't handle multi-layer security, it doesn't create and manage content on the fly, it doesn't offer workflow control," I tried to explain. This may mean nothing to you, but he was supposedly the expert. He wasn't and he wanted to go home.

"What you're trying to do is impossible. You can't make software perform with such a level of adaptability." chipped in his colleague.

"You're thinking about design software on a workstation creating output with a certain, fixed design, content and functionality. I'm talking about software on a server that lets you control this on the fly." I added, exasperated that they'd not even got this.

I left the room with a mark of 40%, the lowest possible score that they could offer so that I didn't fail the module and cause the university statistics to suffer. Others had submitted ridiculously simple projects such as random lottery generators, the sort of stuff I could program up in under an hour, and had received double my mark.

You may think that I was destined to become a software developer, but I felt too young for it, and imagined a life sitting behind a screen going blind, fat and bald. I apologise to any software programmers that meet that specification. Instead I chose to train as an I.T teacher, which while only utilising 1/10th of my knowledge and ability, would offer a dynamic work environment. Plus, I like working with kids. My teaching ethos I developed early on and it has remained rigid ever since, and no leaning from clueless management will ever change it. I will not dispense information or teach an interface, but instead I present challenges which must be worked through, which in turn offer enlightenment, but only through the underrated process of struggling.

I've always been a popular teacher with students. I'm firm on direction and use dry humour and witty putdowns. I make sure everyone's on board and never, under any circumstances, make someone feel stupid. Sadly, schools are after teachers that teach interfaces to pass exams, giving a firm two fingers to creativity and development. Students hate it. Teachers hate it. Management hates it. Everyone hates it.

My very first motorcycle was a Honda CG125, a so called bullet proof commuter come pizza delivery vehicle that wasn't in any way bullet proof or able to carry anything, especially when hills were involved. It was really cheap and when I purchased mine it was only a few month old. For the new version, Honda had taken a simple bike and built it down to a price. Quality was awful and immediately it began snapping spokes. I can remember quite vividly when four (or was it more?) snapped on my way through the Tyne Tunnel, causing the rear to snake all over the road. The bike couldn't go fast and I remember a day of horrendous wind when it refused to go over 25mph on the flat. The end of my tether came when the carb began requiring daily fettling to make the engine start once it was up to running temperature.

I upgraded my license and purchased a Suzuki GS500, mainly because I couldn't afford the more expensive Honda CB500. In my eyes the GS500 was going to be a cheap runner that would offer the fuel economy I still needed as a thrifty student. For what I saved in fuel, I ended up spending on trying to fix its many problems. The brakes never worked and were downright dangerous. The carbs had idle issues that the local mechanic tried repeatedly to fix and rear swing arm rusted so badly I expected impending rear suspension collapse. The carbs had given up again on one cold winter night and I'd taken it apart in the university bicycle shed using tools I'd borrowed from the campus engineer. It was dark and I was miserable, but at least I was partially intoxicated by the petrol that had leaked out of the tank and carbs. Having cut a wire, I used a gas powered soldering iron (handy things to have) to put it back together, and then there was an almighty boom and I was flung into the fence on the other side of the shed. With my ears ringing, I'd learned about the flash point of petrol vapour. I wouldn't be doing that again. That month I finally did the right thing and sold the bike on.

My next motorcycle, a Suzuki SV650 V-Twin, was a wonderful machine. As I'd little in the way of money I bought an insurance write off that had been repaired but not perfectly as it steered slightly left, but that I could live with and I spent the next few months tinkering with parts and fitting unnecessary crap like exhausts that spat fire on full acceleration. The torque was fantastic and propelled the small thing and me to 60mph in about 3.5 seconds. As I was young and it was fast and nimble, it was only a matter of time before it got me into trouble. Undertaking an undercover police car in the single lane Tyne Tunnel was such an example. It was great fun and as a commuter I'd have kept it, but then just before I began my teaching practice year down London I took it to Switzerland with a few friends and its ergonomic deficiencies nearly broke my neck. I decided if touring was to become a focus, I needed a different bike.

At the same time I was starting my first full-time teaching job down in Harpenden, on the London fringe, I was interested in bigger trail-able bikes that could double up as a hauling wagon back to Newcastle. Using my first pay check I purchased a BMW R1150GS motorcycle, my first with off-road potential, and then began trail riding. The BMW

R1150GS was good, really good, but it was heavy. Once on its side I'd difficulty getting it back up, and once the panniers were loaded with touring gear it became near impossible. Towards the end of that teaching year, during the two week easter break, during which I turned 22, I initiated my first real challenge on two wheels.

The challenge was to drive through the non-touristy areas of Morocco on a solo expedition. I would aim to tackle routes not possible by car. I would rough it, camp out, cook stuff myself and acclimatise to living on the road.

I travelled down with two other BMW riders I'd not met before and we did insane riding hours. On the last day, one of them got pissed off with me for holding them up when my GPS bracket failed and I grabbed the brake as I tried and failed to prevent it falling onto the road. It did and that was the end of it. Anyway, the last day was 16hrs long and by the end of it I couldn't remember the pin to my debit card. I'd been using it for three years, that's how knackered I was. At an ATM the bank locked it and I was up shit creek. I could still use a signature at petrol stations and used it to buy food and fuel, which got me to a police station where I used their phone to call the UK embassy. I was ready to give up but they came up trumps, had I thought about Western Union they asked? Indeed I had not! I phoned my mother, who was in pieces worrying, and three days later (it was a bank holiday and weekend) I'd a few hundred quid transferred, which I hoped would be enough to wing it and back, so long as I lived cheap. As I had no money at all for the three days waiting on the transfer, I slept on grass verges at the side of motorways. Then I was on my way, determined not to be defeated.

All went well up until a week when crossing a point in the

deserted, cold and baron Atlas mountains where I made the mistake of trying to make it through a snow drift using horse power. The bike sank into mud underneath the snow and began sliding down the mountain face as I desperately tried, and failed, to turn it around by rotating it on the cylinder head (boxer engined BMW's have two opposing cylinders sticking out on either side). This was one of the rare times I cursed God.

There was nothing around for goodness knows how far and being 22 years old and new to "adventure riding" into the middle of nowhere, I was worried. I began calling for help across the mountain range. Darkness fell and I switched my torch to SOS mode, noting that I'd used all of my water up in sweating with my efforts to turn the bike around. I felt exactly what I was – alone.

A few hours later it was dark and I was in my sleeping bag as the temperature had fallen to around freezing. Then came panting, not my own, and I very nearly shit myself as through the darkness a young Moroccan shepherds face became visible through the thin moon light. He'd seen my torch earlier and had travelled from another mountain face to offer assistance. Together, he pushed and lifted on the back on the bike while I pulled on the front and worked the throttle. The rear wheel covered him with freezing mud but after exasperated efforts, the bike eventually broke free from the snow and I made it back to the rutted track. I loaded the bike back up and the Shepard sat on the rear as I navigated to his dwelling, a ramshackle stone that came with a complementary fanged toothed dog and flee infested sheep. It was an experience I wouldn't soon forget, largely because in the morning I was nursing so many bites I felt diseased. It took at least a week to rid the flees from my clothes.

I published the report on a BMW motorcycle forum and the members chastised lack of judgement and poor hindsight, but I ignorantly shrugged it off and began thinking about the next adventure.

Somehow two years went by before I knew it was time for another challenge. By then I'd downsized the wheels for something more agile and less likely to pose a problem when it became stuck in soft stuff. With a friend I met on Horizons Unlimited who would ride a KTM 640 Adventure, I drove a Suzuki DRZ400 to the passport departure gate at Kent, to be queried by the French authorities if I knew my passport had expired a week earlier. I couldn't believe it! - and felt so idiotic. They let me through and I felt the Moroccan authorities would too, or a backhand would sort it. A few days later, after a numbing ride through France, Spain and down to the Ceuta border crossing, I discovered I was wrong. My friend went on and crossed the upper Sahara himself, while I had to take a slow drive back to the UK.

Thoroughly pissed at myself, I spent little time finding another ride. The DRZ400 was poorly geared and wasn't a mileage eater. I needed something in between. I found a well used but fully kit loaded BMW F650GS Dakar and went for it.

It was summer and hot, really hot. I made Morocco with nothing more than a fine from the Spanish police for traffic filtering, but on the way south through Morocco over shot a bend and hit an oncoming Toyota Hilux which ripped my panniers off and damaged bits of the bike, and my leg. But I was still going forward.

Close to the start point I was advised by several Moroccan locals to 'forget it', advising the route was driven little and I could be out there for days without seeing a sole. I was completely focused on doing it no matter what.

It began badly, starting with my damaged panniers falling off the pannier rails. The temperature was 40c and I wore black biking gear and a black helmet. I tried to make the panniers secure but ended up ditching them. The panniers featured a well built into the walls so I lost a lot of water capacity. I pressed on. By midday, in 50c heat and high humidity I was exhausting energy I never knew I had. I'd hit proper sand, which was fine and dust like. The bike sank over and over and had to be repeatedly dug out. Progress was dire and both engine overheat and oil lights illuminated. My water ran out. I still remember crying in desperation, the bike having sank in the sand and then falling on my leg as I tried to dig it out the sand. It should've been a text-book disaster but I persisted and made it the following day, very thirsty, and very euphoric.

Before reaching the tarmac at Erfoud, I came upon a small auberge in the middle of nowhere, where I slept the night and ate a makeshift omelette. The following day I became ill, with my innards draining out my backside. Over the next few days I developed a complete inability to control my rear, and making my way north through Morocco, would shit myself without any notice. Many of my clothes were in the panniers I'd been forced to ditch the previous week. Things became rather smelly.

After two days of feeling really, really terrible, I made it back to Spain, where I became deliriously ill. I couldn't hold down any water, it literally went in and out in sixty seconds, and I hadn't ate anything in days. Things start to get hazy from there, but I do remember late in the evening when I pulled up at the side of a petrol station unable to drive any further, and collapsed. A few hours later I awoke and admitted myself to the nearest hospital where they stuck a drip in my arm and took a blood test. The ward was full of elderly people on life support and with no partitioning it was a real sorry sight. I had no energy to do anything. I couldn't even remove my t-shirt. I was instructed to a bed in the corner where four nurses assisted. I felt so ashamed at my smell, which they duly noted.

I fell asleep but awoke with a sudden need to visit the toilet, I had seconds before my fresh hospital clothes became soiled and I was determined to not let that happen. I lunged towards the toilet at the far corner of the room, with my drip in tow, but I tripped up, hit something and blacked out.

The next morning a young female doctor arrived and informed me that I had Cholera. She asked why I hadn't gone to hospital in Morocco. I didn't have an answer. She gave me antibiotics and left.

I must have slept for 18 hours, perhaps they'd put something in the drip, and I awoke around 05:00hrs to darkness and many life machine beeps. My grandmother had died the previous month and it was the first time I'd watched someone die, an awful experience that hit me hard, and in the darkness I panicked, removed the drip, donned my motorcycle gear and ran out the front door. My bike was where I'd left it. I got back on the highway and rode.

During the night my mother had sent the name of the antibiotics and they were, at that point, available at any Spanish chemist. I bought a load of them and kept going.

Things were looking promising but a little short of Bilbao the bike broke down with a broken water-cooling propeller. As it was a bank holiday and I had to be home for work, the insurance arranged repatriation and the bike was left in Spain to be fixed.

A friend, Gavin, picked me up from the airport, and alarmed at my appearance, his first question was whether I wanted to go to hospital. At home, on the scales, I found I'd lost two stone.

Two weeks later, and £400 spent on repairs, I flew out to Spain and drove the bike back to Newcastle. The next week someone stole it.

The insurance paid out a few month later and with a little extra I finally bought my dream bike, a second hand BMW R1200GS. It still stands as the best bike I've ever owned, and I drove it to Greece and around the islands there.

Now with a steadfast job, I aimed to get out of renting, and over the next couple of years I saved a £12,500 deposit for a house, and In 2009 I bought one, leaving behind my student lifestyle. I had to sell the bike to do the place up.

Despite having a solid job my quirkiness prevailed and the following year I bought a 1992 Royal Enfield, then began the laborious process of transplanting in a 400cc diesel cement mixer engine into it. This required a measure of welding and engineering, for which my garage served as a workshop.

Utterly simple to fix, light weight and parts easily found around the world, the diesel Enfield offered 160mpg, 60mph top speed, unfathomable vibration, and real head turning character.

I tried to make Greece on it in November 2010 ,but it went through its forth fuel pump and I spent two weeks in Genoa, Italy, waiting for a fifth to arrive from the UK.

In April 2011 I vowed a ride to the south of France and Spain, where I'd meet up with a Greek friend. It was a nightmare from start to finish. On the first day I made 50km down the A1 when the front frame cracked. Using two heavy duty ratchet straps I was fortunate to be carrying, I held the engine roughly in place then drove back at 20km on the hard shoulder. Determined not to miss the planned two weeks holiday I sourced thicker metal, had it welded and set off again at midnight, sleeping on a grass verge for a few hours before putting in the hours to try and mitigate the delay.

I made a further 100km, whereafter the alternator fell off. Damaged, I stripped some of the enamelled wire from it and soldiered a fix. In the middle of France the air filter welding cracked and it fell off I to the unknown. I bought a sponge and mesh from a local supermarket and car garage and zip tied it in place.

Later the key on the crankshaft used to rotate the flywheel snapped. I pushed it to a small DIY shop and used a grinder to made a new slot in the end of the crankshaft, then hammered in a bolt between it and the groove on the flywheel.

Throughout the trip the bike leaked oil with much going on the rear tyre and my clothes. I knew if I ever got it home it was back to the drawing board.

In later part of 2011, four years since my daft excursion

through the sand and nearly two years since I'd bought my house, all appeared well, in the sense that my life was stable and normal, but to me I felt like I was passing time and not living at all.

My friend Paul theorised that my job wasn't demanding and I was avoiding female courtship because I didn't want anything getting in the way of what I wanted to do. Over several weekends at the pub we concluded I was bored and in need of a challenge. He said I could try signing up to a match making website. He said I could try changed job.

Instead I typed that innocent question on Facebook, and overnight the direction of my life was transformed.

I would quit my job, sell everything and hit the road. There was nothing for me here. I had to better myself. I had to search for a better life. I had to live.

Paul's said I was "doing the trip for all the wrong reasons".

There was only one way to find out.

Chapter 3

Preparation

It was November 2011 and I thought, at a push, that I could be ready to go by mid-January. I had to move quickly and not waiver, and the night after the Facebook replies came in I typed up a resignation letter for my job, and handed it in the following day. My boss didn't do a good job of accepting it, and begged if I could at least stay on until the end of the teaching year. I thought on it and concluded that building up my finances, further testing of the Royal Enfield, and having more time in general was good planning. I agreed to end my contract at the end of July.

Not surprisingly, money was my primary concern. The burning question, one which litters the internet almost as much as porn, is just how much one needs for a journey around the world? I deemed the question irrelevant. The way I saw it, I needed to raise as much as I could.

As I had no intention of coming back, and more to the point, would have nothing to come back too, and that made we want to be entrepreneurial. From December 2011 to February 2012 I set up a website whereon I could blog and update readers with my progress. The website would use the web software

I'd been continuously working on ever since that final year at university. Driving content and people to the site would be an excellent way to show off and exemplar my programming skills, which ultimately I hoped would kickstart a career change somewhere down the line. Just as it was time to move on from the U.K., It was time to move on from secondary school teaching.

I also planned to write a book during the journey, the one you're now reading, and it would squelch my insecurity by proving that I could write with a decent prose. None of this would bring in money for the trip, and in January 2012 I focused on liquidating everything I owned. At that point, the bank balance stood at a mere £2,000.

I continued to work on the Royal Enfield to solve some of the long standing issues but by early spring concluded it to be a lost cause. The diesel bike had to go. What I required was two wheels that would be cheap to run and dependable. For my sins, I bought a scooter, a modern Honda PCX 125cc. It came from Leeds, cost £1,500 and it's single previous owner had put just 1,200 miles on the clock. My modifications were minimal; I fitted an aftermarket accessory called a variator which increased the top speed from 55mph to 65mph, a higher windscreen, a top-box on the back, charging circuits for my electronic devices, and brackets to hold the stainless panniers from the Royal Enfield. Whether my choice to take a scooter was doable or ridiculous, I knew it would be good on fuel, offering about 100MPG (imperial) ,and that it would carry even more gear than my previous BMW R1200GS with its big panniers could manage. The only problem was the 7 litre tank offered a mere 110 mile range. I planned to solve this with a 5 litre fuel can under the seat.

Meanwhile my house, which I'd had on the market since January, had attracted minimal interest and I continued to drop the price. The U.K. housing market was piteous, with completed sales being very low. The rental market on the other hand was much more buoyant. Would I consider renting instead of giving the house away for a song? If I were to let the house out my trip balance would be significantly lower, but possibly still enough. If I sold it I was laughing. I left it for the time being.

Sitting on my drive was an old ex-wedding car, a Mercedes 250D in pearl white with 17" black alloys, and in the garage the now defunct Royal Enfield. Both required fixing if they were to sell, which I did and sold at considerable loss. The bank balance now stood at £4,300.

The month of May arrived and with it I focused on asset liquidation. My cherished Yamaha digital Piano had to be worth something. That made £450 on eBay. I then collected everything I hadn't used in three months and gathered it in the spare room, included things such-as a drill-based fuel pump and a wetsuit. Selling all this on Gumtree netted a further £500. My mother owed £2,000 and my brother owed £250. Work owed two pay checks at £1,500 each. Adding this up gave roughly £11,000.

There was a problem with the £2,000 owed by my mother, in that she didn't have it. Financially imprudent, she'd used several credit cards to fund a house renovation and a few holidays n Spain while barely working. In doing so she'd racked up £13,000 of debt with no method to pay it back. My £2,000 was to help transfer one of her cards for six months. If declared bankrupt the creditors would probably come after her house. A bailout was inevitable and would require my assistance. Having put down a large deposit for a cheap house in a not-sought-after area, I'd a mortgage with a low APR. A better *loan to value* (aka higher deposit) opened up lower APR rates and also cheaper additional borrowing. You can probably guess where this was going. I began an additional borrowing application for a mythical £13,000 car which would be used to pay off her credit cards and release the £2,000. My problem was I'd be forced to rent the house instead of selling it. There was also the minor issue of committing fraud.

From late May I switched focus again to planning and equipment. Potential routes were volatile with changes every couple of years. Information was sketchy in places, such as was the Russian/Georgia now open to foreigners? At the time of writing it was no longer possible to take a ship from Siberia to Alaska, and so if going via Kazakhstan, Mongolia and Russia, shipping would be required from Japan or Vladivostok, a port in Southern Russia. Another option was to head south from Kazakhstan down what is known as the Koraram pass. This required going through China and Pakistan and passing borders with Afghanistan. I'd heard doing the route as a solo traveller was risky with no means to turn off and take a different road. The final option, which was the most popular, was to travel through Iran and then either through Pakistan or via Dubai (if no visa could be obtained) and then to fly the bike to India, which would be expensive. Going through Russia would miss out much of Asia, something I wasn't prepared to do. From India I'd go to Nepal and fly the bike from Kathmandu to Thailand.

My friend Paul was to marry a month into my trip and requested my presence at the wedding. As I'd fallen in love with Greece the years before, I decided I would ride the bike to Athens, spend a few weeks travelling around the islands and then leave the scooter at my mates while I flew back for the wedding. On the return I'd ride eastern Europe with my mate on his Ducati for two weeks and then set off eastwards through Turkey. Spending a few weeks in Greece would be enough to iron out any problems and I could swap kit in the UK and bring it back with me on the return flight. It seemed like I had a plan.

Inevitably there would be paperwork for this trip. A *Carnet de Passage* is a requirement of several countries to allow importation of a vehicle into their country. The system is managed by ATA in Switzerland and outsourced to a local company (typically the automobile association) in each country. For the U.K., this is the RAC. The value of the carnet is based on the vehicle value multiplied by the maximum "risk" factor for a country as determined by the local company. The highest for my planned route was Iran at 500%. I reckoned my scooter, once it had covered Eastern Europe would be worth just £1,000, so the carnet value was £5,000 plus RAC fees of about £200 and a £375 refundable deposit. For those without that spare cash, insurance is available whereby you pay 10% of the carnet value and 5% is released back to you when you return the carnet. The final figure was hence a little over £1,000. During the journey, the carnet is stamped in and out when you enter and exit border crossings. Forgetting or missing a stamp can cause major problems, such as the host country may come after you for the full amount (so £5,000 in my case), or you might be unable to enter the next country. The insurance option doesn't indemnify you.

I began the process a month and a bit before leaving, as recommended on the RAC's website. Communication was very poor and despite my valiant attempts to get it sorted I ran out of time and had to leave without it. Thankfully progress improved and the document was delivered to my mothers house where I would pick it up on my return for the wedding.

For a Brit., few visas are required in advance for entry into foreign territory. They're unlucky that where required, they are expensive. I required a visa for Iran, Pakistan and India. The Iranian visa cost was €150 plus fees and couldn't be collected in the U.K due to the closure of the Embassy, so I would have to apply and wait in a foreign country. The Indian visa was close to £100 and would be granted for three or six months depending on how the wind blows. It would start as soon as it was issued. The Pakistan visa would cost over £100 and would only be granted if I had the Indian visa in the passport. Rejection was possible due to my choice to travel solo, and they may request an interview down at the London embassy. A transit visa was equally unlikely because the south of Pakistan is tribal land and known to be dangerous. In addition, I had no idea when I'd get to India. The entire process seemed laborious and arcane with problems. Instead I left it all and planned to apply at the appropriate Embassies/Consulates in Athens. I also hoped doing this would work out cheaper.

American sanctions against Iran meant visa/mastercard withdrawals were no longer possible, so I'd need to draw out Euros or U.S. Dollars and change them in the country. In the U.K. I used only a single debit card and I'd never had a credit card, believing in spending only what I had, a lesson I certainly didn't learn from my mother. Carrying a credit card for the trip seemed a good backup however and I arranged a small meeting with an advisor at my bank, Santander, whereafter I walked out with a backup debit card and my first credit card.

Blogging and content creation was going to be a major part of the trip and I required a laptop with suitable battery life and power to make it happen. For my first time I bought into Apple, specifically a Macbook Air for its ultra portability and strong aluminium body. Unlike typical laptops of this size it featured a high performance CPU, plenty of memory and a solid state (no moving parts) hard drive, which was good to counter vibration. I complemented it with a 750Gb USB slim-drive housed in a military grade case.

All my online based accounts used different passwords. Remembering them was impossible so to gain access I intended to lock them away using a master password which I'd use for nothing else. While bespoke programs were available for the task, I opted for a generic solution that was portable and accessible on anything. I chose a password protected OpenOffice spreadsheet.

I wasn't a fan of health insurance, or any insurance for that matter, and I left on the trip without it. On the return for the wedding, my mother was so worried I bought some just to alleviate her fears. Thanks to the scooters 125cc engine size I managed to get it for £100. A bigger bike would have seen that figure rise into the £300-400 bracket. All health insurance policies have wording in the small print stating they don't cover countries the FCO advises against travelling to. My health insurance was thus void for Iran and Pakistan. I didn't tell my mother this.

I'd reluctantly registered with a G.P and met a nurse to discuss injections. After that I re-visited every other week to be stabbed with various needles that promised protection against Hepatitis, Typhoid and other various nasties. Two were at cost; Yellow Fever, which is mandatory for entry into South America (it comes with a yellow certificate card) and Rabies, which doesn't stop you getting it but helps cure it. Believing prevention to be better than cure, I committed to a non stroking of dogs and fox policy, and would try my very best to stay clear of biting bats.

Malaria was a hot topic. I'd need two types of tablets and there were two reasons why I left with neither. First, I didn't like what I read about the side effects. Second, Malarone, one of the tablets, would be very expensive for the duration I would be in South Asia. Surely I could get it cheaper in India? I spoke to a guy from Thailand and he said nobody bothers, instead they cover up and use plenty of deet. Like my visas, I chose to sort it nearer to the time. I certainly wasn't spending £500 in the U.K on Malarone tablets.

For navigation I'd been toying with a Nokia N8 smartphone for its world-wide mapping. Whichever mapping solution I used, it had to be off-line based. The Nokia software was painful to use and unreliable in real-life. The de-facto for any traveller is Garmin, so I switched to an iPhone with Garmin Onboard software and set about creating a mount, rain protection and charging system for it. I ran a lead down under the scooters headstock to connect headphones, allowing for music on the move.

In addition to the 5v power I wired in a 16.4v charger for the Macbook, a USB charge lead and a 12v point for AA battery charging. The majority of my electronic devices would run on AA batteries and that was no co-incidence. A portable shaver, a wireless mouse, a head-torch and my DSLR camera could all run on Sanyo Enloop AA batteries. These low-leakage batteries were considered the best available, and that made me think that I'd arrived at the best choice.

The head-torch I chose was made by Felix, model FL21. A plastic bodied IP65 rated torch with a flip down light defuser, it ran on a single AA battery. Efficiency was high, as was brightness, and when I ran over the first with my car I loved it so much I bought another.

Camping was to a major role in my trip for I certainly couldn't afford hotels or even hostels for the duration I would be away for. I was divided on what to take. I had experience with a Goretex bivi bag, the ultimate in light-weight and portable sleeping, but it sacrificed practicality and was impossible to get changed in. When it rained it was equally unpleasant, especially getting out to take a leak. Where's my boots? - the grass is sodden... oh, they are outside, and soaked like everything else. I considered a hammock but thought I'd get bitten by dangerous spiders. I tried a Vango tent as recommended on Horizons Unlimited, but upon assembly in my living room found it to be small and impractical, with little usable room. Then I came across a picture of a U.S Army cot bed, as used extensively in the 2003 Iraq war. The British Army also bought them and had made a mosquito shelter that fitted on top. I'd have to waterproof it, but I'd be off the ground for greater comfort and have protection from water drainage and curious creepy crawlies. All I had to do was find one. The mosquito shelter I sourced quickly but the cot bed was difficult. I asked my brother who was in the British Territorial Army to ask around and a month later I purchased one under the table from his Warrant Officer. Back in the living room I erected the bed and shelter and marvelled at it. It took a bit longer to assemble then a good tent but the comfort and practicality were unbeatable. Although made from aluminium it and the shelter still weighed a hefty 10kg, and packed it was still some 20cm wider than the bike panniers on my scooter. I purchased a 7 by 9 foot tarp to sling over the top and a couple of ball bungees to tie it to the bed legs and parts of the scooter. Lastly, a down filled sleeping bag certified to -20c would serve for cold conditions.

For cooking I assembled a petrol stove, two army mess tins, a cup, knife/fork/spoon, a tin opener and a mesh sieve with the handle cut off. While testing the stove, a cheap Chinese thing from eBay, the seal on the bottle blew out and the pressurised fuel caught fire. My garage nearly went up with it. I bought replacements, plus spares, and would check it each time before use.

I packed a small medical kit with bandages and sterilised wipes and added a sealed tub containing various antibiotics and sudacream. My mother, thinking ahead, added diarrhoea tablets, while my sister kindly donated packs of condoms of a make I've not seen before, which made me think she got them from a clinic. My luck being what it is, she can have them all back when I return.

Motorcycle clothing is mostly poor quality rubbish and I can say that having spent so much on fancy gear that is neither well made or fit for purpose. For solid dependable gear, stick with what works – Army gear. For the bad weather I purchased Army Goretex jacket and pants and black leather Goretex boots with high rise ankle support (I also carry wax and a brush to keep them in good condition). The gloves I chose were made from wool, were fingerless and cost £2, making them no good in rain or cold conditions. I remedied this with a pair of handlebar muffs. These may have looked silly but they enclose hands and controls and work well. Experience told me motorcycle trousers were impractical, so

I'd go with jeans for riding. I'd wear a motorcycle jacket with minimal armour and plenty of pockets, a size too big for better breathability. On the generic side, I'd pack three pairs of boxer shorts and socks, four t-shirts, one long sleeved t-shirt, an army jumper, a shirt, leather flip-flops, two pairs of jeans, one pair of light trousers, one pair of dress pants, two pairs of shorts and swimming shorts. Extras would include thermal bottoms, a wool hat and a neck warmer.

I carried out quite a bit of research into helmets and ended up purchasing a Nolan N102, a flip-lid that promised good quality and a quiet design. I paired this with Sennheiser CX300 headphones, and for the first time in ten years of riding I could hear the bass.

For washing I purchased a collapsable bucket, potentially the greatest thing ever made, and would fill an aluminium drinks bottle with laundry liquid. For dishes I'd carry washing-up liquid and a brillo pad. These would work better than sponges at scraping burnt food from the pan base. I'm an expert at burning food.

All this, plus packets of food and bottles of water would be packed under the seat, in the two panniers and/or into a 70 Litre waterproof canoe type bag that would secure on the back seat. Also stored under the seat alongside the 5 litre fuel can was a swiss army knife, a SAS survival book and bike related items like epoxy resin glue, a mushroom puncture repair kit, tyre pump, and enhanced tool kit. The things I bought and could do without, but would carry anyway, included a compressible pillow, a foldable aluminium chair and a tripod for the camera.

When June arrived I felt confident that the scooter and

equipment were ready. I felt able to sort the visas in Athens. The only remaining problem was money. I had enough to get going, but I was at risk of running out if I didn't the house letting become problematic and if the money from my mother didn't come through. Luckily, last minute style, I found a tenant for the house. Letting would pay for the mortgage and add £3k to the trip balance, if it all went to plan, and so long as the additional borrowing I had applied for to bail out my mother went through I could expect to have a budget of £13k (after paying for the Carnet de Passage document). In the meantime I'd begin the journey with £6k in the bank and an expectance that the rest of the money would find its way in drips and drabs.

Chapter 5

Departure

Konstantinos Tsakias is, as if the name doesn't suggest, Greek. I've known Kostas since university, some ten years now, and I've watched him change from a part punk, part communist, who hated the law and those responsible for enforcing it, into something simply older, but not necessarily any wiser. Our friendship at university was an unusual match. Whereas I worry about everything, he worries about nothing. In the early years he sported a punk Mohawk haircut dyed orange and his favourite t-shirt read 'No school. No job. No problem.' During uni he lived on biscuits and was addicted to heart-attack inducing Greek ice coffee. His ability to scrape through each year was bordering on farcical, and his laptop DVD drive was fused with garlic and wouldn't open.

Kostas is a great friend and a unique character whose faults never cease to put a smile on my face. I also adore his mothers cooking. His inability to take anything seriously makes him the worst person to partner with for a motorcycle trip. Then there's his wheels, a Ducati 600 Monster, known for its unreliability when maintained. Kostas doesn't maintain it.

My journey would begin with travelling around Greek Islands using my scooter and Kostas sitting on the back. I wasn't entirely sure how, as he'd be sitting on top of the 70 litre bag, so about a foot above the passenger seat. He'd also have his own backpack and I had no means to carry it. Despite these misgivings Kostas assured his employer would grant him leave and so all I had to do was drive down and begin island hopping. Marvellous.

Thursday 26th July was my final day at work. After teaching at the same school for nearly five years, it was all over. The risk excited, and at the moment I walked out the door for the last time, I held no regret. I was ready. To celebrate I went to the pub with Paul and drank way too much beer. Despite the flow, it was quite a sober event, for we both knew that this was an almighty change that would lessen our contact with one another.

The following morning I made an emergency change to the scooters configuration - I switched the variator back to the original unit, as I hadn't tested the aftermarket unit and was concerned with reliability. Unrelated, an email came in from a fellow PCX owner in Tanzania, Australia, who wrote that his subframe snapped due to the bad roads. It was the first I'd heard of it happening and hoped it was one off. My PCX would endure far more hardship!

The top-box contained my sleeping bag and a few other bits, but as the lid was designed to open like a mussel, storage of items above the half way point would try to fall out. In front of the top-box, resting on the passenger seat and the panniers, was my very wide army cot bed which I secured with two ratchet straps. The 70 litre roll bag was perched on top of this, which was less than ideal as the bag was much wider than the sleeping kit, and when I sat on the bike the bag pushed into my back. Further more I couldn't open the top-box as the lid would hit the bag. To get into either side panniers I'd first have to remove the bag and the army camp bed. It couldn't be any worse than the Royal Enfield. I'd make do.

I carried out a final check and the tenant who'd be renting my house arrived and I transferred the keys over. My personal belongings were now either on the scooter or in a four foot cubed area of my loft. It was remarkable how little I now owned, the only significant things now being a pair of Tannoy speakers I couldn't bring myself to sell and a few power tools. No man should be forced to sell his power tools.

At mid-day I drove to my mums house. The scooter, being fully laden was surprisingly manageable, but a caveat came to my attention. When going up larger curbs the scooter would "beach" on the stand. I studied the undercarriage a few times expecting the sump to be bruised, but the stand was taking the impact, so I didn't worry about it.

My mother was on holiday so I had the house to myself. In the evening some mates had arranged a gathering, whereupon I was bestowed with a few leaving presents. These included an inflatable penis and a pack of 80's porn poker cards. They insisted I carried both through Iran and posted pictures of my arrest, torture and raping on Facebook. I left a little early, shattered and coming down from the adrenaline of quitting my job, leaving the house, leaving my life. The thrill was replaced with worry. I'd set off for the Dover-Dunkirk ferry early in the morning, a long motorway drive down the backbone of England.

On Saturday the 28th July 2012, at 07:00hrs, without any fuss

42

or fanfare, I departed Newcastle. The weather was good, and as I took the slipway to join onto the A1, the first song selected by iTunes was Billy Joel's Allentown. The grin on my face was unmeasurable.

I'd underestimated just how slow the original variator was and found myself trundling down to France at 55mph. Trucks began queuing up behind my rear before overtaking at 0.5mph. I would have to ship the aftermarket unit to Greece and fit it there. It took over 8 hours to drive from Newcastle to Dover and I made the ferry with 10 minutes to spare.

It was still light when I made France but the evening was approaching and with it I'd be driving at night. Something I'd learned about France from prior trips was that it valued its motorway parks and rest areas as much as I valued being able to wild camp in them. I found one, parked up for the night and got a brew on. While the water boiled I looking at my luggage. Even this early on I knew some of it could go. I ditched a large beach towel, several pairs of boxers and socks, and repacked the space in the panniers and under the seat so well that in doing so I pretty much emptied the 70 litre roll bag. Now I could continue without the pressure of it pressing against my back.

In the morning Belgium came quickly and all was working well. Making good time, I reprogrammed Garmin to avoid the motorways and began a more laid back route. In Belgium everyone appeared to live in spacious modern houses with big gardens and double garages. In four hours of driving I never saw one flat or terrace house. The roads and towns were so pretty, clean and maintained. High standards also applied to the picnic areas, these being to an even higher standard then the French managed. That evening I pitched the army cot bed and mossy net for a second time. During the night I awoke to the pattering of rain and threw the bike cover over the top. It was a good fit but I expecting to suffocate. I awoke in the morning dry, pleased with my non aching back, pleased to still be breathing. When it came to my choice of camping gear, I'd faired well.

While driving in Belgium the heavens opened and I pulled over too slowly to prevent water ingression into my new Panasonic camera. The rear screen failed and being that it had no viewfinder I could no longer see what I was shooting.

The little European area of Luxembourg was interesting and worth the day I spent in the capital. I wasn't expecting a Switzerland level of perfection, nor the green richness and the quaint stone marvels. It was however an expensive place and the hostel wasn't cheap. In the evening a big band played in the town centre and I sat for an hour with a beer.

Driving gave time to think, and with a lot of driving time came a lot of thinking. Every so often my heart would race as I asked myself whether this around the world trip was a big mistake, but as quick as the thought came another part of my brain would counteract it and I'd calm down and forget it. These flutters came and went.

I drove on and made Munich, Germany, where I pitched at a packed out campsite full of tourists for the beginning of the annual beer festival. Foreign eyes peered through my transparent mosquito shelter, and that made changing in it awkward. I began chatting with two British bikers who'd blasted down on similar bikes to what I'd owned two years before for a tour around the Germany BMW factory. The conversation went well, better then the second that I had next

44

with two male campers from Holland, on the left of my rig. I made the mistake of noting their small tent looked "rather cosy" and they took offence. To my right was a man and his bicycle. Sleeping in a cheap and worn tent, he'd little belongings and was obviously living out of the bike. There was a story here, and the guy looked miserable, so I decided to stick my nose in. The guy was German, called Yatz, and 50 years old. He'd been living on the campsite for several weeks after his wife had booted him out of the family home. Rooms in Munich are expensive so he'd little choice. His difficulty was compounded by having to get up every morning at 04:00hrs for the long ride to work. I offered to buy him a beer and despite language difficulties learned the greater story. He'd had an accident cycling in the Italian Alps, was hospitalised, and while in hospital had fell in love with an Ecuadorian nurse. When his wife found out he computed the campsite and new love of his life was worth more than his marriage. His wife would take him back if he denounced his new love. Problem was he couldn't. I suspected he didn't want to either. Yatz was having his own little adventure.

From Munich I drove over the Austrian alps towards Italy and passed through a beautiful and charming place sporting a deep blue lake. I've since tried to locate the place on a map, but as it was a little spec on the GPS and I didn't save the name, I've been unable to find it. It was perfect for a respite, offering swimming and leisurely strolls through clean and crisp air. Sometimes you know you have to revisit a place, and this is one of them. I stripped on a park bench and swam half the lake, then put my gear back on and continued on the long drive south.

As pleasant as middle Europe was, it reminded me of England, and hence I can't remember any significant points of interest because England didn't interest me at all. The fun would begin at Europe's edge; Greece. Subsequently the few days it took to reach and cross the Austrian Alps and into Italy were long and fairly monotonous.

Unsurprisingly I hadn't yet turned into a complete miser. I'd have to learn to control my desire for creature comforts and to stop wasting money on snacks. I still felt a need to shower every day, and I didn't suffer being wet very well. When it poured one evening I splashed €34 for a room in a little Inn. It was outside my budget by a long way, but that was the price of a heated, cosy room. Still, I felt like I'd hammered a toe. The difference,was my money wasn't being replaced. When it ran out the fun stopped. I had to make it go further and for longer.

I reached the outskirts of Venice at night and had difficulty finding anywhere to wild-camp. Perhaps it's because so much of the land is drained swamp.When I tried to discretely camp by a river I was noticed by a bunch of gypsies on the other side who went wild. What they spoke I couldn't understand, but I smelt trouble. It was late, dark and with no-one and nothing around there was a possibility I'd be turned over. I played it safe and left. Garmin came up with several campsites and I set off for the first on the list. I was repulsed by the £22 commanded per night but was out of options. In fairness the toilet facilities were hotel standard, but still it was way to much. Then again I've always found Northern Italy to be overly expensive.

The following morning I set off on the coastal road towards Accona where I'd catch the ferry to Patras, Greece. €132 bought a ticket for myself and the scooter on a slow boat that would take 20 hours and offered 'deck' space to sleep on.

Once aboard I forced myself to socialise, as it'd been far too long since I talked to anyone. A single woman sat at the table next to my camp bed (which I've brought up from the scooter) and I introduced myself. Finishing a degree in Florence, Italy, she was travelling to see her parents on Greek island Paros. As this was an island I'd be visiting we swapped emails and agreed to meet up again.

The weather was changing. It was humid, well into the 30's and I managed little sleep. I and the majority of the passengers awoke at 06:00hrs, in no small part because the crew began innovative vacuuming in the hope people would buy coffee and breakfast. As it happened I'd done a little innovation of my own by stocking up at a Lidl before the boat had set off. Unfortunately the milk I'd bought for my Muesli had leaked inside my 70 litre bag and saturated my spare clothes. The smell of festering milk lingered for the rest of the ferry trip.

Athens was a paltry 180 miles from Patros and driving off the ferry I was instantly back in love. There's something about Greece, it has just the right amount of dust, just the right amount of wear and tear, and everything looks dated. Then there's the people. Greeks have a passion for life, and while they mightn't reach their desires, they present energy in everything they do. Whether it be the way they eat, the way they socialise, drive or argue, there's energy in abundance.

I'd learned just after setting off from England that Kostas had booked a ferry for the weekend I was arriving to party island Ios. At the time he thought my scooter did more than 56mph and I'd be able to join him. I had the option of joining him the following day, otherwise I could stay at his over the weekend. The option was nullified when I found the ferry was fully booked, but I was happy nonetheless.

Kostas had called a friend named Stella to let me into his flat and hand over a set of keys. When I pulled up Stella turned up a few minutes later. She's the same age as us and rake thin. A pretty wee thing, she tried hard with her English and at the same time I tried not to damage her confidence by turning off my Geordie accent and speaking slow. Did I mention how thin she is? Looking at her, I wonder where her internal organs are stored.

The key opened the door to Kostas's flat and we let ourselves in and my jaw dropped. There was an unusual décor to this Athens flat. The owner had gone mad. Essentially Kostas had a vision, or an acid trip, and painted the walls an orange then graffitied over it in huge colourful letters the kind found on 80's subways. His leather sofas were non ergonomic and bright red, which apart from being tasteless also give an impression he was running a brothel. In the corner sat a broken bottle fridge and several emergency exit illumination signs. Kostas hadn't spent his money wisely. His place hadn't air conditioning and net-less windows only aided mosquitos to pass freely between outside and in. The bathroom sported a ceramic toilet that was somehow rusting and a decaying shower curtain half hanging from the rail. The connecting kitchen featured thirty empty or half-empty bottles of liquor in the corner. I liked what he'd done to the place, even if he'd lowered the resale value and made in unbearable to live in.

Stella was being polite and helpful and asked if I'd like to go to the beach and meet a few of her friends in the evening. Over the weekend we visited some excellent spots along the Athens coast line, swam in the sea and hung out at a few coffee bars. Meanwhile Kostas drank away on Ios.

48

The weekend passed and Kostas returned from island Ios on which he let up that he'd asked work about a week off but hadn't any confirmation as such, but that it would have to wait a week or so. I was annoyed, but I've learned to accept this from him. He doesn't plan anything. The island hopping would have to wait a week. I decided to spend the time fixing several items of equipment that needed my attention. Top on the list was to have my water damaged camera repaired. Being a Panasonic with a European warranty I put it into an Athens dealer to be fixed. To my disappointment the entire repair department was on holiday. You'd think they'd have staggered the holidays, but then this is Greece. I'd have to wait four weeks for the camera to be repaired which would mean no picture taking on the islands. I was on the trip of my life and I needed memories, as did the website. I travelled to a camera outfit situated close to the Athens parliament and bought a similar unit to cover the period. I'd sell one afterwards.

Most of the Euros I'd taken out in the U.K were spent which meant drawing off my cards. Only then did I learn about my mistake with the charges. Santander's debit card charged a minimum fixed fee and a percentage on every transaction while my credit card waved the minimum fee but charged a percentage and instant interest on cash withdrawals. I'd done a bad job on preparing a travel worth visa card. I explained this to Kostas and he arranged to supply me with Euros until I returned from the wedding. While in the UK I'd sort out a debit card more suited for travelling.

The top-box on my scooter had to go. It was ineffective at storing anything and I couldn't open the lid with something behind it. With it ditched I now had the option of using the

49

rack to carry the camp bed, which in turn meant the side panniers could be opened. The 70 litre bag that had sat on-top of the camp bed was now sitting lower down. Lowering the weight on two wheels mattered more than having it. It would transformed the convenience and effectiveness of living life on the road.

Greece in early August was too hot for motorcycle gear and few of the bikers wore helmets. At night many drive without lights and owners not seeing a need to swap out broken bulbs, and with no MOT style test many were in a state of disrepair. The driving style I found fairly aggressive and nobody indicated their intention to turn. I drove with assertion and kept my eyes on what was in front, rather than checking the mirrors and blind-spots. The mood was infectious and it wasn't long before I rode with my helmet flip-lid up, shorts and a t-shirt. Then I ditched the helmet.

I had an opportunity to sort the visas so I set about enquiring with the Indian, Pakistan and Iranian consulates about applications, hoping I could apply, do the Greek Islands and then pick up my passport on my return. The Iranian consulate couldn't provide a visa but helpfully noted it was easy to accomplish in Turkey. The Pakistani consulate hadn't a clue, stating that I could, and I use the words of an officer there, "definitely maybe", receive a transit visa on the border. The Indian consulate directed me to a third party processing centre that was asking about €100, which was non-refundable and which could only be granted for three months and with various bank statement printouts and a letter explaining why I wasn't applying from my home country. After thinking it through I decided to delay the visa process again, this time until Istanbul, Turkey, where I knew for sure I could apply for the Indian ($52 dollars) and Iranian (£150) visas. The

Pakistani visa wasn't a surety but from what I read online the closer one came to the country of entry the easier and cheaper a visa became. It made sense to try in Turkey, or even Iran.

Mid-week I decided to go ahead and begin the island hopping. I booked a ferry to the small Greek island Kythnos for the Friday. Kostas would join a few days after I'd left. In the meanwhile with Kostas at work I had to entertain myself for two days. It had been a couple days since my last swim in the ocean and I left Thursday morning to follow the Athens coast line and swim at multiple points along it. For the first swim I used my diving goggles to swim alongside many blue/yellow stripped fish. I worked out that if I came in from behind rather than down onto them they were unafraid. This was my first free dive on larger fish and I swam among them at a distance of just a foot. I'd a big grin on my face. For the second swim I decided a challenge was in order. Out to sea was a small rocky island at what I judged to be half a mile out. I could just make out a few huts and tiny boats on it. As I'd been swimming this distance every other day back in the U.K. I judged it doable. I set off in ferocious sun, and I wont lie, it took a lot longer than I'd anticipated. My left knee was in pain from overdoing breast-stroke and the lack of suntan cream on anywhere I hadn't managed to reach on my back had left those areas somewhat crispy. My face was toast.

When I reached the island I looked back over to the mainland, whereon I realised another error on my part; I had no landmark to aim for, and it was a big coastline. I could only hope things would become clearer as I became closer to the shore. The swim back went a little quicker, probably as I had the tide on my side, but when I reached the shoreline I couldn't see the bike or anything memorable. I was at completely the wrong point, and unable to determine if the

51

bike was to my left or right.

"Crap.", I thought out loud.

I chose to go right and began walked the broken shore line in just my swimming shorts. The sun had baked the concrete all day and my feet literally burned like a stone baked pizza. I couldn't stand on an unshaded area without hopping. The suntan lotion had long washed off and subsequently my once pale white skin took another hit.

After 20 minutes of walking and cussing I gave up and flagged down a taxi. The bemused driver and I doubled back a couple mile and with two pairs of eyes found the scooter. I drove back to Kostas's flat, downed a couple litre of water and lay down dizzy with sunstroke. On Thursday I drank several more litres and didn't urinate at all. I didn't sleep much as every body part was cooked and putting weight on the skin caused such pain.

The following days were spent in soreness as my skin began to heal, but then I couldn't let stupidity get in the way of my adventure. I'd a ferry to catch.

Chapter 6

Greek Islands

Kythnos, a small fishing island situated west of the Greek mainland, has a small population of around 1,500 people. It isn't a tourist destination even for the natives, but the idea of visiting a remote island where I could feel a little lost suited me fine. The boat arrived early morning at 10:30hrs but due to all the tightly packed vehicles that were remaining on it for subsequent islands, I couldn't find my scooter, and the steward couldn't get past the tightly packed to search for it. By the time it was found several seniors were venting their frustration as the boat was being delayed. One pushed the back of the scooter while I was putting the front bag on, just as well really, as the ramp was starting to lift as I powered off the boat and into the port.

The port was a shoe horn in design and featured a small beach with a few restaurants, ferry agents and little shops. Back in England the people on beaches tend to have pot bellies and horrible skin. Here the people were toned, looked healthy and had deep tanned skin. I was jealous of the males with their six packs. My stomach wasn't bad, but I wasn't ribbed either. I wondered if a heavy diet of fish was the answer. Perhaps I needed to follow the trend and do what every other Greek does; smoke. I'd decided well before the trip to do something about it but for all the swimming and gym sessions the effort hadn't visibly shown. Packs of Jammie Dodgers hadn't helped my cause.

I'd already decided to wild camp (Greeks call it free camping) and to ride all the major roads on the small island. The sun was powerful with temperature in the high 30's, and with my skin still recovering from the burning I upped the cream to factor 50 on my face and covered up as best I could. I stuck the helmet on the back of the bike, donned my trusty sun-hat and fake Ray Bans, and set-off on one of the two dusty roads.

As I ventured higher and further away from the port the remoteness calmed my worries and I felt, for the first time since setting off, a sense of peace. I stopped under some leafy shade and cooked some pasta. After I road the rest of the road, briefly admiring a few deserted beaches. The heat hadn't helped my brakes, nor had the load the scooter was carrying, and alarmingly the front wheel began disconcerting sliding on even minor corners. I nearly lost it twice. The front brake became very noisy as it overheated and reduced its effectiveness. Apart from that everything was peachy.

The last beach was positioned south at a place named Agios Dimitrois and I was expecting it to be more populated. When I say populated, I mean it would actually have a population count above zero. By the time I arrived the sun, now lower in the sky, had made the sea popular with the local Greeks, and many had came out to enjoy its diminishing power. I joined them, my first time in the sea since the silly swim at Athens.

However much I, like everyone else, dreamed of small and secluded places, the reality of it is best served in small doses.

By the end of that day I'd travelled all the island had to offer and felt a strangely crushing need to move on. I needed to learn to relax. Would it come with time? With it came small panic flutters. I was fighting myself over the unknown that was to come, and while trying to be positive and of the possibilities, I couldn't help but worry all the same.

The sun began its fall beneath the horizon and produced glorious deep rays over the sea. I propped myself against a tree on the curved sand dune, hat on my head, ready to enjoy it. The beach was mostly empty, but a stunning young female in a pink bikini was relay running the sand only several metres away from where I sat. As I watched her I missed the fantastic sunset and my worries all but disappeared. I fell asleep and didn't awake until the next morning.

Sifnos is a slightly larger island situated a little south west of Kythnos and appealed because of a popular and recommended campsite. I still hadn't acclimatised to living without a shower every other day, and left Kythnos in the morning itching from the sea salt. The island also had a reputation for excellent beaches and after short ferry hop I set about trying to find a one suitable for free diving, where I'd hope I could swim alongside tropical fish. Wearing a white vest to protect from the searing sun, I spent a few hours scouring the island for one but to no avail. The campsite was situated at the port of Kamares, and the owner was friendly and customer service was good. The toilets, showers and facilities were clean and the in-house shop matched the prices offered by of the local community. That didn't mean commodities were cheap, far from it. As it was high season the camping ground was packed out and I had to squeeze my foldable camp bed into an area offering little shade.

On the second day I explored east and south of the islands port. Many of the roads were rough and my venerable scooter struggled with its desperately poor ground clearance. I hammered on regardless. Typically the little roads I followed would lead upwards and end at a small white church watching out over the sea. Nobody was ever around, and usually the church would be unlocked and I'd enter for a short peak. The churches were built on the best locations on the island, a nod to the importance of Christianity in Greece.

Knowing that I'd done little for the website I knew I had to work on a few videos. Doing so would increase traffic, but I'd also an interest in learning how to do it well. Attaining footage of myself and the bike required setting up the camera, riding back, shooting the footage and doubling back to collect the camera. Then there was the syncing of the audio captured on the Zoom H1 microphone, as the camera didn't feature a microphone input. Having spent the best part of half a day sorting three minutes of video, I knew that a cameraman would be needed if I were to keep the standard high and time consumption low, so I gave up.

Prices on Sifnos were a little cheaper than Kythnos and I usually went by the price of a bottle of water. For these two islands, 1.5 litres cost €0.80 and €1 respectfully. In both cases it was high. Fuel was really expensive at nearly €2/litre, the highest I'd paid so far. Fruit and veg, was disproportionally high at double the price of the U.K.

The social scene was sparse and at night I found myself at the Pirate Cafe, which while expensive (beer was €5 while the bar next door charged €2.50), offered a friendly atmosphere. The owner's wife was American and they lived in Thailand when the Greek tourism dropped off. Nice life. I wandered into the main town of Apollonia and found the crowd in the main street to be full of young couples, which led me to believe the island was a Santorini for locals. There were only a few bars and while they stayed open late they were all empty. After that I became a Pirate Cafe regular. It seemed to be the only place where I could chat to people. On the second evening I met an older couple from Wales and they offered useful advice on where to go and eat. As it was a Friday I was determined to see if the town really did come alive in the early hours, and I kept drinking. The bar staff reckoned by 02:00hrs the town would be heaving. So at this time, and intoxicated on the beer they were serving, I fetched the scooter and drove up to find out. Again I left disappointed.

Paros is a large island situated north east of Kythnos. It's positioned in the middle of so many other islands and has become a central hub for reaching other islands. Paros is popular with Greeks during the summer but still has a large bustling crowd drinking winter and ferries to the mainland are frequent and run all year. It seemed a better bet to find people to talk too.

Many Greek families use Paros as a primary vacation spot, yet on arrival I quickly discovered the place to be overrun with slightly post-teenage French, which to the dislike of the local business, were being thrifty with their money. The French were happy sitting on the promenade with supermarket booze until one of the islands two club opened at 03:00hrs (yes, you read that time correctly). Beforehand the smaller bars tried to tempt them off the streets with cheap 'happy-hour' liquor, however it had little effect.

Most of the activity was around the port of Parikia, where I wasn't, at least not to begin with. Instead I spent the first day at Naoussa, the islands second largest town which is situated to the north of the island. It was here that I stayed at a shameful campsite. The toilets and showers at this site were vile, clearly they were washed down once a month, with piss.

The main part of town was splendid, but the views and authenticity was diminished by the amount of tourists. At night I found no genuine bars, just coffee outlets. I avoided the big club for it seemed hideously pompous for an economy in deep recession and charged an equally hideous €12 entrance fee. There was a good reason for this; because Greeks don't order multiple drinks. Why would they when a cocktail cost €12? The club would ensure a massive queue developed outside to give the impression that inside it was packed out. It was all part of the exclusivity, the brand, and the enticement to join the other very important, selected individuals who'd queued because they weren't worth it. Sheep to the slaughter.

The next day I moved away from the town and slowly along the east coast where the beaches and rock pools were stunning and void of tourists. It felt more as what Greece should be, and I thoroughly enjoyed cruising the easy going road by myself. By the end of the day I was back at the port of Parikia where I'd originally came aboard the island and began sniffing around for something fun. I wondered into town and discovered the price of a beer was less than 50% that of other local islands, and much cheaper than in Naoussa. This was a good thing and I intended to make the most of it. Before beginning the evening festivities I should've found a campsite, but earlier I'd had a look around the more eastern side of the island and found it quite bare and open; perfect wild camping territory. One such area was *Palm Beach,* a small stretch along the south east coast and it's remote sand looked ideal for a wild camp. I'd filled my solar shower for the first time and was keen to give it a tryout, plus I was living life too comfortably, so I was keen to force a little suffering on myself after I'd drank a bit too much beer. I parked the scooter at the port fully laden and took my backpack and helmet on a trek to find a suitable bar. I was largely disappointed, finding mostly restaurant or taverns, but I did happen upon a bar called Entropy. Entering, it was 21:00hrs and empty, but I got chatting to the owner, an American ex-pat, and settled into the cheap €2 happy-hour beers on offer. Several young French turned up, then some very friendly Greeks, with one in particular who kept ordering group tequilas. On round five she ran out of money and I bought the next two. Then she borrowed from her mate for the next. I expected my liver to file a personal injury claim. An older Denmark expat called Leon, a carpenter, turned up and then several linguistic Americans. Behind my back, 'ping pong' beer had begun between the bar owner and a young lad and his brother from Holland. I began talking to a Nigerian girl whom, as I recall, sold tourist crap (wrist bands and such). She had a thing about the British for their exploitation of Nigerian resources and subsequent suffering in the local populaces. I did my best to mediate and affirm that the U.K government/big business and the general public are separate entities and it didn't take long to win her over. At 04:00hrs I should've had to drive my bike to a wild camp area, which at my level of intoxication was nigh on impossible, but by fortune the several Americans in the bar owned a property and offered a spare room to crash in. By 05:30hrs I was at their house, which had an incredible slipway into the sea. In the darkness we stripped, and with star constellations clear in the sky we went for a lazy float in the Aegeon sea. The night was exactly what I was looking for.

I slept for just a couple hours and yet awoke with a fresh head. I was worried about my scooter, or what was going to be left of the equipment on it, so I departed and hurried down to the port. Everything was fine. The Americans had mentioned a small boat cruise the following day which I said I'd try to make, but I wasn't sure how many days I could afford to spend on Paros. Potentially I would leave a few days later and go back to Athens to start the two week stint with Kostas around Eastern Europe. That was all based on whether Kostas secured the time off work. Before then, I simply had to squeeze in a day on Antiparos.

Antiparos is exactly what the name suggests. It sits right next to Paros and the short boat ride doesn't take long at all. Antiparos secured a reputation in the 70's for attracting hippies and offering a chilled out vibe. Since then tourist exploitation has took some of that magic away. It's still quiet, and a great place to disappear, which is probably the reason behind Tom Hanks and Madonna buying houses on the island.

Once the small ferry docked I ventured without delay onto the *official* nudest beach, in hope of seeing beautiful topless young women. Instead, viewing material came in the form of naked German men in their 50's, and I quickly found myself in the sea rather than on the beach.

I booked into the only campsite at Antiparos, which was fair enough. Rooms, if you could call them that, were simple partitions made from bamboo cane. It was sound, but again I felt like the magic it secured decades ago was amiss. Now it was relying on a bygone reputation, one which was dwindling ever further thanks to high prices and showers that merely pumped warm sea water. The sea behind the campsite was walkable to a huge distance and the area clean with an untouched feel to it. It was quiet, chilled and a positive, beautiful place to find myself at.

Later I drove the scooter around the other side of the island, which didn't take long, and looking up I spotted a small white church at the peak of the island. Getting to it looked like a challenge but I set off on an hour of off-road trail riding knowing the view would be worth it. I reached the little church in the later afternoon. On a crumbling wall, a large Greek flag donning and flapped in the wind. The view over the island and the surrounding sea was spectacular.

That evening I was tired, the previous night on Paros had caught up, and I had only a single beer at the campsite cafe before going to bed. While lying in my mosquito shelter I received a text message from Kostas stating that he couldn't secure three weeks off work all in one go. Instead he's join me tomorrow for a week around the islands, go back to work for a week and then take two off for the Eastern Europe trip. This was unfortunate as I'd hoped for three weeks rather than a bad dash, but there was nothing to be done. The time we'd have for Eastern Europe was cut. At least it would give me a chance to meet up with Maria, the girl I'd met on the boat on the way to the first island, and to visit some smaller and secluded islands dotted around The Cyclades. After Eastern Europe I'd fly back for the wedding.

The following day I returned to Paros and awaited at the port for Kostas, who arrived by super-fast ferry without his Ducati and a very large backpack. I queried how on earth I would carry all my gear, and him, and his backpack on my scooter, but he just jumped on top of the big bag on my passenger seat and it was done. The scooter was now taller than it was in length, and handling became flagitious. We stayed the night at

61

the campsite to the left of the port, downed a few at Entropy the bar where I'd met the Americans et all and ended the day visiting Maria over at her parents tennis court, where we played chess.

We left the following day in search of small islands neither one of us had visited before. Kostas was keen to expand his island repertoire, and so was I, so we left the mainstream and went in search of the secluded. The adventure was on.

Koufonisia is an island made from two two small islets, a term used to describe two islands technically adjoined but with a small area of water passing between them. In the case of Koufonisia, one islet is sparsely inhabited and the other mostly empty. A small island, it's usually missed on the map as it's size is even smaller than Kyfnos, the first island I'd visited. It sounded like a perfect place to explore.

The boat from Paros was small and the water choppy. I rarely get sea-sick, but by the time we arrived, in the latter part of the evening, I was suffering.

On the boat we heard rumours that said the islanders didn't like free campers and would throw their gear into the sea. Giving this was our plan, we set off in search of an isolated stretch that would offer a low profile. It was dark and the road began with tarmac, diminished into dirt, then degraded into stones and rocks. I required a dirt bike, which I didn't have, and the heavily laden scooter received damage to the lower body, plastics and to the centre stand. The spring on that was ripped off and it noisily trailed and bashed on the ground as we edged forward towards the far end of the island.

When we saw it, we knew it. A perfect alcove faced out

towards the sea. The weather had eroded the land flat while the walls give us protection from being seen. There were no dwellings, land exploitation or human activity. Here, genuine undisturbed island rock met the barrenness of the open sea. It was raw, and quite perfect.

We used my petrol stove to cook a tuna paste mix devoid of any taste then headed into the small area of town, leaving our belongings and camp gear to the mercy of whoever, if anyone, were to happen upon them. The town offered little, but a small outlet offered tubs of the finest ice-cream I'd tasted yet. The one tavern on the island offered poor quality draught beer, we sank one and then left.

By the time we got back to our cove it was dark. Really dark. The moon wasn't anywhere to be seen and with the scooters headlight switched off neither of us could see our hands held out in front of our face. What natural light there was, it came from the distant stars, and looking up, we'd the most brilliantly crystal clear view of the universe. The detail and clarity I shan't forget. I'm sure Kostas, like myself, didn't sleep straight away, but lay on his back for hours in sheer awe. When my eyes finally submitted, the air was crisp and I fell into a deep sleep.

Breakfast was a half-tin of sweet-corn and green beans used from the evening supper the night before.

Now that it was light we could see how thin this part of the island was, a mere 200 metres or so between the sides. On one was a gentile decline and a sandy beach. On the other, daggered cliffs and a long drop into the clear sea. The question we were both asking each other, was who had the bottle to tombstone it. To find out if we'd live through it, we opted to check the depth of the sea below first. Entering the crystal clear water and using my diving goggles, we determined the depth to be a good 10 to 15 metres. While in the water we found a number of caves, some of which passed through one another via underwater crevices. We tried to outdo each others bravado by seeing who could make it through without scorning the jagged rock or touching any of the spiked ball fish clinging to the sides. The sea was pretty rough and added to the challenge.

Back on land and again looking at the long jump, the sun was baking hot and the wind picking up. We guessed the height to be between 20 to 30 meters. I went first and dithered for several minutes before leaping off. I let out a girly shriek on the way down, fully warranted it was. The impact, and it really was quite an impact, tore a large scab from my leg and slammed my backside like a train. Kostas was next and aligned himself for the jump. Treading water, I looked up at his small face knowing that it was worse than it looked.

"It's fine! Get it done you big girl!".

He dithered for an eternity, and then bottled it.

In the late afternoon we spent an hour on the beach on the opposite side of the island and then made our way back to our campsite to see what was around that area. Amazingly, directly below our alcove appeared to be a semi water logged tunnel leading to an inaccessible part of the island. It was like something from *The Famous Five*. Inspecting it, the rough sea would engulf the tunnel with a wave and then subside, letting us briefly peer through. We scaled the cliff to the side of our cove and found another larger cove that had been dug out of the island, only the cove was closed to the sea other than through the tunnel. It was down to sea level with its very own beach, quite unique. Only one thing was on our minds; could we get through the tunnel?

After the previous bottling Kostas had yet to redeem himself and this time he led the way with an inspection using my new camera. From the sand I pleaded at him not to do this, but he ignored my woes and swam out to the tunnels entrance. He reported back that light from the other side wasn't so far away and that the tunnel was thin but sufficiently deep enough that we could stay away from its jagged top. While relaying this vital information, water entered my replacement camera.

That day the sea was too rough to swim the tunnel and we decided to revisit later in the day once the wind had calmed down. In the meantime we went back to town and picked up some sausages. As my previous effort to make a "pasta bake" using my petrol cooker and mess tins didn't turn out for the best, I put Kostas in charge of making some sort of ambitious casserole. Somehow he did a surprisingly excellent job, but throughout I scorned him for breaking my new camera. I told him the "food was shit" and that he was a "complete pansy for not jumping the cliff" earlier that day.

In the late afternoon with the wind having subsided we both swam through the tunnel. Kostas went first this time and I followed with reluctance, expecting to have lungs full of seawater by the time I exited the other side. With the wind down it was a straight forward and less daring exercise than it had looked. As my head came out the water on the other side I found Kostas several meters away haplessly swimming with an unusual stroke. Was he in distress? In fact he'd needed an urgent turd, and with pants down was swimming and excreting at the same time. Key to his success was to swim and squat faster then the current would bring the poop back on himself. Hilarious!

I very much enjoyed Koufonisia but we wanted to continue around further non touristic islands and the next was Amorgos, and a small boat left Koufonisia for it at 17:00hrs that day. With a few hours to spare, Kostas made good by tomb stoning the cliff he'd bottled the day before, then we packed up and left. The three hour boat ride was unpleasant and we arrived nauseous and sea-sick, but this was offset by the great memories we'd brought from Koufonisia.

Amorgos is a fair sized island situated further away from the Paros-Naxos Cyclades, and one of the most western islands in that particular group. Primarily a fishing island, a small amount of fame came in 1989 when a French film called *The Deep Blue* was made there. From then it built a reputation for clear seas and volcanic stone type beaches that give the coastal water an iconic deep blue reflection. Its economy is based on fishing and some tourism during the summer, but it's by no means a popular tourist destination. I'd learned about Amorgos while researching free-diving areas, and what stuck out was a shipwreck on the coast.

Amorgos had a major town called Chora, or Hora to the locals. The port, where we disembarked, was a busy spot and offered fabulous scenery and iconic cuisine from locally sourced fresh fish. It was the perfect place to moor a luxury yacht, and that was why many had done just that. Those with money came here to wine and dine, and that made it expensive, so we left it for later. Although the sun had yet to set, time was getting on, and our first priority was to find a campsite and take a shower. The island offered two close to one another and the first we checked out seemed fine. It was also cheap. I set up my cot bed and noted that like Koufonisia, the island was strangely mosquito free.

As Kostas had to be back at work the day after the next we had the following day to explore Amorgos and then we'd take a morning boat to the island of Naxos and then an evening boat to the mainland. My itinerary and timeframe were different as I'd another week or so before heading back to England for the wedding, however Naxos was a hub for getting to other islands, namely Mykinos and Santorini. We both booked tickets to Naxos at the port, put on our best attire, and drove the winding road up to Hora. Near the top we parked the scooter and then continued through the intertwined alleyways expecting to find some sort of atmosphere. It was dark, save for a few underpowered candlelight bulbs, but it made for a pleasant walk. On the "street", where taverns pumped out jazz and locals sat zombified, we discovered there was only two bars to the place, and neither were jamming. At one of the many outdoor restaurants we tackled and failed to eat a monstrously large pizza. Bagging some for the following breakfast, we downed a couple beers at one of the homely bars and eventually left. The night was fine, but we both wanted a bit more Mykinos zing to the evening. Amorgos was simply the wrong island for it.

The following day we drove the island and stopped at a few of the pebble beaches along the coast. Most of the Amorgos coast was cliff, high above sea level, with beaches reachable by a sharp decent. Compared to Koufonisia, we found the islands shores lacked character as there were no caves, no challenges, and no diving opportunities within easy reach. Despite this the one particular area of interest to us was the shipwreck and having toured the island all day we sought it out. Crashed by pirates in 1979, we swam around the decaying wreck and I dived below and through its collapsed middle section. Unfortunately the sea was badly polluted. The shore line, difficult to access, had made cleaning troublesome and so it hadn't be done. Flotsam was everywhere and we didn't stay long.

We spent another night at the campsite and in the morning caught the ferry to Naxos the large sister island to Paros. Kostas had to be home the day after that and I would spend a few days on Santorini. I'd yet to decide whether to fit Mykonos into the itinerary. I'd spoken to a French girl back on Paros and she'd given me some of the prices she'd been paying over there. It would be correct to say my eye brows had been raised. I was on a finite budget not a two week holiday, and I had to be sensible. At the same time I was in search of fun. It was a shame the fun wasn't coming cheap. Hell, I was finding even the ferries to be expensive.

Naxos, a family island, isn't a favourite with those preferring fun and nightlife, but more than enough Greeks visit it to make it a busy and happening place. On arrival we checked into a campsite Kostas had learned about from his mother and then joined others at the peak of the port where the sunset refracted over the stones and people. After the sun dipped below the horizon we drank a few beer and relaxed in the port region. Being fairly large, Naxos is well equipped with many taverns, restaurants and bars, but it's chilled out and not an island for night-life.

The following day we drove the entire island, stopping at many of its beaches. Away from the port Naxos was pretty barren, but you don't need much more than two wheels, sun, your health and good food. I thoroughly enjoyed the day.

Trouble began in the evening when Kostas couldn't find a ticket back to Athens. Being the end of August, the holidayers were on their way home, and the flow of traffic had reversed meaning all the boats were full. Luckily for him a company had chartered an additional boat an hour after the first.

I wasn't so lucky. The ferries were following a loop, because that's where the money was. With ferries transferring to different routes, tickets to Santorini, which was against the flow, were minimal. I could find one for me but not the scooter. The situation was worse on Santorini and it looked that if I got there with the scooter then I could become trapped, unable to leave. It was the same story for most the week. No travel agency could guarantee anything. The same went for Mykinos. I couldn't afford any delay into the Eastern European trip so with reluctance I made the decision to spend the remaining time I had left (while Kostas was working) exploring a small Greek island at the southern point of the mainland, rather than finding myself stuck in the Cyclades. I joined Kostas on his return to Athens.

While Kostas went back at work I put the second broken camera in for repair, had the aftermarket variator that I'd sent over from England fitted, and drove to the small island of Patroklos where I spent a few days lounging aimlessly on its coastline. It was sound, but after experiencing constant companionship I found it difficult to revert to a singular existence. I'd plenty of time to think, and I released how nihilistic and laid-back I was becoming. The trip still had it's objectives but I wasn't so worried about reaching them. I wasn't worrying about money, not yet, and I wasn't worrying... about anything. I found myself wanting to speak and socialise with the locals more than I wanted to drive my wheels.

Chapter 7

Eastern Europe

As my scooter was considerably slower than Kosta's Ducati 600 Monster, I pushed ahead a day early towards the first Eastern European country on our list, Bulgaria. The long motorway bore was occasionally disrupted by a wobble caused by one of my wheels rolling through a sunken section of tarmac, and the reason for that was the sizzling heat. Boy it was hot. In preparation for this I'd ditched my Nolan full face helmet and bought a cheap open face replacement. My riding was changing, I was no longer so interested in listening to music on the go, preferring the noise and wind instead.

I headed towards the capital of Sofia at 60mph knowing that Kostas wouldn't be far behind. At the Bulgarian border vehicles turned on their headlights and religiously respected the 60km/h limit in built up areas, and disregarded it entirely outside them. Aggression, acceleration and harsh braking took over. The worse driving I'm seen yet came when an underpowered 4x4 vehicle two cars in front of me overtook a lorry and couldn't pull in due to another lorry being in front of the first. The driver ended up playing chicken with an oncoming van, which waived first, slammed on his brakes, left the road and flipped into a ditch.

What a contrast to Western Europe. Exiting a main road with a tight angle proved troublesome as my scooters top speed would result in a queue of impatient Bulgarians sat right up my backside . I frequently heard the screeching of tyres as drivers realised last minute I was braking for the turn. When I finally made Sofia I began looking for a hostel I'd heard about and was shunted at traffic lights by a lorry. The camping bed took the brunt and nothing was broken, but my neck was sore. The driver reversed and left. Nobody stopped. Several got on their horns demanding I got out the way.

I finally found the excellent hostel called *Hostel Mostel.* It was cheap, friendly, had hotel like quality and a large base of travellers all converging in its large ground level lounge. While socialising I received a text message from Kostas. The chain on his Ducati has snapped. Deja-vu, we'd had this the year before. He was being recovered home whereon he'd fit a replacement the following day and try again. Over a hot chocolate I scorned his existence. An hour later I received another message from Kostas. Sadly the mother of a very good friend of his has unexpectedly passed away and he'd attend the funeral in northern Greece which will delay his arrival another day or two. I knew he and Miltos were close friends and I was sad for him.

I parked the scooter up in the hostel area and walked around the centre of Sofia. Ultimately parking the bike up was a better way to explore an area as I didn't have to worry about it. Plus it was safer.

I honestly couldn't believe how cheap Bulgaria was. The price of petrol here wasn't much more than £1 per litre. Food cost nothing, like a quarter the prices back in England. Beer worked out at a little over £1 a pint, whereas I was paying the equivalent of £5 or more in Athens. If Asia was even cheaper then this my money would stretch further than I thought.

Walking around the Park National Palace of Culture I appreciated the remaining Russian influenced architecture and ended up at a large concrete monument. A young kid came over and asked something in his mother tongue. My English seemed to offend him. It wasn't the first time I was seeing such a response from the locals. On the locals, I was wondering where they all were. Sofia was empty, especially devoid of young people. There was a reason for this but I'd only learn it later.

Back at the hostel I met an Iranian called Ali who began offering tips on my upcoming excursion through Iran. His first, was not to go. He was pretty negative about his country, especially the political side of it. I got the impression he'd absconded from the military or something along those lines and that going back wouldn't be good for him.

On the second day, with Kostas now in Northern Greece, I took an organised trip to the Rila Monastery. Despite its uniqueness I couldn't help but feel disappointed at the installation of shops selling bottled water inside the centre temple. It was a shameful, showing the lengths people will go to to extract money from tourism. On the third day I joined a group of tourists for an organised tour around the city, as organised by the University there. The students tasked to lead the trip didn't turn up, and I, like the rest of the tourists, ended up doing a walk on my own.

Later that evening I joined a bar crawl with three 18yr old lads from Kent. It started well enough with an Armenian palatially drunk on spirits and loud rock music. The *kids* had come to Sofia expecting night-life, but the city was deserted and the subsequent bars reflected this. Too many times we walked a long corridor to find we were the only ones in the place. The last bar looked a better bet, certainly seedy and low drum enough to meet my expectations. Manned by three beefy leathered doormen, they rejected the 18yr old lads outright, took one look at my trainers, and said something in Bulgarian. Fuck off, probably.

In the morning, and with no news from Kostas, I decided to drive over to the black sea coast and to the city of Varna. Several fellow hostellers had commented on this being a particularly worthy destination, and all noted the availability of semi-naked massages offered on the beach. On the drive eastwards I stopped at a little picnic area to the side of the motorway. The picnic area featured trees, benches, grass, … and three MIG 21 fighter jets!

European investment in Varna was immediately evident. The centre of town was modern and dwarfed Sofia in terms of the amount of people and things to do. It felt like the real capital. A little north outside of the centre was the black-sea and the sand and resorts that come with it. One of the more infamous is the *Golden Sands* resort, and it was here that I arrived late in the evening. The place looked fun. Entwined between bars and the odd club were huge casinos and non Western Europe tourists. I had a quick look around and then spent too long trying to find a very difficult to find hostel. The days riding caught up on me and after a pizza I was in bed and fast asleep.

A little after midnight I was awoken by the arrival of Kostas. I was impressed that he found the hostel so easily for he'd no map or GPS. I was even more impressed that he'd done twice the distance I'd done that day. Kostas had visited Sofia the year before and so had pushed on.

In the morning we took a stroll down to the Golden Sands resort. The daylight exposed the place for what it really was. Among an awful miniature Eiffel tower, the Kebab King shops, with the same logo as Burger King but with the name changed, were tattoo shops and outlets selling so called poppers and fun pills. The place was tasteless, tacky, and full of gangsters, or at least people dressed like gangsters. The place sucked. We left with no intention of going back.

The more time I spent in Bulgaria the more I came to believe that Bulgarians don't like foreigners. In my experience, only those who work with tourists are helpful, while the rest are stubborn and arrogant. I'm generalising, but asking for directions, which one might expect either a shrug of shoulders or a shake of the head, would instead warrant anything from a scorn to a stern tongue lashing.

Average wages in Bulgaria were just €300. According to a few elders that I managed to speak to, the biggest problem facing Bulgaria was the young leaving to find better and higher paying jobs in Western Europe. This was why Sofia seemed so empty. There was disparity between the retail shops found in Varna and the average wage, being as hardly anyone here could afford the items on offer. Varna came across as a town that has procured investment, and while the E.U has ploughed money into improving the road infrastructure, it's hard not to feel a bit cynical over it benefiting the foreign investors and their BMW X6's than the local populace.

Kostas and I didn't think much of the first hostel with it's tiny rooms and smelly carpets and so we shifted to another about 5km from the city centre. Run by a gentleman from Birmingham and costing just £5, we had a great room and a very pleasant stay for the night. A previous builder back in the U.K, the owner was one of the many foreigners that had bought property at the start of the new millennium for nothing, expecting a housing boom when Bulgaria joined the E.U. When it didn't happen many pulled out, putting further pressure on house prices. Subsequently there are many empty properties available for low prices. Closer to the coast the prices go up, but slightly inland dwellings are available for a song. The owner commented on corruption and mafia dominance, both apparently rife. His little tourist business was too small to attract attention, but bigger businesses are a target for protection rackets and the like.

Varna had a decent, if unusual, night life. For the evening we were recommended a restaurant called *Alba.* I will state on record right now that they served the best food I've ever tasted. Multiple courses for two cost under €15. I can't even remember what I had, it was that good. Afterwards we tried to find bars and clubs for a few social beers and the bread crumbs led us to the beach front. Playing English hits overdubbed or re-sang in Bulgarian, the young danced wildly in what looked like a lax martial art. A few a few too many cocktails later, I was outside urinating against a military boat parked on the inner promenade, as you do, then we called it a night.

Believing Varna had little else to offer, and with not much more than a week left, we mounted the wheels and headed north up the black sea coast towards Romania. Just after the border we stopped at a small but pretty village built along the beach where we had yet another pizza. The people here were friendly, going out their way to show us where a working cashpoint was. I was determined to spend at least five minutes in the black sea, it would be the only chance I'd get, so I did, and came out surprised by the lack of salt content.

I'd a stereotypical vision of Romania being a country of ragged gypsies being pulled along by horse and cart. The reality was far from it. The roads, the people, the way of life, they were all clean, organised and European like. It felt modern.

We drove towards the capital Bucharest and made it in time to check into a popular hostel, one at which I felt way to old. Run by teenagers, it was like a university bar full of freshers. Washing dirty linen in my collapsable bucket took my mind of it, then we hit the old city, which by no coincidence was where the pubs were. Walking and taking in the sights, Bucharest was just another large bustling European city. Full of advertising and relatively high priced, I wasn't too concerned with spending any further time there. The following day I was happy to move on.

We made poor progress towards the final city on our jaunt, Budapest, and ended up wild camping at the side of a road quite high up on a pass. In the dark and using the light from our head-lights we cooked a quick pasta soup. Large trees cast shadows around our site and looking down over the side of the pass afforded a view of a small town. I was happy here, but Kostas was worried about large paw marks on the ground, which was more his problem than mine for not bringing suitable camping gear. I rested in my raised army cot, feeling quite comfortable and safe.

On the way to Budapest we planned visit Bran Castle, know for hosting the fictional character Count Dracula. As a child I'd read the books and the curious place called Transylvania but then that word had vanished. Until a week before I'd had no idea it was a state in Romania. The castle was functional and less of a show of power and more of a lookout. It's position, like all castles, was chosen it's a tremendous view over the land and the road below, a road that would be used in any attack. The castle is now operated by a company set up by the inheritors and is charging too much for entrance, but then the more I was on the gravy train the more I felt like I was being overly keen to bitch and bemoan at every possibility, especially when I had to dip into the pot.

There was a second castle for which I'd copied the GPS co-ordinates from wikipedia. Either wikipedia lied, or I'd made a critical reading error, and in entrusting Garmin we ventured into the middle of no-where. It was actually a pleasant enough drive loosing ourselves like that, but the calmness terminated as abruptly as the small road we were travelling along. Without any warning at all, the tarmac road ended in a potholed mess. I hit it at about 50mph and found the front brake too eager to lock the wheel up. The scooter part jumped as the weak suspension and heavy load jostled it in the air. My iPhone left its holder and went bouncing onto the road. Feeling like a wide-body aircraft after an emergency landing, the scooter came to a halt and I walked back to pick up the phone. I turned it over and found it still navigating, but with the words 'You have reached your destination' on it's now smashed screen. We hadn't. I turned the now broken holder on my scooter upside down and taped the phone into place.

Although we asking the locals, we failed to make the second castle, and without maps or any knowledge on its whereabouts, we gave up and continued towards Budapest. An hour or so later I lost Kostas in my mirror, which meant he'd either stopped or had broken down. Usually he'll give a petrol low thumbs-down warning so I expected the latter, especially given the condition of his Ducati. Curiously I turned around and back tracked, and then found him at a petrol station in what appeared to be a state of mental breakdown. His bike was venting steam, but there was no way for it to be a water leak. In fact, the hose connecting his tank to the carbs had split resulting in a massive petrol leak. As it ran down onto the extremely hot exhaust headers on his bike and boiled off, I had two questions. Why had he stopped alongside a fuel pump, and what was the flash point of petrol?

I was genuinely impressed at the speed at which Kostas was ripping the luggage from his bike and the speed at which he found his swiss army knife. Perhaps it was some sort of fortuitous planning, doubtful, but he had the tank up in no time. The fuel line had ripped in two, a combination of having never been replaced and the heat of Greece. He called me over to squeeze the line, which I presumed would relieve him to source a knife or scissors to shorten and reattach it. Instead he went hopping off to the toilet.

On reaching Budapest we checked into a quaint hostel run by a flamboyantly homosexual of which name I tried successfully to forget. I've nothing against people of either sexual persuasion, but why do some gay's insist on speaking like Julian Clary? He employed a young lady called Victoria who we began befriending but it had been a long day and we hit bed pretty early. We'd managed to avoid the rain but in the night it came down hard. As we looked out the window in the morning we weighed up our options and left to tour the city. As I only had my army jacket which I didn't want to wear

79

around the city I wore the only alternative I had, a cotton jumper, which became very damp. We crossed the centre river in the city, walked up to the palace and then came back down. At night we tried to crash a student club like thing situated on an island in the middle of the river. It was expensive and had an organised, manufactured feel to it, but we did well to persuade Victoria to recommend and join with us to a huge rock like club not far from our hostel. It's customary to have Kostas sing Marti Pellows 'Wet Wet Wet' on a karaoke and I was very happy to find the club had a room just for that. After several beers I was organising a small crowd for what I promised would be an excellent performance. I was lying. Victoria had high hopes, but just as the year before, he was a disaster. His cringe-worthy monotone vocals were awkward, but not as much as the pained expressions coming from others in the room. Honestly, the CIA could have used it as part of their no-sleep interrogation program.

Soon after Victoria had to leave and we stumbled on into another room heaving with bodies. I perched myself on the side of a stool and another beer went by. While Kostas left to get another round, a Hungarian bloke, shorter but stockier than my own frame and dressed in heavy leathers, came over and spoke in a drunken and broken English that I couldn't piece together. I did the usual polite smile and shrug and then unexpectedly, out the blue, he punched my shoulder. I didn't second thought hitting him back, so I did, and slammed my first into his shoulder at half force. He returned it with a lot more force, I felt it that time, and gave it back much harder which moved him back a step. Expecting to have my arse kicked, he moved closer.

"You van't to dance?"

Ok, so I'd just pulled a drunk Hungarian homosexual. Could be worse. Expecting he wouldn't take rejection well, I put my arm around him, the lucky guy, and steered him towards an unsuspecting Greek who was just being handed two fresh pints at the bar. I introduced him, picked up my beer, turned and swiftly faded into the crowd.

Time was not on our side, we didn't have anywhere near enough to see and experience all that the countries we were passing through had to offer. Kostas had to leave for Athens in the morning, which would take him back through Romania and Bulgaria. Being as I had a few more days, I'd head first to Serbia and then make my way south. Before that I spent a day on an underground tour. Carved out by thermal water, long labyrinths of caves and tunnels stretch many miles under Budapest.

Having rode to Belgrade the next day, I found a hostel that was nothing more than an entrepreneurial lad using his deceased grandmothers flat to make some quick cash. That was fine by me. After dumping my gear and parking the scooter in the corner of the condo lobby I walked around the centre of town and ended up at the fort situated on the river mouth. Prodigy were headlining there in the evening and sound checking earlier on. Security were clearing the place out so I couldn't stay and watch from the sidelines. Although I didn't have the chance to speak to many Serbians, the ones I did were very friendly. I made a note to revisit for a few weeks, on another trip, in another life. but instead I opted to spend the extra day I had in in Kosovo. The drive south was slow and dull and upon reaching the Macedonian (FYROM) border I learned that I needed Green Card Insurance for entry, or I could spend €50 for the one day it would take to drive through. I had to stick to my financial rules, didn't I? In retrospect, I made a poor decision. I chose instead to backtrack and travel into Bulgaria via a mountain pass marked out on my GPS. This was to turn into a classic motorcycling mistake, one which involves coldness and rain.

I turned around at the border, tracked back and took a road right on the beginning of the pass. It began to rain and I stopped to cover over with my Goretex army gear. The scooter gradually gained altitude as the pass rose but the rain came down harder and the temperature fell. My progress on the winding and now water logged road was dire.

It soon became dark, and with no street lights the blue high-beam indicator light on my scooter dazzled my vision. I couldn't mask it off as the cluster panel was sodden and the tape wouldn't stick. Through the rain my dismal headlight did little, while the screen on my open face helmet in combination of my breath and the coldness of the outside air, quickly condensed over. The rain now poured and remembering back to what the front tyre was like on the Greek islands, and with such an imbalance of weight towards the rear, I was overly cautious and dropped the speed to under 30kph.

It was late, dark, cold and wet when I nearly ran out of petrol. I managed to find a small pump still open but it had no petrol left. A Serbian man offered to show me where the next was, all I had to do was follow his car. He drove too fast and I remember my anxiety. After many years riding I developed a sense for what the wheels could take. It was too fast, the water was lying on the road, and my front tyre had diabolical grip.

Suddenly I was going down the road sideways. I'd barely

touched the front brake and now I was clinging to the handlebars waiting for the 50mph slide to stop. It was the best crash I could have hoped for, for the road stayed straight, it remained empty, and the damage was only to the plastic bottom on the scooter and holes to my Goretex waterproofs. I was very, very lucky. After calming down, I gingerly made my way to the pump and filled up. It was 23:00hrs.

The rain worsened and with it parts of the pass suffered small landslides, distributing small rocks across my path. I edged forward and was quite miserable, tired, cold and wet by the time I made the Serbian border. A small crossing, the officers took pity and allowed me an hour in their building to dry and thaw. Midnight came and went and I knew somewhere I'd have to wild camp in the miserable weather. My camping gear was mostly wet and the rest of it would certainly be by the time I'd erected it. I drove on and and into Bulgarian and began looking for somewhere offering a roof where I could doss for the night. With no lights in the rural area I could see little outside of my headlight path. I came across a small abandoned petrol station, its old and rusting roof offering relieve from the rain. I inspected the building with my head-torch and found wild dogs using it for the same purpose. I knew wild dogs in Bulgaria may carry rabies but I wasn't too put off as my camping shelter was pretty solid. Then one of the dogs made a horrific noise which echoed off the roof and pierced the silence of the early morning. I freaked out, got back on the bike with expedience and drove on.

At about 02:00hrs I found another disused petrol station and with my will now broken, decided to check this one out as well. It looked more promising with a large semi-circle of disused buildings and a large forecourt. As I sat under the roof and weighed up my options in my blind spot I suddenly spotted a car with no lights moving slowly around the rear. Although dark, the moon gave off enough light to make out the words POLICE on the side. I began fumbling with the GPS as if lost. Tyres slowly crunching over broken glass, they pulled alongside.

"This is a very dangerous place Mister!". They looked very concerned. I doubted they wanted a tourist incident on their watch.

"I'm lost, is there a motel or something?" They paused for thought, spoke to one another and replied with a no, however if I continued onto the E95 road I might find one there. I thanked them and drove on, miserable after driving for some 14 hours.

It was around 03:00hrs when I made the highway and it was still raining. By now I really didn't give a damn where I stayed, so I parked up on the grass alongside the first petrol station I came across and unfolded my shelter to get some sleep. By the time I'd erected the poles and stuck the rain cover on top my down filled sleeping bag was wet. I managed three broken hours of sleep, as around 06:00hrs an entourage of vehicles began filling up with fuel.

As idiotic and unnecessary as the whole thing might seem, it was my way of ensuring I could take the discomfort. I had to move on from the hostel and hotel mentality if I was to fully experience the life of travelling around the world.

Two days later I was back in Athens. I'd made good time and arrived only half a day after Kostas, whom having no waterproofs and no camping gear, had hit the rain and endured it. Like his bike, Kostas was a wreck. We couldn't help but laugh.

Chapter 8

The Wedding

Up till this point I'd thought of everything as a kind of holiday and a trial for the scooter and the equipment. As a holiday it had worked well, I felt much more at ease and had settled into a travelling mentality of less stress, less planning and less worry. In a way then the ten days I'd spend back in Newcastle was an opportunity to swap out kit, but it was more than that. It was closure on a part of my life.

Before I'd set off Paul asked me to Usher at his wedding. Many years ago I'd had reservations about his girlfriend at the time, Charlotte, who came across as defensive and awkward, but after a short time it was clear Paul had, as usual, made a sound decision. I was becoming an every increasing gooseberry among my friends.

On the wedding day I'd never seen Paul so stressed, so terrified with nerves. It was funny really, all he had to do was say a few words and sign a few cheques. I mean, it wasn't like he was giving up his career, life, possessions and heading into the unknown.

There's another couple, Gillian and Steve, that Paul and I are close to, both we knew well at school. Gillian I've known half my life, we grew up in the same street at a teenage time of sexual curiosity, and that's probably why today I feel I can talk to her about anything and everything. We left the newly wed, her husband and the entourage and took a stroll down a pebbled path and hung over a leaning fence where we talked, especially about the future.

My friends were increasingly entering long term relationships, were married or had spawned children, but like always my brain wanted adventure not stability. My focus was on the trip and its objectives. I'd set aside the triviality of how lonely my heart really was.

I said goodbye to some of my longest friends not knowing when I'd see them again, and got on with it. The following morning I began to sort out the equipment.

The two broken Panasonic cameras that had been repaired in Athens I'd brought back with me on the flight. As the manual joining of the audio and video streams from the camera and mic were laborious I chose instead to turn to direct capture, which meant finding a camera with mic input. I scoured the net, did my research and found Canon selling refurbished 550d DSLR kits on eBay for £350. I added a battery grip on the bottom so that I could power it from AA batteries, just as with my other electronic equipment. I was concerned at how big and inconvenient the new kit was compared to the small cameras, but I hoped the results would prove worth it.

The problem of my bank Santander ripping me off abroad was annulated by opening an account with the *Yorkshire* buildings society. This debit card came with 0% fixed and 0%

percentage fees on transactions carried out in foreign currency and the card wouldn't automatically block abroad pending suspicious activity. It would be a much better card for travelling with.

My iPhone 3GS with its bluetooth GPS receiver was accurate but would occasionally loose pairing. It made sense to upgrade to an iPhone 4 with its integrated GPS reception, so I did and transferred the Garmin software over. A compatible bracket was purchased on eBay, which would slot into the same holder already attached to the scooter. All the leads were the same.

The bike cover that had doubled up as a rain cover wasn't going to be good enough in the hotter climates I was heading into. Instead I envisaged a large canopy that I could string up between standing objects like trees or which at a push could simply be thrown over the top of the mosquito shelter. I purchased a large tarp and added it to the collection of items for the outbound flight.

My winter gloves were waterproof but when wet became heavy, soggy and not at all warm. I decided to switch to handlebar muffs (these cover your hands and all the controls) and a pair of cheap cotton gloves. I'd a pair of handlebar muffs already stored back at home, unsold as I didn't know if I'd need them. The gloves I sold on.

I sold the big full face helmet. I wouldn't be needing that.

That was about it. I felt I had the equipment nailed.

It was great to see my family even if it were only a few months since I'd left. As I'd aged I'd became closer to my mother but I still acted like a complete child and couldn't talk about anything serious without breaking out into a Chinchilla impression (we used to have one and it would grate its teeth all the time). I still loved tormenting my younger brothers and would go on like a complete tit doing so. Back when he was about seven, the second youngest brother Adam would start any conversation designed to torment with the words "And so,", which is exactly what I now do to him. The youngest Al would clamp himself around one of your legs making it surprisingly difficult to move or to lean over to do anything about it. This I now do back, and I'm nearly thirty!

Leaving this time was harder on my mum. She drove me to the airport and we hugged, but I was intentionally formal rather than show emotion, which I knew wouldn't help her. I waved goodbye not knowing when I'd next see her, but knowing that pending success, it wouldn't be any time soon.

Chapter 9

Turkey

Back in Athens I attached the replacement equipment and left the following morning. It was to be a motorway slog up Northern Greece towards the gateway of Asia and my progress was slow due to multiple punctures to the rear tyre. Having done a little over double the expected mileage, it was bald and easily susceptible to glass punctures, the worst kind to repair. Being thrifty, I'd tried to stretch the life of the tyre to Turkey where I hoped the price of a new tyre would be cheaper. As usual, I paid the price in a different way. In the souring heat I found myself on the ground trying to mushroom plug what was essentially small splits in the rubber.

I'd not done much research into Turkey, I was way too excited to get into Iran and viewed the former as more of a stop-gap until I got there. I passed over a single bridge separating Greece and Turkey, the armed guards on either end still a reminder on the cordiality between the two countries, and onto Istanbul.

I ended up in the nightlife part of the city, quite late, definitely dark and ultimately lost. Eventually I found a hostel

I'd heard about, but the bike would have to be left outside on the street and the lady running the place advised thieving here was a problem. Not taking any chances (my big U-Lock had fallen off onto the motorway some days before), I located several additional hostels close by and ventured on to find one better suited to my needs. The thin and densely packed roads were hell like with no evidence of planning, and the entire network came across as a mess. As I'd furthered into the centre the roads congested with taxis, tourist buses, lorries (many just stop in the lane to drop things off). Then there is the one-way system, where if you miss your turning there is usually a significant time penalty, especially with the frequent traffic jams. Unusually curbs were much higher than anything I'd ever seen in Europe and prevented mounting the pavement to carry out an illegal traffic manoeuvre, my first choice when I'd made a navigational error. Drivers were impatient and discourteous, while pulling out and cutting up was accepted practice. Unlike large cities in warmer climates where scooters and two wheels dominated, the opposite was true for Istanbul. Here the car ruled, because the car was safe.

My plan to find a better hostel backfired as all were located on busy streets offering no place to park my scooter but eventually I found myself on the other side of town closer to the historical side of the city and paid a rip-off €30 to secure a room for the night. I'd looked into campsites but all were 30km out. It was late and my motivation to try something else was as deflated as my rear tyre. I paid the price.

I was going to be in Istanbul for a while sorting visas for Iran and India so I had to start the process without any delay. After breakfast I visited the Iranian consulate with a visa application code I'd secured from a tourist company inside Iran for $30, paid the $150 fee and left my passport in what was a swift and straight forward process. On the form it asked for my religion and any military experience. I was advised atheist and yes were wrong answers. On the way out I was bemused with two Norwegians who'd thought they could get their knackered €200 euro scooters in without the requisite visa reference code or a Carnet de Passage. Good luck on that one. I left to find a Honda dealer.

Finding a dealer proved troublesome. I'd saved a list from the Turkish website but could only positively identify three that were reasonably close. The first was around 8.5km from the Iranian consulate and took over an hour to reach the place where it should have been, and wasn't. I enquired at a car mechanics and several employees had a go figuring out what I was after and the actual location but none of the Turks spoke any English and I left none the wiser. The next dealer, some 22km away if my GPS chose to be truthful, was in the opposite direction to the way I'd just came. The traffic was persistently gridlocked and it took just shy of two hours to reach the dealership, which thankfully existed. Luckily the dealer had the tyre in stock but I'd have to wait four hours until they could fit it. I put on my Hugh Grant accent, so quite British well-to-do, daft and polite, the stereotypical voice what they hear in the movies. You know it's going to work when it catches a smile and here it did. I'd have to follow the mechanic a backstreet fitter in an hours time "if you can keep up" and in the meanwhile walked down the road to fill my stomach with McDonald Chicken Burgers, which were the equivalent of 70p in Turkey. Later at the backstreet dealer I negotiated a deal to change the front tyre as well. It had let me down in Bulgaria and wasn't worth the risk.

It was 16:00hrs by the time I rolled out on new tyres and I still had to find another, cheaper hostel. While at the garage

I'd used their wifi to source another at just €10 a night and which offered free motorcycle parking. It sounded great as a hold up while the visa applications were processed and on arrival I booked in for three days to begin with. I began talking to a Kiwi called Daniel who'd been on the road for 14 month and sank several beers listening to his stories. The beer would also help later, as the non air-conditioned and fan-less 30 dorm hostel room was, I assumed, going to be noisy, smelly and claustrophobic.

The following morning was Wednesday and I awoke with a bad head. At home I couldn't drag myself out of bed but now travelling I'd be up early at around 07:00hrs, hangover or not. I spent the morning washing clothes, sorting camera pictures, faffing on Facebook and updating the website. At 13:30hrs I left the hostel to meet a Turk named Fanul who'd made contact several months earlier on a Honda PCX scooter forum. Finding his place took longer than I'd predicted and included my first crossing over the Bosphorous bridge. As Fanul later explained, Turks called the two sides Europe and Asian side. I felt uneducated not knowing Istanbul essentially splits the two lands.

Although Fanul rode the same Honda PCX scooter as myself, the month before he'd locked the front in the same way (and on the same tyre) as I'd done in Bulgaria, and sent the poor thing into a barrier. His scooter was a write-off, although curiously he'd decided to repair it. Fanul came across as well spoken and educated. Until recently he's ran a large car dealership/servicing and although this was no longer operating he still owned the premises outright. It was here that I saw the remains of his scooter and all the new parts he's bought to repair it. It would probably cost him more to repair it than what it was worth, but he felt a bond to it, very much in the same way I did.

We visited a picturesque location overlooking the European side of Istanbul and devoured a very reasonable lunch at a nearby restaurant. Later I met several of his friends and arranged to go to place on the coast called Sile with one of them in the morning. I had to be at the rendezvous point at 07:30hrs, a tall order.

That evening Fanul had his first beer with me in as I recall four years. He explained the reason, a previous session involving eight beers, Turkish Raki, and waking up on a beach (having driven 40km to get there), and not remembering anything. He and his mates would repeat it every other day and eventually he'd called it a day. I felt guilty for he was drinking because he knew I did and he wanted to do his best at being a host. I was finding a similar pattern away from the tourist train; Turks were very accommodating to their friends and guests. We had a second beer, which he instigated and after that he grinned and said "another?". For his sake I declined, hoping Jack hadn't been let out the box.

It was a fun night and we all have our issues. I certainly had mine and Fanul had his, like driving on a suspended car license. I hadn't see that coming, but the beer had let out a few secrets. A friend of his was keen to meet me before I left Istanbul, curious as to why somebody would travel around the world without reason. Fanul explained his friend was released from prison two years prior citing mental health reasons. Originally he was jailed for entering a hotel and shooting a man in the head, in what was not a clean operation as he did it in front of a girlfriend who he let live. Fanul said he'd be the friendliest guy I'd ever meet. I hoped my answers to his

94

questions would keep him that way.

I awoke the following morning at the usual 07:00hrs. My iPhone alarm failed to go off and I missed the day trip to Sile, which I hoped I could reschedule for the following week. Instead I spent the day walking the historical museums and mosques and wrote a blog entry in a nearby park.

Time drifted by and the next day I picked up my passport with its new Iranian visa and at 10:30hrs left to find the Indian consulate. I drove to the other side of the river where I finally found the place and took the stairs up to the top rapid style hoping to beat a large party that were waiting for the lift. Closing at 11:30hrs, I had 12 minutes to secure a bank that would change for US dollars, of which I needed 55. The first bank said sure but they were way to slow and I stomped my legs in frustration. I ran out, over the busy road dodging traffic and scanned for an alternative. Yes! I found a small broker offering a diabolical exchange rate. I didn't care. I nearly got swiped by a car crossing the manic road again and reached the consulate top floor covered in sweat and panting with literally seconds to spare. The security guard had seen it all before, took a look at his watch, shook his head but opened the door anyway.

Istanbul as a large and busy city wasn't for me. Too crowded, the traffic made driving miserable so that I usually didn't bother but took the tram or walked. The food was generally excellent and most things were cheaper than Europe. At the Orient Hostel where I'd now stayed eight days I'd made many new friends including three Americans, one being young archaeologist by the name of Charlie. At just 22, Charlie took a group of us around a local museum where I realised a curiosity of the periods. Thanks our young guide I learned how to spot the differences between Roman, Classical and Byzantine statues. Back in 2000 I saw a Clint Eastwood film called Space Cowboys and now I remembered a passage from one of the actors which read "Whoever designed this Byzantine piece of shit is probably banging rocks together in Siberia." I hadn't thought about it at the time, but twelve years on and I'd learned Byzantine work was considered lesser quality than that of the Roman period where stone carving skill was valued greater.

People were here from all walks of life. An American I met called Steve Boitano was a freelance press photographer and was making his way to Syria. I half fancied joining him. Later I'd view pictures of him dodging bullets alongside rebel fighters.

One evening I joined two American girls around my age and over a few too many drinks became close to one of them,co in what could have easily turned into a relationship for she was looking for it. Later I found myself, at around 04:00hrs, in a king sized bed in the middle of their apartment. Her mate was on the other side on the bed and had pulled an Australian traveller who'd rode by bicycle from England (missed the surf). He was out cold from the drink and that wasn't good enough for her, so she began quite violently shaking him and slapping him in the face. After a while he woke up and thereon ubiquitous intercourse began. Me and the other girl were cuddled up, and she was quite embarrassed by her friend who full on didn't care. I on the other hand, kept a sly eye open.

I also bumped into an Italian by the name of Andrea Ciani. Andrea had set off from his hometown of Treste and was aiming to reach Tibet by bicycle. Like me he'd dropped everything for an adventure, and I instantly liked the guy for his great sense of humour. Andrea was up for stupid challenges, and after a few drinks he had no problem walking down our busy street with a trainer stuck to his ear. Although fun he was a determined individual, but then he had to be; his cycle was simply unliftable due to all the crap he was packing and he'd some arduous inclining terrain to cover. I had no idea how he'd manage it.

Both waiting for visas, myself and Andrea were quite sick of drinking and waiting. I broke the week up with a nights camping some 30km away outside of Istanbul but found I couldn't hack the solitude. I'd ran out of interesting things to do and rather than look at monuments I felt a desire to be active, to be moving. Our visas arrived on the Thursday and we'd both planned to leave straight away. Ready to depart, several of us had a go trying to lift his rear wheel off the ground but gave up and then waved him off. He had a head start tracking the coastline east while I first picked up a parcel from the local post office and would then set off to find him. It took me an age by road but I found him 25km outside Istanbul drinking tea in a small promenade cafe. Unlike Istanbul the area was green, relaxed and undeveloped. Andrea told me a firefighting wagon had stopped him along the way and donated a load of ration pack style food. Hearing that I wondered if cycling was the way to do it. We drank several Turkish teas and camped on a grassed area by the sea. In the morning we packed up, had another tea, shook hands and departed. I would head towards Cappadocia, he would stay North and continue towards Uzbekistan.

A short visit to Cappadocia was assured being as it was on the way to Iran and I'd been told to visit the place no matter what. I was afraid that it would be full of tourists like Istanbul when

I really wanted to get away from all that. As it turned out, it was full of tourists, but that didn't matter for the place was something not of our planet. Cappadocia has suffered limescale erosion in a way that is both creative and purposeful. It looks stunning, like mother nature was given a paint brush and told to take her time. In creating what she did she opened up opportunity for shelter from the rain and cold, and thousands of years ago humans dug out parts of the unique hill-tops and called them home. As the erosion is ongoing many of these shelters were abandoned and are now available for the curious to inspect, and tourists come from far afield to see this unique architecture for themselves. Big business followed, with many of the abandoned dwellings re-enforced and turned into hotels, restaurants, or renovated into museums.

I awoke to strange and unexpected noise. As I looked up through my tents canvas I could tell the sun had barely come up. It was still very early. I rolled over and read 06:00hrs on the iPhone. What is that noise!?! I unzipped the tent on one side and crawled out. And what I saw was amazing.

Very early in the morning, when it's cold and the air hangs with dew, hot air balloon burners roar and these majestic light weight vehicles take to the sky. It so happened that the campsite I'd chosen was very close to the field they all took off from, and as the sunrise began the rays filtered through them all in a brilliant array of colours.

I left in the early morning to cover some of the 700 mile distance to the Iranian border. The aim was to do half that, which I did, and there was nothing of interest to note about it. That night I stayed at the far end of a large service station car-park, hoping to be undisturbed. I was now on the D400.

The D400 is a long road of varying quality that skirts the Turkish, Syrian, Iraq and Iran borders. If I'd realised this earlier I may have chosen the much busier northern route into Iran. The road skirts the Syrian border with frequent lookout towers. The day before Turkey had banned Syrian air traffic into its air space and vice-versa. As I looked right over the baron fields separating the two countries, I began wondering if this particular route into Iran was going to be 'unsafe' as someone had commented on Horizons Unlimited. But if it was, I didn't feel it. Not yet.

The quality of the road deteriorated as it climbed into the mountainous regions separating these countries and with it the temperature dropped. Heavy open cast mining was frequent as were slow moving trucks full of shale. Frequently I found myself trying to overtake uphill on gravel, the 125cc engine being helpless and typically leading to a sharp cut in to avoid the next bend. Military helicopters occasionally flew high and slow overhead.

This area featured some of the best scenery I'd ever seen, but tension between the Kurdish Iraqis and the southern Turkish was high, and it's not an area I'd really want to pass through alone at night. I'd certainly be wary on wild camping here. It wasn't long before military checkpoints began. At first they were reasonably lax but closer to Kurdish territory that changed. Soldiers with M16's and and APC or two blocking the road were curious as to why a Brit would be riding a bogged down scooter in this area alone.

Darkness came at 18:00hrs and the temperature dropped to near freezing. I stopped to add extra layers of clothing and then continued to climb at no more than the 35mph permitted by the 125cc engine. The area continued to be heavily mined and overladen trucks come down at reckless speeds on the gravel roads. I was slower than them and would pull over to let them by and then would sit coughing in the dust storm that followed. I wanted to stop but needed a flat area that was less exposed so I kept going in hope of finding one.

The traffic reduced to nil and sometime after 22:00hrs I ran into the largest checkpoint yet. It was so utterly black I barely saw it coming and drove up with my headlight on which illuminated soldiers hidden under camouflaged netting on the side of the road. An officer appeared to my left and hissed at me to turn the light off.

"Terrorists are watching us right now!", he motioned his finger upwards towards a high mountainous region.

"Why you here?!", he asked with authority.

Hoping to relief the tension, I told him I was crazy British tourist on an. He smiled and said he'd only been to America. Then he got down to business.

"Are you carrying a gun?"

"No", I replied, "But perhaps I should get one?".

He laughed and then did a 360 around the scooter. "You're going to Iran on that?" he asked incredulously.

"Yeah. I had one of those APC's parked over there but you Turks wouldn't let it pass through customs. So I downsized." He continued grinning.

"The backpack. Open it.". So I did, showing him the contents.

"No C4, TNT?"

"Nope, ran out."

"What is this?" he said, pointing to the rear Army cot bed assembly.

"Camping gear".

And that was that. He told me the area was unsafe so I fairly pointlessly asked if I could camp near his check-point. It was worth a shot.

"No way", he snorted.

If I wanted somewhere to stop he said a small village ahead might have something to offer, but I knew he knew it didn't. It was a good three hours to the border and I wouldn't be making it that night, so somewhere up ahead I would be wild camping. My GPS was off, probably blocked by the Americans, and I had no phone signal. It was pitch black, very cold and for the first time on the trip I felt an inkling of vulnerability.

I drove another hour and pulled off the side of the road onto a large gravel patch in the side of a bend. Being selective about where I crash for the night my first criteria was no dogs as they wake their owners up. I couldn't hear any. It was so dark. In the silence I could hear a river running in a gorge far down from the gravel edge, while the moon displayed the outline of a shear cliff face rising high up from where I currently was. A forest and further cliff edge faced on the other side of the road so that the road was the only route in or out. Without my head-torch I discretely assembled the camp-bed by not much more than touch, doing away with the mosquito shelter, and then hid the scooter and camp-bed using the dark green tarp. This I primarily carried for rain, but here it did an excellent job at lowering my footprint.

Dawn came before 06:00hrs and I was up with it. By 06:20hrs I was back on the road, covering the final distance to the Iranian border.

Chapter 10

Iran

My heavy scooter was suffering from altitude sickness and was crawling its way towards the Iran border at a miserable pace. It took a few hours and when I finally arrived I blew all my remaining Turkish coinage on chocolate bars thinking I was in for some heavy paperwork.

The border crossing I'd chosen, which was the lowest possible route into Iran, was of a curious design as the customs for both countries are housed in the same building. Unlike a typical crossing featuring no-mans land between the exit/entry points, here was simply a door stating Turkey on one side and Iran on the other. By mistake I went through it and began queuing to get back into Turkey even though I hadn't left it yet. The whole process took an hour and was the first time I had to use the Carnet de Passage document. I was expecting a full inspection of the bike and its contents. The Turkish customs officer picked a random pannier and asked me to open it. He took out the diving goggles on the top, put them on and shouted to his friends on the side of the road to take a picture.

On the Iranian side, entry required several eloquent signatures from people in civilian clothing. Meanwhile I had several 'helpers' desperately flapping to be involved in the process and fending them off was troublesome. I made it look like I was loosing my temper with them which seemed to work. After that I had to give fingerprints (a requirement for British nationals) and fill in several forms. There was no inspection of the scooter or any of its contents and I was waved on my way. The helpers ran after the scooter, it was in fact money exchange they were offering. I told them I'd already changed in Turkey, which I hadn't, and drove away promptly, missing the insurance office by mistake and aiming to clear the border hassle. As I drove out I half expected I'd be followed or something like that. I'd seen too much western TV.

My first point of contact was a lad called Hossain, an Iranian who hosted motorcyclists entering his country. Residing in Urmia, about 30km from the border, it would be an ideal place to see Iran first hand, to meet young Iranians, experience the culture and plan a route using the local knowledge rather than just the tourist book. I arranged to stay at his house with his family for a few days.

On the relative short road to Urmia I had my eyes opened to how modern Iran was. Despite crushing sanctions and lack of foreign business Iran still appeared modern with a clean environment, well tarmacked roads, pizza shops and LED traffic lights. The cars were dominated by the older Peugeot 405 which I remembered from the 90's and some other internal brands, while the usual manufacturers were missing.

My visa ran for 30 days but could be extended with relative ease. I found the Pakistan embassy in Tehran was closed over the Thursday/Friday Islamic weekend and wouldn't open till the Saturday. I needed details on the visa application and planned for Hossain to do the talking.

Over the next four days I was given a tour around Urmia city centre. To begin with I was uneasy with my nationality being as it is, but it quickly became apparent that everyone, and I mean everyone, would be exceptionally helpful, polite and interested in where I was from, if I was married, my religion and why I didn't ride a big motorcycle! I can't describe how warm the people of Iran were, and how willing they were to accommodate and be a good guest. I drank much tea, shook many hands and throughly enjoyed the warmth, a warmth that I hadn't experienced anywhere else on the planet.

Eating with Hossain's family was done on the floor and they happily slept together in the one room while insisting I had the spare to myself. Breakfast centred around a delicious selection of nan bread and fresh jam and butters while lunch was more western than i'd envisaged. Halal burgers or kebabs aplenty! Also somewhat different to Europe I didn't see any overweight Iranians, the younger generation especially being rake thin. Of course that could be the lack of alcohol, and by lack I mean non-existent, but either way the populace seemed to be in better health than the norm.

With Islamic rule in force, females had to fully cover up their head although the burka was optional and rarely was taken up. In this part of Iran especially the young were rebelling in there own way, defying the government by letting their head scarf slip backwards a little, pushing back against rule and order.

It did seem that anything I construed to be "fun" wasn't allowed, because socialising between male and female groups was not tolerated. So how did young Iranians have fun?

Hossain took me to a basement where young smoked fruit tobacco pipes, drank tea and played little games. One involved a pea size ball that is hidden and shook in the hands with the aim of guessing which it's currently in.

Hossain and his friends took me to a car track where people would come and try handbrake turns. On the way there I found the car I was in inside a wedding celebration involving several other vehicles and very cheerful individuals hanging out the windows. There must have been six abreast at one point going down the single road and inevitably there was a crunch as one collided with another. At the track, the cars with there limited engines would take ages to accelerate to the end of the run and then perform an unspectacular slide. It was here, for the first time, that I was confronted by a group of hostile guys who weren't happy with the UK government and wanted to vent. Being unable to speak Arabic I could only guess what was being said. Hossain's friends said they were uneducated, but I felt that they sort of agreed with some of what was being said. I couldn't blame them. The western led sanctions had hit the population not the Government.

Despite the limitation on vehicle brands and engine sizes Iranians are true petrol heads. As one of Hossain's friends told me, they spent a lot of time and money customising their cars to make them stand out. This can involve colourful LED lights or wacky horns that whip the air. Driving is manic and aggressive. The best and sometimes only way to get across roads is to step out in front of cars and presume they will slow down. They do, but its dangerous if you don't have your wits about you. Driving a scooter is equally hazardous. Lane keeping is generally ignored and roundabouts are a hilarious contortion of sharp acceleration and braking. Everyone uses their horn. It is not unusual to see cars driving the wrong way down a lane or even reversing backwards with traffic approaching the rear. As it's dangerous, scooters and motorcycles are much fewer than I'd expected, are restricted to 250cc, and only a few models are available. The majority are copies of old Hondas, made in Iran of course.

From there I visited an antiquated theme-park featuring very old rides from the 80's. I felt like I was in a time warp. Roaming around in Hossain's car, his friend would occasionally get him to stop near an old lady, would pull his hoody over his head to thwart being seen, exit the car and would then do a mad dance in front of her, before getting back in the car and making a getaway. It was innocent fun, if different.

It goes without saying, though I'll say it anyway, that there's a marked difference between the media of Iran and that of Europe. Here television is strictly controlled, no satellite is allowed and content is highly critical of the Americans and British, who are frequently portrayed as the devil's workers. Internet is restricted, filtered and slow with wifi uncommon and media websites like Facebook and Twitter blocked. Yet the young are crafty and eager and the majority use proxies to get around the limitations imposed by their Government.

The young are very open with foreigners and keen to talk about the two topics the British FCO strongly advises talking about; religion and politics. Iranians are interested in the cultural difference between other foreign countries not just their own, and are educated far more about the western world than the western world is about Iran. Iranians could distinguish the difference between a government and the people - something the British are yet to master.

The Iran government aims for the country be self sufficient and most of what it consumes it produces in-house. Anything else is taxed so high that ordinary Iranians don't have the option to buy it. Petrol and gas come from the Iranian ground and is unbelievably cheap. As an example, 7 litres cost the equivalent of $2 USD. A residence card permits 60 litres per month at half this rate. Low prices don't just apply to fuel but food and accommodation. With the exchange rate being what it is, Iran is currently one of the cheapest places in the world to visit.

I owe a lot to Hossain for opening my eyes to the wonderful country that is Iran. Unfortunately it wasn't possible to secure a visa for Pakistan as they'd changed the rules and I'd have to go back to my home country and probably go through an interview. I left Urmia pointing south towards Istafan.

From Urmia I had a solid two day drive to reach the popular city of Isfahan but along the way I stopped at a dry salt lake and side tracked to visit Takht-e Soleyman, a world heritage site. This was another wonderful area featuring a large sedimentary rock created by a natural spring, a fort, and natural hot water springs. I arrived rather late and climbed the rock said in folk legend to have been a former prison. The fort cost next to nothing to enter as Iran didn't change a tourist entry rate.

Night fell and with nowhere to stay I chose to wild camp not far from the rock but still away from the main road. I found a large boulder and using my green tarp created a shelter for the scooter and to sleep under. Meanwhile on the other side about 150 metres away I could see two people stopping any infrequent vehicle passing on the road I'd came along earlier. They were armed with AK47's and dressed in civilian attire but it was too dark to make out if they were genuine police or something else. Bricking it, I quietly crawled into my shelter and lay in silence, realising that seclusion could make the situation worse.

As usual the best spots to camp were to be found in daylight, and in the morning not far from my location was a fabulous natural hot spring in which I could bathe and wash clothes.

After packing up I continued towards the city of Araq and a few hours later I found myself in the town centre wondering why Hossain had recommended going there. I fancied a cheap hotel for the night but found only the one at a pricey $80/night. I spent another 30 minutes riding around and ended up asking two Iranians if they knew of any alternatives. With typical enthusiasm and helpfulness they insisted they get their car and that I follow them. I did, only to be taken back to the hotel I had been to. Sod it. I left Araq knowing that the day after I'd be in Isfahan. The day passed in a blur, the cool wind and easy going roads passing the hours by. In the evening I found a superb spot not far from the main road but which was high and tricky to reach. The poor scooter barely managed navigating the rocks and as back in Greece I ripped the centre stand spring off trying. This time I lost it, so held it up with a bungee rope.

Now away from the high ground around Urmia, the temperature was rising and I could ditch the cold gear. I threw away the handlebar muffs and fleece. I wouldn't be needing them anytime soon. The road to Isfahan was long and offered landscaped views over undisturbed land. It was a very easy going ride disturbed only by the occasional car wreck on the side of the road or my stopping to dump the fuel can contents into the tank.

109

When I reached Isfahan it was late evening and the traffic was heavy. I pottered around not knowing really where to go. The locals proved helpful and directed me towards an area where I found a hotel reputably popular with backpackers and those on a tight budget. As standards go it was a bit of a dump, the room being only slightly bigger than the single bed inside it, but it was enough. I left to find some grub and outside the hotel things were immediately better. I wandered over the centre bridge and into one of the many perfect parks that run alongside the dry river bed and noted how everything was super clean and organised.

In the morning I planned to go back to the quiet park I'd discovered over the bridge, where I'd work on my blog backlog. After yet another superb breakfast made from some sort of tomato omelettes, I crossed the bridge and found a park bench where I could put pen to paper and play catchup.

It probably looked like I was writing a book, or I was a journalist, and it didn't take long for my presence to draw attention. An elderly guy sat down and after a while asked if I was busy, his way of saying he wanted a conversation. I didn't - I had to get the writing done, so without looking up I said I was and he left without further word. I wrote for another 30 minutes at which point a young lad who I figured was around the age of 20 sat on the far corner of my bench. He didn't say anything but quietly took a call on his mobile then after a few moments asked if he was causing a disturbance. By now my motivation to write was nearing a collapse and I said it was no problem. The older guy was still lingering around in the distance, I presumed he'd be back soon enough. In the meantime I began conversing with the young lad. Like all young Iranians he was eager to talk about religion and politics and early on in the conversation he asked why I'd come to such an expensive city with so little to do. Then the bombshell, he added that he disliked his country because he was gay, and described how he and his family sitting down to an evening meal had laughed when the president said on national TV that there were no gays in Iran.

I was finding it remarkable how open Iranians would be with foreigners. Knowing that I had no connection with the government here was another example of someone venting like I was a psychologist. As I was on my best behaviour, I listened like one and said little. Without fear of reprisal, he talked about his desire for liberty and freedom and concreted my understanding that the everyday Iranian didn't hate America or her allies because of the sanctions but blamed their Government. Of all the young people I'd spoke to all would do almost anything to move to one of the countries their Government damned. Moreover, these people wanted change and the amount of these people was growing. As the young replaced the previous generation I could foresee a loosening grip. Perhaps Iran would have its second revolution.

Being in a public place and being a part of such topics could easily have made for trouble with the authorities. I became a little on edge as some of the park dwellers were staring. The young Iranian explained the park was an unofficial gay hangout scene at night and as two women passed by he mentioned they were undercover police looking for women failing to wear the headscarf *appropriately*. It was ready to move on, at which point the elderly Iranian came back and sat down on the middle of the bench. He began talking about his visit to England in the 70's and his desire for his country to change. Much of what he said came from deep inside him but it ended up coming out as a ramble. He wanted me to come back to his house but frankly I couldn't suffer the abuse on my eardrums and I tried as best I could to respectfully decline the offer. This offended him and he excused himself. The young Iranian explained to decline such an offer was indeed deemed offensive, but then what else was I to do when I had my own schedule and itineraries.

Over the next two days I explored more of the city and was ripped off by a Jewish store keeper when I bought a shoddy backpack at a bad price. Perhaps I was taken aback by seeing an orthodox in Iran. Isfahan featured an opulent main square complete with horses in a royal style dress, perfectly maintained hedges, water fountains and pavements clean from chewing gum. It was delightfully maintained. At night further green parks were are beautifully lit, a real treat on the eyeballs.

After a few days in Istafan I realised why I felt so at peace with the place. It was the lack of advertising. No billboards, fliers, posters, touts, audio sales pitches – nothing. It was so easy going. I loved the layout, the food and the people.

A traveller heading north had offered his tourist map of the Fars province. It was a mistake to travel without a Lonely Planet guide. For all the criticism they receive for curtailing the thrill of self discovery, the benefits are ten fold when on a budget, alone and without reliable Internet.

Finally, early one morning, I left for Shiraz, the touristic capital of Iran. Leaving Isfahan I exhibited heavy traffic, but it gave me time to pause and think on how highly I regarded the place. Once the traffic subdued I found myself climbing into the higher terrain to the west of Iran. Isfahan's tentacles hadn't spread far, and as before the land soon turned baron. Looking down into the valleys below, sand swept through untouched lands of nothingness. While my progress on the incline was slow, the scenery was breathtaking to behold, and there was no traffic to worry about. The air was noticeably fresh and being that it was still early in the morning, the sun had yet to overcome the cold altitude. It was brisk and I felt alive.

95 octane petrol was now a thing of the past, as were frequent petrol stations, and I kept the 5 litre fuel can under the seat filled whenever possible. 85 octane petrol was causing a little irregularity with the fuel injection, but power was so minimal to begin with I couldn't make out the difference.

Hours went by, then a day. I slept by the road, cooked pasta and pulled up at small villages to pick up boiled eggs.

About 50km from Shiraz I slammed on the brakes to make a sharp turn to my right. I'd spotted a sign with a name on it recommended my new map of the Fars province and thought it might offer a decent picnic site. It did, but I was far more interested in a ford and adjacent stream that looked suitable for a challenge and some video footage. An abandoned campsite nearby offered no clean water to wash my backlog of dirty linen and so I moved onto setting up the tripod and testing the scooter's capability in water. I was very aware of the scooters low ground clearance. Pockets of the stream were deeper than the air intake, but a bit of throttle and I'd get through. This was true for going over but on the way back it drowned and I had to drain the cylinder by removing the spark plug.

Afterwards I tried to reach a place called Lost Paradise.

Although the name was probably appropriated by an overly keen government worker, I was willing to give it the benefit of the doubt, and having estimated the distance I thought I'd enough petrol to make it. I was wrong, the road was twisty and I had to give up an hour in knowing I'd be grovelling for fuel off a local if I didn't. 50km later the scooter was running on fumes and the fuel can was empty. So was my petrol stove bottle - I'd emptied that with about 5km to Shiraz when the engine died.

Shiraz is the capital of Fars province and in the 1700's was the capital of Iran when it was ruled by Karim Zand. Mr Zand built a large palace in the city and the city prospered, but the ruler of Tehran overthrew the province and the palace with its gold carvings and sculptures was used instead to house political prisoners. The cleverer of these would scrap decorative gold off the walls and send it by bow and arrow over the high walls to family still living outside the prison. I learned all this from my first guided tour. It was so cheap to enter (no extra for tourists, must be the only country to do this) that I felt a moral obligation to give something back.

In what came across as more openly planned than Istafan, Shiraz was equal in beauty with stunning parks and attractions unmolested by tourism services. In one park close to the centre I found holidayers from elsewhere in Iran with little red and blue tents and exotic tea making facilities. It was fine to wild camp here, nobody would disturb or shuffle you along, and I sorely considered joining them. It was, in hindsight, a shame I didn't.

I spent three days in Shriraz and it became one all time favourite places. It was even cheaper than Isfahan, a points not missed out on the locals who were keen to point this out, plus it had an even easier going and laid back feel to the place. I befriended the cheap hotel's owner and insider knowledge led me to an all-time great for breakfast. Featuring the same style of tomato something omelettes that I'd never replicate, I'd engulf these and other Iranian breakfast specialities for under a single American dollar. It wouldn't get any better than that.

The backpack I'd bought in Istafan had already disintegrated but I found a genuine Iranian army replacement, a retro design and semi waterproof which was a good fit around the handlebars.

One evening there was a large commotion outside of the most unusual book store I've ever seen. Roughly 3m cubed, the walls were surrounded by piles of books stacked as high as the ceiling and in the middle one man trying desperately to serve a mob of people through a roll up shutter. A single bulb hung over his head and the customers were in a frenzy as he tried to pull out books with twenty or so others on top. Perhaps the new Harry Potter was out.

The route south of Shiraz was slow and surprisingly cold. Along the way I ran into a few hostile Iranians at a petrol station, where several repeatedly said "English f*king Iran" while making a fist and finger poking into it gesture. The crowd began to grow, as did my nerves, and I promptly packed the fuel can back under the seat and made a speedy exit. I doubt I was in any real trouble, but then I was in no doubt had some Iranians had been really hit by the sanctions and it only took one with a smaller brain to apply blame directly.

From Shiraz I was in two minds whether to go east to Fez or

to begin making my way south and out of Iran. Part of me wanted to go on exploring Iran while the other part needed a good conversation. It'd been a while since I'd had a laugh and I really did need to converse. I chose to head south towards the port at Bander Abbas.

As luck would have it, a social cookie come out the jar when I passed a heavily laden cyclist with panniers on the front and rear and luggage on top of that. At first I waved as I went past, but then I turned around to say hello. At first the guy seemed in a rush, but we begun talking and then stopped for a few biscuits. Kevin Downey, an Irishman, was cycling with a plan to travel the world over a timeframe of about two and a half years. Compared to cyclist Andreas I'd met in Istanbul, Kevin had much less equipment and looked like he was living it day by day. We were both in-need of overcoming the solitude that had come from travelling Iran and after sharing a laugh and taking some pictures we shook hands and agreed to catch up at Bandar Abbas, where we'd both be making for the ferry to Dubai.

I drove for another hour and before dark, then pulled off the main road and covered a bit of distance over the hills to a remote spot. I'd hoped to reach what looked like the perfect hill peak, but the scooter didn't have the gears for it. Among the rock bashing I had to compromise for a spot further down, but in my uninhabited area I was still able to play music from the iPhone as the sun sank beneath the horizon. As I unfolded the cot bed and mosquito shelter I saw my first snake. Black and about two foot long, it slid away before I had the chance to identify it in my little SAS survival guide. The sun sank away and I was left to another clear night under the stars.

In the morning I took a little longer than usual to pack up and get back onto the main road but I was on my way by 08:00hrs. Fifteen minutes later and incredulously I passed Kevin riding his wheels. I pulled over and enquired how he'd done it. He told me he'd rode into the night, then slept above a kebab shop in somewhat calamitous conditions, and had got back on the road early at 06:30hrs. Why the rush? Well he wanted to reach Bandar Abbas quickly as the day after he'd be 26yrs old. There was nothing out here, but unluckily for him he still had 150km to go. Despite his tenacity, I knew he wouldn't make it.

I then had a bright idea, and to my surprise Kevin was all for it. I took a large bungee rope, attached it to the back of my scooter and handed him the other end. I'd tow him to Bandar Abbas in four hours. All he had to do was hang on.

It quickly became apparent that the skinny tyres and top heavy bags on his bicycle were not suitable for towing at 40kph. So I accelerated to 50kph. Kevin would later note that going through one of several pot-holed tunnels was among the most scariest moments of his life. Half way it began raining. Filthy trucks spat out mud and sand from the road onto both of us. I had my screen to protect myself from the spray, but Kevin didn't, and by the time we reached the town he was a mess. We found a value hotel which 'offered him' to clean up before he went upstairs. Despite his condition he was delighted and grinning.

Neither of us were ready to hit the ferry to Dubai which left twice a week and the next slot being the following morning. I'd heard about an unbelievable amount of paperwork required at both ends from two brothers driving a Tuk Tuk from England around the world. They told me it took seven hours to sort paperwork on the Iran side and twelve hours in the UAE. Meanwhile our rather brilliant hotel was costing a little over $20 a night, so neither of us felt in any hurry. As I got to know Kevin more I found we had a similar sort of humour and mentality. It was a bit of a relief after the loneliness of Iran. Despite meeting new people every day, I missed good banter and that made me realise how much better the journey would be if I had someone to share it with.

In the town we found a very cheap ice-cream shop and ate very cheap fresh pizza, and while sitting at a table watching the traffic an Iranian named Ali introduced himself. Speaking good English, Ali seemed trustworthy and easy going and I assumed he talked to foreigners whenever he got the chance. He'd a house in Bander Abbas but usually lived in the UAE, and as of that moment was figuring out how to get his paramotor back over there. He'd befriended a French lady driving a Winnebago with her two small kids, lent her the money for the crossing (because the Iranian ferry company demanded USD) and thus his transport problem was solved.

While talking we got onto the subject of Kevin's miniature guitar he carried on the back of his bicycle. Ali offered for us an impromptu jam with another Iranian guitarist and his friend. It was a great night. Ali brought some beat box type of thing and I'd a tambourine. Some time into the evening we did the unthinkable and bought cans of illegal lager, which was delivered by a secret source on a scooter. The 8% strength was enough and by the end I was calling Kevin, Scott, and singing him happy birthday. He turned 26 that night.

In the morning we met two French cyclists in town (Kevin had bumped into them before). They'd just returned from a small island between Iran and the UAE called Qeshm. Kevin was meeting another Iranian he'd couchsurfed with in Sharaz named Roozby, plus an Australian cyclist named Brad and a few of his friends. Ali was also thinking about borrowing a bicycle and coming along as he was siding against putting his paramotor in the Winnebago and might instead stick it on the ferry to the UAE later on. I was in.

In the late afternoon a little boat docked at the port and we were on our way. With no ramp, the scooter had to be lifted on, and I removed much of the luggage to make it easier to lift. They managed with relative ease. At the other side making it off the boat was more difficult, the gap being as it was a good meter down to the wooden jetty. Six members of staff worked together and it made it down in one piece. The guys wanted paying for carrying Kevin's bicycle and my scooter. We hadn't paid anything as the so called captain of the Bandar Abbas port had just waved us on after we'd paid the passenger fare. We played dumb and left the arrival port without paying anything else.

I followed behind Kevin like a support vehicle, but he was quick enough and besides I had no timeframe. Away from the port and beginning to track the coast in an anticlockwise direction, dusk arrived, and before darkness came in its entirety we pealed our eyes for a quiet beach. Time was working against us and after riding and driving five mile into the rural island, now unable to see anything, we set up camp on bulldozed land. A pungent smell of rotting animal corpse was drifting over, or rising from directly beneath us, but without care we cooked and drank 3-in-1 Nescafe coffee sachets, which both of us were hooked on.

The moonlight was just enough to see out over the coast and the outline of an abandoned gas platform. It had broke its moorings in a strong storm and drifted to shore the month before. The road between us and the coast, the one we'd came along, was now used by 4x4 Toyotas travelled at speed and with lights off. All were carrying a cargo of big barrels in the rear; petrol from Iran to ship over to UAE or alcohol to ship back over to Iran. Smuggling was big business here and the island thrived on it. The police were paid off and the smugglers used flares to warn of any impediment, typically the product of a Government ordered crack down.

During the night we were awoken by a small fox. A timid thing, it came into the camp and grabbed a pair of my shorts before making its get away. I gave chase and it dropped them, but it kept wondering if it could get back to them before I could. Not long after it returned and made off with Kevin's water bottle, but he gave chase, his Irish accent bellowing with curse, and he got it back. Hilariously, in the morning we found his tent was missing several pegs.

With the sun rising we hit the beach, my first since the Red Sea of Romania. It was great to be back in the water, except for one of the things in it, a fish with a peculiar diet of human nipples. Later Ali came trundling along the road and after setting of an hour later we were joined by Roozby from Shiraz and Brad the Australian. I was the only motorised vehicle in the group and in the humidity I wasn't complaining. We rode until the afternoon and stopped at a restaurant for lunch. A plan was made to carry out some fishing and myself, Kevin and Ali doubled back half a kilometre to a small village made from authentic brick and mud to find some tackle. Rejoining the main group, we set up camp on a large sandy area, which my lardy scooter had trouble reaching. As I was rocking it backwards and forwards to free the tyre from the sand some kids came over offered help, but actually they just wanted to rev the throttle. Our camp was complemented by several more Iranians and another French couple in what had become a rare travelling community. Food was shared around. Kevin got his guitar out and sang a few Van Morrison hits. Ali had a bottle of home brew spirit, strong stuff that I could barely touch.

In the morning the group rode on with Brad eventually departing to travel up North. At mid-day we reached Qeshm roof, the highest point on the island, where we built a shelter from the sun using my huge green tarp. Myself and Roozby climbed to the peak which afforded a terrific view in all directions.

We'd made a three quarter circle around the island when we began to plan for the evening. Doing as the locals do, we stopped at a stall in a dusty village and Ali went off to find to a wood crafting shop to have two pieces of wood made to accept the line we'd bought the day before. Ali had a nearby uncle and from him he sourced some squid.

The young son led us to a rather magical place. It was dark when we arrived at a floating jetty but the sea was calm and there was plenty of room for all four of us to try our hand at the shoals swimming around the wood. Out to sea the pressure release flame from a gas well lit up the sky with the effect of a large candle and cast enigmatic effects back onto the few moored boats in our beautifully tranquil spot. The fish were abundant and unwrapping the line from our wooden handles, we attached four hooks and a small weight and cast off.

I caught my first fish. About 20cm long, and a catfish, it was good only for cutting up to try and catch an upgrade. From the boy I learned catfish had barbed fins and spikes that had to be snapped and then cut off. Kevin outdid my effort by catching two. The boy caught around twenty.

At Ali's uncles house we ate some of the fish we'd caught and then slept at a guest house which was opened to accommodate our arrival. People here were Islamic, the men dressed in full white robes and the women in black. All were exceptionally lovely people. On dressing with respect I acknowledged it was harder for the cyclists when they were riding in such heat, but Lycra cloth and exposing the chest area to me seemed avoidable. Roozby the Iranian didn't appear to care. He was either oblivious or daring, but it had already gotten to Ali who felt embarrassed by it.

Our group discussed and chose to take the second port back to the mainland, which I was in favour off as there would be no height difference between the boat and the peer. It was about 10:00hrs the following morning when we accidentally came upon a small fishing village with a memorising sea front of iconic boats; some were colourful, some were rotten, some had sunk. A young boy of no more than 10yrs of age rode a 250cc Kawasaki dirt bike through the mud baked streets while little children hung outside little convenience shops with big grins and flapping hands An old woman took a carrier bag of rubbish, crossed the road and dumped it over the wall and into the sea.

Making it onto the ferry, which was nothing more than a barge with an engine attached, the skipper found himself blocked in by another boat with a constricted and clearly inadequate space to make it through. He went for it anyway. There was a large jolt as the two collided.

I arrived back in Bander Abbas before Kevin and checked into the same fantastic and cheap hotel. He and Roozby arrived later and Roozby began persistently asking for a massage. I persistently refused.

At 08:00hrs the next morning I began the extraneous paperwork required to get the scooter on the ferry from Bandar Abbas to Sharjah in the United Arab Emirates. I spent several hours going from office to office, photocopying documents, paying fees and racking up further cost on top of an already expensive ticket. Everything had to be paid in US dollars, but it wasn't as bad as I'd heard or expected it would be. Although everything was slow the process was straight forward and relatively easy to follow. Kevin joined at 17:00hrs but by then I'd met two French cyclists, a South Korean traveller and two French motorcyclists making their way to Australia. Ali had failed to get a flight back to Dubai and so was also joining us.

The boat departed at 23:00hrs, an hour later than planned, and that was a very sad end to my first Iranian excursion. Based on my empiricism so far, Iran would be hard to beat.

Sleeping that night was tough on the thin wooden benches, and the supplementary food wasn't much better. At around 04:00hrs a religious man with what appeared to be six wives following him around took it upon himself to awake the entire ferry to prayer. He cussed and cursed as most the men didn't want to get up, but his damnations did the job and the men then began climbing over and onto us and our benches to try and get a place in the small prayer room. I left the air conditioned inside and moved onto the deck outside where the chaos inside was replaced by heat and diesel fumes. I got another hour in after that. It was a rough night.

Chapter 11

United Arab Emirates

The ferry docked at Sharjah around 10:00hrs and I and the two French motorcyclists on their Yamaha 125's began the paperwork process to see us out of the port and into the UAE. Sharjah port was it's own municipal Government and even went so far as to use the Carnet while at the port. I had a feeling I was going to be hit with relentless charges. On this I was right.

The game began by having to identify and locate many offices dotted around the port. As the port was large we drove our vehicles to cut down on the effort. The UAE heat was unexpectedly hash and we spent most of the time waiting outside portable cabins for a piece of paper, which none times out of ten required a stamp from another office. Noticeably everyone was going slow and being largely unhelpful. There was a reason for this. At 14:00hrs they could start billing overtime.

The price of the ferry ticket was 8,000,000 Iranian Rial, or $267 USD and by the time I'd all the paperwork complete to permit security to open up the gate the cost had breached $500. By now I was disgusted with everything, and especially ireful with a fat Indian man who demanded $50 for unloading my scooter from the ferry. My case was strong – I rolled the bastard thing off the ferry myself!, but he didn't care. If I wanted his stamp, then I'd pay his fee.

My entry into the UAE was hence entirely negative, and it was about to get worse. Starving, I hit the nearest fast-food joint, a KFC, and in a moment of my tiredness forgot to wash my hands before devouring the greasy chicken. A silly mistake given all the stuff I'd been touching over the past 24 hours, the ferry and port germs went down my neck.

To minimise the Dubai price shock I'd arranged my first couchsurfing request at a place closer to Sharjah than Dubai and in an area dominated by Pakistani, Bangladeshi and Indian workers who were lucky enough not to be in the, shall be say "slave", labor construction trade. I experienced unbelievable hospitality from my Pakistani host. I was holed up in bed for two days in close proximity to his toilet as my backside drained my internal liquids away. That was not nice.

Kevin was also couch-surfing but was at a well-to-do young Arabs house in Dubai centre. The rent on the apartment would have cleared my bank balance in three month. I met them for lunch one evening and found his host to be a complete arse. All he could muster was a cheap comment on my functional Casio watch, but then I'd prepared myself for a materialistic mentality from the locals and offered a polite fuck you smile in return.

After a few days Kevin and I left our couch-surfing hosts and decided to sleep on the beach at Jumeira 1 in Dubai. Having a laugh was more important than a regular shower, and the beach was clean and vacant. Also vacant were seven large beach houses along the front. These massive houses were mostly complete but had been abandoned when the financial crises hit Dubai the years before. To our left a huge building was under construction. It looked like a very expensive hotel with its all glass auditorium style design, but it was to be a private dwelling. The owner had also purchased all the abandoned houses on the shore front. Indian and Bangladeshi workers arrived early to work on it and were bussed back to their camp in the evening. We used their rusting tap each morning to shower and saw first hand the squalid conditions they were working in. Slave labor indeed.

For a cheap traveller, Dubai was a stop gap, and while creatively impressive, I did not belong here. The roads were made for cars and services like hotels and restaurants for business. One thing was clear; people didn't come to Dubai to live cheap. During the daytime I researched ships and other methods to break out, even looking at Yemen and the possibility of getting a 'fixed' visa for Pakistan. Kevin was trying to find a Yak or a considerate container ship that would afford him passage. Neither of us wanted to fly.

Up the road leading up to our beach was the Bikers Cafe, a Harley Davidson bad-boy themed joint that lacked any of the requisite authenticity. It was convenient and a good place to chill at, but still in Iranian price mode I found the spending hard to stomach.

Further travellers turned up, including a new french cyclist, the two french cyclists we'd met in Bander Abbas, and the

126

French lady driving her camper-van with her two kids. This was unusual and when the owner of the cafe found out he quickly called his photographer and began creating marketing material. We were interviewed, telling our stories one by one, then pictures were taken with our transport in front of the premises. Then we were told for as long as we were here all food and drink was on the house! Bingo!

The owner of the cafe was an indigenous Emirate, and this quartile make up around only 7% of the UAE population. The guy was of course wealthy, and apart from 35 other restaurants, he owned 62 cars and properties in capital cities around the world. I only briefly saw one of his cars, a modern Bentley, but the rest were, I was told, equal or more expensive. I was curious as to why he'd shown such hospitality towards myself and the other travellers and why he hadn't shied away from the general public who would, I figured, be canvassing the life out of him for money, jobs and contacts. He explained how he felt old values were being lost in the UAE and how he came from a traditional family that still believed in being a great host. He recited an old Arabic proverb that said if you meet a hungry guest and have only the camel on which you ride, you must kill the camel to feed your guest. We talked for a while longer and the guy came across as very noble, patriotic and down-to-earth individual. I concluded that if I'm not chosen to own a good size of money, then I want people like him to be chosen instead. Inshallah.

Breaking out of Dubai was the priority but the only option I could source was to send the scooter by plane from Dubai airport to Mumbai in India. I'd looked at getting a Pakistan visa 'fixed', but information was sketchy and unreliable, plus I'd still need a boat. A few days were spent at Dubai Cargo Village working on the prices and learning about the process, which I was determined to do without any agents. To my dismay the prices were higher compared to the previous year. Flying the scooter over to Mumbai was going to work out at $800 USD. I had to suck it.

The day came when the scooter was to be part dismantled and crated, but before I could begin I had to visit two Dubai offices to get clearance forms which verified I had no road fines to pay and which would allow the vehicle to be exported. These required two colourful stamps from two different places and I spent the first two hours running around clueless. At 11:00hrs the crating of the bike began. I removed the front wheel, the panniers, handlebars, mirrors, screen, GPS bracket and mudguard and with this done the size was considerably smaller. This was a good thing because the chargeable rate went on metric volume as well as weight. Paperwork went on and on ending with customs and dangerous goods checks.

It was the later part of the afternoon when I nearly snapped. I was in the customs building about to get a final form complete when an agent lied about needing his services to do it. He spoke to the authorities on the desk before telling me this and so I paid the 100 dirham fee (about $36 USD) he was asking. Then I found out otherwise, that he'd just asked something which would get the customs officer to shake his head. Deception. I blew up and stormed back into the Dubai custom office demanding to know who had lied. Being brash with authorities isn't exactly acceptable in Dubai and I had a good chance of being arrested, but it was a long day and I was worn down. The agent had guilt written all over his face, plus he was Indian which probably worked against him. The customs officer blasted him for his deceit and the agent fee was reimbursed.

The process went on into the evening. At 18:00hrs the scooter, now crated and shrink wrapped, kept failing the industrial x-ray check. An hour later it passed. I left at about 20:00hrs, exhausted but with the airway bill in my hand. The bike would leave for Bahrain the following day and then fly from there to Mumbai at the end of the week. I caught a taxi back to Bikers Cafe where Kevin was waiting and tucked into another free meal. My flight to Mumbai was booked for the following evening at 22:30hrs.

The following day I passed a few hours seeing the new James Bond movie and then shook hands with Kevin. It had been quite a journey so far. I was off to begin Asia and he had an agreement with the skipper of a ferry that would dump him somewhere near Indonesia. Perhaps we'd meet again, it was a small world after all.

Chapter 11

Mumbai, India

Stepping out of Mumbai airport and onto Asian soil was a key moment on my journey around the world. I had mixed expectations for India. Many had warned about the chaos, unfriendly people and a place not for outsiders. Others had compared the place to a cocktail of spice, sweet, sour and bitter flavours. All I knew was my plane landed very early and having not slept I crashed near a window near the airport exit while I waited until 09:00hrs for my hostel pickup to arrive.

While the taxi touts did their best to secure another dump white tourist, at 09:00hrs I was in the back of a rickshaw beginning for the first time to see what India was with my own eyes. It was eye opening. Among the people, so many people, bared a sensory overbearing amount of rubbish; real filth and disgusting overflowing refuge containers. The roads flowed with juices and the stench was at times nauseating. Coming from Dubai and the cleanliness of Iran before it, India was a real, genuine shock.

I was told the paperwork formalities to release the scooter from Mumbai airport would be troublesome but having gone through the process at Sharjah and Dubai I applied a level of ignorance to how bad it could be. I began the next day when the customs opened, which was Monday at 08:00hrs.

The effort on day one, calculated in terms of hours rather than by my stress level, came to thirteen. I had never witnessed such stupidity or idiocy before, which included photocopying of random, pointless pages of the Carnet de Passage and then writing the details by hand into several books and into a typed letter. At some point I visited everyone in the damn airport to get some sort of stamp. Most came with fees, and the total to take the scooter from Dubai to Mumbai soon crept over the $1,000 USD mark. Everyone was shafting, including *Gulf Air* carrier who charged $120 additional 'dangerous good handling charges' on top of what was paid at Dubai, making it one of the most expensive couriers to ship cargo with.

If I were to fully describe the process in its entirety, every other word would be an adjective and the others would be damning. I'll side rail that writeup by stating I will never, under any circumstances do it again. Categorically, I'd rather die then allow the people working there the pleasure of witnessing the inflicted mental torture that their nonsensical formalities, the corruption and the time wasting process inflicted upon my soul. It was a truly hateful period of my life.

At the end of the day they closed the office and told me to come back the next day for part two. I was exasperated but had no choice and finally at 14:00hrs I rode the scooter down the ramp and onto India soil; and into ungodly traffic that made Istanbul look like a leisure cruise.

For the first time I'd picked up a second hand Lonely Planet guide and as I read through its write-up for Mumbai I could only smirk at the inaccuracy. Sentences came full on with praises like 'a concoction of sensory imposing experiences' when a greater truth would have read "dull, impoverished, hassle bound and to be avoided at all costs."

Mumbai had a very dirty beach, a dirty port and dirty streets that were always full of people and trash. The rich lived in the suburbs away from all this and the city was an obvious explosion of poverty and the quick-cash elite. Situated close to the airport, I was at the only hostel I could find and it was overpriced and the most depressing I've ever been too. The people there were all waiting for connecting flights or trains. Everyone wanted out.

On the Friday I visited the city centre close to Churchgate train station which gave me a chance to try the train for the first time. I was genuinely impressed by the industrial frankness in its design and operation. Forget padding, seats and even doors, this was more a moving metal cage jam packed with bodies. The lack of seats worked well, nobody wanted to be away from the doors anyway, it was way to hot for that. The lack of doors served to process the in and outgoing passengers in record time.

Churchgate showed a little forward planning, at least there was a field for locals to play cricket on, but many of the so called 'attractions' were largely out of reach to the general public, including the University building, closed since the Mumbai bombings of 2008. The port featured a very expensive hotel frequented by world leaders and a large monument left by the British to remind the Indians it was they who ransacked their country.

Above all I was dismayed with the people. Corruption seemed rife and engrained into the way the people thought. With a free-for-all attitude, everyone went about ripping everyone else off, threw rubbish into the streets and had absolutely no regard for the safety or warfare of others. I hated the disheartening lack of self-respect for the environment. I hated the fact people were living under bridges amongst piles of filth and bloated rats fatter then their own impoverished children. I hated that man could sink so low.

The Government seemingly didn't bother emptying bins and subsequently refuge free-flowed everywhere. Clogged streams running alongside roads were mere cesspits and crossing over a railway bridge, which authorities had the audacity to charge for, I noticed rats running along the iron beams unafraid of human attention. The sheer amount of people in Mumbai was staggering with minimal personal space and privacy. At times it felt suffocated by it, and as I pushed my way through resistant crowds I wondered how a disease endemic hadn't unfolded.

The transport system strangely works. Manic rickshaw drivers ferried people around in what were the most dangerous roads I've encountered so far. To drive and survive you must be bold, aggressive and cunning.

On the weekend a famous politician named Bal Thackery died and the police ordered the entire city to shut down. I was eating in a cheap restaurant when the door shutters began to roll down and a commotion began outside. The people in the streets were worried and moving fast. Expecting something to kick off, I made my way back to the hostel on an extremely busy train and joined others in the lockdown. The day the hostel ran out of food reserves and I couldn't buy any elsewhere since everything was firmly closed. I joined another guy from the hostel and together we went scourging the back streets where we found a guy quietly selling dodgy soft apples, his eyes pealed for police. It seemed ridiculous that a city with the population of Australia could shut down in such this way, but shut down it did. As for the dead politician, his ideas included amassing a team of Indian suicide bombers and forbidding Pakistan-Indian marriages. The locals said he was a "God Father" in Mumbai, an untouchable figure which no-one dared query and held him in high regard.

With my scooter ready to roll I left Mumbai first thing Monday morning on what was to be a a drive south towards the promise of something beautiful – the state of Goa. On the way out a petrol station refused to fill the fuel can under the seat, more stupid rules, but in the ever constant rush hour traffic I made my way onto the highway, greatly concerned that I was going under a truck. Even as a seasoned traveller, having buses and taxis just inches from my handlebars, then them slamming on brakes and cutting me up was a nerve racking experience.

Somewhere outside of the city I stopped at a restaurant and asked if I could pitch my shelter at the side of the dining area. Thinking I was out of the big city life where the Indian's would have lost the ripoff culture, I didn't ask the price of the Chicken Birani and was suitably ripped off. That was a turning point for dealing with people here. From now on I planned to be on the defensive with everyone. It was that or my wallet would soon run dry.

"India, a place you dream about, until you get there." - a post someone wrote on my Facebook wall.

Chapter 12

Goa, India

An ex Portuguese colony, Goa I was told would defy typical India with its rich beaches, resorts, partying and package holiday tourists. Situated on the west coast, half way down the country, the land was supposedly swampy, somewhat tropical, and cleaner than the rest of India. It would also be less populated. After the mad rush of Mumbai it felt like I'd be taking a holiday.

The drive from Mumbai to Goa was mostly trouble free and enjoyable. It took two days but probably could have been done in one if I'd set off really early. Instead I pitched my camp besides a dusty restaurant that looked like it mainly served haulers and buses. It wasn't long before my scooter began to stir a crowd. I felt some negativity from some of the locals, or apprehension, either way I was uncomfortable and on the defensive, expecting trouble to stir. Trouble didn't, but a couple of the locals spoke broken English and said if I'd stopped further ahead down the road I would have had it. Once outside of Mumbai there were little police around, and many Indians have a distaste for Goa and the tourists that go there. As one of the Indians at the restaurant put it, "Goa is not India."

The open platformed restaurant ran christmas lights along its width and was wooden with plastic table and chairs. It was raised off the ground and the entire area was, as is typical in India, a dumping ground. I'd set up my camp in a corner a little out the way of the colourful lights, which turned out to be a good decision as the restaurant owner left them on when he closed for the night.

I expected an easy sleep as I was out of view and 50 metres from the main road but during the night heavy haulage increased and the truck noise, much louder than European regulations allow, was deafening. At some point I awoke to the arrival of an Ambulance which unduly parked it's just 10 metres away from my tent. The rear door opened and ten women dressed in head scarfs climbed down then after a short pause a female doctor followed. The driver began changing a rear offside flat while the women stared in my direction as if they'd witnessed an alien. Half an hour later they were on their way and the commotion replaced once again by wild dogs rummaging under the stilted restaurant for food, and the frequent drive-by of noisy trucks.

The following morning I made Goa and knowing nothing about the place headed for what I would later learn was the worst part of it; a tourist trap called Calungate. Here, the thickest British subjects live out their annual holiday without attrition or remorse for how they go on. Whereas a few year back they'd have gone to Majorca or another area of Spain, Spain is now expensive, so they come to Goa where beer costs not much more than $0.50 USD a bottle. After a few they project their filthy mouths and allow their minuscule brains of the leash. For the benefit of man-kind, and personal satisfaction, I'd have happily executed a good portion of them right there and then.

The centre of Goa proved very popular with Russians and they outnumbered other nationalities by a good measure. Most hung around Calungate or Baga and the local economies had adapted to suit. Calungate road, leading to the overcrowded beach, featured tattoo shops and hard liquor stores amidst hassling street sellers and pungent smells of rotting rubbish. Apart than the smell it rescinded the beach resort I'd visited so many months ago in Varna, Bulgaria. The Russians seemed to enjoy it, but alas I did not.

Calungate featured only the one hostel but this was really just a hotel that had put aside a small room and filled it with eight bunk beds. The room had zero ventilation and the fan inside pushed around the deoxygenated, damp air making all that stayed in the room ill. Having experienced this so many times before and knowing that this is what makes backpackers ill more often than dodgy food, I took my mosquito shelter and assembled it next to the pool on a sun lounger. I told the disgruntled manager that I had the god given right to breath and he argued no further.

In the morning I ventured out to a nearby fort, which was nothing special, and then on to a lighthouse that afforded superb views across the Indian ocean. Afterwards I found a restaurant with wifi and began to plan the places I'd an inclination to visit. My first priority was to get away from these kind of tourists and to find real Goa. Bring out the hippies! As I worked my laptop I could hear British scum and their filthy mouths swearing away at the bar. "The f**king kitchen was worse than the f**king bathroom, f**king c**t spewed everywhere!", a leather skinned woman in her late forties mouthed off.

The following day two interesting Germans arrived. The first, younger than myself, had travelled to India on her transitional journey to become a nun, and before doing so she would go see the Dala Lama speak. Named Serena, she sported a shaved head and taught me the essentials of Buddhism. If there's one religion I knew nothing about it was Buddhism, but even calling it a religion is incorrect for there is no god or requirement to worship. All that is extra and unnecessary. What is required is a belief in what Buddhists call 'reaching enlightenment', where one has no desires. Serena was easy to talk to and was open about her past even more so. I was interested to hear about her ideas and discover the mind behind such a radical departure from my kind of standard life. I learned that before Buddhism found her, she was suicidal, hurting herself with a knife, and in her earlier years she'd suffered sexual abuse. This was her way out.

The second German was a little older than myself, in her early thirties. Sadly I can't remember her name but she too was more interesting than your everyday Joe and a common bond formed which led to some deep discussion. At the bar, we talked quietly and I listened more than I offered. Serena discussed the importance of forgiving, and I came to understand I'm of an unforgiving nature. By the end of it, I felt a little of that enlightenment she carried within her. It was a fabulous conversation.

The older German girl left the next day but Serena had a bit of time before the Dala Lama talk and I offered a ride-out on the back of my scooter. That day we met up with two Australians who were around for a week or so and agreed to tag together. One was an expert in Chinese medicine and had done a lot of volunteering in poor Indian villages while the other had done a lot of weed and was curious about yoga. Both were fine, and we moved from the awful middle Goa area and north to the little village of Arambol where we rented two cheap wooden shacks, two extra scooters and chilled out on the beach. At night the place was a haven for travellers. The genuine real-deal, they came with all sorts of instruments and when the sunset was over, jamming began. Others brought brooms with wicks soaked in paraffin, set them alight and danced to the fire. Few things I can remember with absolute clarity and vividness, but swinging an ignited stick over my head and around my body, while others whooped and danced and clapped is one of them. This was retro Goa like from the 70's, and I'd managed to catch and experience a rare glimpse of it before it was lost for good.

The Aussies swapped their small scooters for small motorcycles, both of which were better in sand than my own. Over the next few days we tracked the northern coast to the very top of Goa, discovering little bays with disused wooden boats, paddy fields, empty beaches and lots of foliage. We drank beer in moderation and dined on the cheap. It was a time of great relaxation, and Serena relished it even more than I. She was so happy taking pictures with my camera and so content with her current situation that I found her happiness impressionable and almost infectious. We shared a wooden hut on the beach front and the time melted away.

All good things come to an end and with the Australians splitting and Serena departing it was time for myself to move on. I had a plan to visit south Goa but only after I'd visited a small national park and waterfall which was a two hour drive inland. On arrival at said park I was told I'd have to be out by 17:00hrs and that I would have great difficulty with my scooter with its inability to off-road or through water.

140

Thinking I knew better, and not willing to pay to share a jeep, I went ahead anyway. I came across only the one significant stretch of water. It was significant in that I drowned the engine in it. Having pushed the scooter out and up the bank I waited five minutes until my heart rate recovered and then deliberated over whether to remove the spark plug and drain the cylinder or to just crank it and hope for no hydraulic lock. I chose the latter. Luck was on my side and the little Honda started straight away. Coughing, spluttered, pouring steam out the exhaust, it made it to the waterfall, where I changed into shorts and swam around the raging downpour. On the way back I had to go through the same water and probably should have pushed it, but instead took a run up and give it all it had. I made it through without drowning the engine, and I don't know how because the air-box was surely below the waterline. Perhaps the wake was enough to prevent water ingression. As I was late returning back to the entrance, I asked a warden with a colonial style moustache if I could stay at a campsite they were building for tourists. It was unfinished and had no facilities, but provided the safety I needed from whatever wild animals was in the national park. Not that I'd seen any.

Having completed North Goa it was time to move to the South where I was told to expect an older and more mature crowd of seasoned foreigners. Inspecting the coast the better of the bunch was at the small village area of Benalium. Here huts and restaurants erected on a six month lease littered the beach while a few select cafe shops offered excellent and cheap food geared more towards European style. As it was low season I negotiated a plot of land for my mosquito tent and saved on the need to pay for a full hut.

Days passed by, on one I filled in a job application, more just testing the water than anything else, and on another I used my Iranian fishing stick to see what I could catch in the sea. Alongside a fellow Englishman, one who flew out to the same place every year, I used my antiquated gear and instantly caught a foot long catfish. With his professional gear it I made a bit of an initial impression, but that was all I caught.

There were a few interesting people and most of them came back to the same place. With hardly anyone else around, myself and an Italian pilot played blues music over the speakers at the hut shackle thing next door to our own and downed beers to the beats. I met a German driving his motorcycle down to Australia and an ageing hippy who had lost the crowd but retained the memories.

My scooter, now battle tested and scarred was developing a noise from the drive chain. The dust, heat and additional weight of my equipment had prematurely worn it. Honda India didn't stock PCX parts, but Honda Thailand kindly offered to DHL a new belt over to Mumbai. I'd be (unfortunately) passing there on my way North so would pick it up at the hostel and have it fitted at a local mechanic. The noise being what it was I was skeptical whether it would make it.

Chapter 13

Indore, India

I set off from Goa with a full stomach; my usual combination of cornflakes with mixed fruit, a cheese omelette and a chai from the excellent cafe beside Benalium beach. Not only was I to pick the belt up at the hostel, I had to go back to pick up clothes I'd accidentally left and to sort out some road insurance (oops!). I drove about 200km and set-up camp before dark in a track off the main road where I remained undisturbed. The following morning I was off early and reached Mumbai in the afternoon. I checked into the same horrible hostel for the night and the following day posted a t-shirt to a friend and tried to sort the road insurance. This required a train-ride to the centre, refreshing my memory on the chaos and rubbish that comes with Mumbai. I'd forgotten it was a Saturday and missed the insurance office by an hour. Oh well, I'd just have to crack on without. I tried to have the new belt fitted at a Honda dealer but they said they were "unauthorised" to touch foreign vehicles. More Indian bureaucracy. I stopped at a local and had it done their instead.

From Mumbai I'd head north, roughly, with a little sidetrack to Ellora and Ajunta caves. These were 400km or thereabouts from the city and with no intention to stay for any longer than

I had too, in the late afternoon I set off towards Ellora. Darkness fell while I rode along the manic east highway and once it began to calm down I began scanning left and right for a wild camp opportunity. I picked up a colourfully lit model Hindu and a type of temple beside it. I could see only three people in the area and lots of dark spots where I could pitch and forget, so I turned off to check the place out. I parked and walked over to the temple. To cross the floor I had to take my shoes off and on reaching the far end I spoke slowly to a gentleman with regards to staying the night. In broken English he said it wasn't a problem, in fact I could sleep on the temple floor in the corner. He asked if I'd eaten and if I would join them for lunch (as they call it, we Brits call it tea or evening supper). It would have been rude to have said no, so I said sure, and asked when, to which he replied an hour, after the 250 volunteers arrived. 250 volunteers you what!?! That's 250 volunteers doing circles around my bike, poking my equipment and asking questions all night. I just wanted a quiet night! Oh god!

Sleeping under the temple roof I thought the tent would bring unnecessary attention so I unrolled just my sleeping bag. The volunteers poured in. Walking 250km over seven days, and some were going the extra distance by doing it without footwear, they were all keen and high spirited. The majority were young, probably around 18 on average. As I was the guest, and I'd put myself forward, I wasn't treat like a foreigner, and hence I was saved from the usual piss-taking and currency conversion querying. When lunch came I mucked in, and to their delight and fascination ate using my hands, just as they did. The food was delicious, although I nearly choked on the chilli/pepper sauce. Plenty of photographs were taken and a little drum and group singing ended the night. I learned that not all Indians are selfish, or

144

robbing sods.

At about 01:00hrs in the morning I found myself wide awake. It was quiet, but huge flying insects were landing on my legs and swarming around my face. I quietly slipped out and erected the mosquito shelter outside.

At 04:00hrs, and way too early the volunteers awoke, and thus so did I. The illuminated Hindu model was turned on and loud and repetitive chanting music began emanating from the centre of it. My sleep was over. At 06:00hrs, and with the sun just poking its head up, I was back on the bike and riding towards Ellora caves, complete with a headache and eyes which wanted to close.

The motorway was well surfaced but the secondary road afterwards was a high contrast to it. Some of the potholes could have devoured my entire front wheel should I be unlucky to drive into one, and I had to cut my speed in half to ensure there avoidance. 'Rumblers' as they call them, and speed bumps to the rest of us, are unusual in design. Instead of one bump they use six or seven, tightly spaced together and significant in height. If tackled with speed the scooter would glide over, but too slow and my spine would feel jarred. I hated the things. The terrain changed to dust and shrub bush and reminded of the baroness I'd experienced in Iran. Here people were few and far between. It was a reposeful place at polar odds with what I'd seen of India so far.

Ellora caves cost a mere 10 rupee for Indians but 250 rupee for foreigners. While 250 rupee wasn't the end of the world it presented a problem when bananas costed 2 rupee each. 125 bananas to see the caves wasn't just and would impression on the locals that foreigners had money to burn. The consequence began as soon as I stepped into the official ground. Here taxi drivers and other touts were doing the 'can I see what a 20 dollar note looks like' and 'take one picture' scams and were persistent and aggressive at it. The cafe wanted paying to keep my helmet in one of their rooms at the back. Zero charity.

Later when walking up the cliff side to photograph the main temple two touts followed from behind. As I paused for respite I could tell from the way they were following and loitering that hassle was inbound. And so it began. "Hello, what's your name? Where do you come from?"

I'd found, so far, that the most effective technique was ignorance, or speaking in French. I lost my temper in the darkness of Cave 15 when two more of the bastards began hustling with aggression. If I was a female and alone I'd have felt vulnerable, and with nobody else around it could have been a different situation. I repositioned the strap on my camera so that it hung mostly over my back and spontaneously pushed the guy as hard as I could into the nearest wall, my fist up so he could see what was going to come if he and his side kick didn't move on.

That the management at Ellora caves condones and accepts these scumbags was another example of India at it's worst. It wasn't just adults either. Later ten kids tried dancing a circle around me calling the 'one picture' act and prancing like the monkeys sitting on the sidelines watching them. Luckily I had no easily accessible bags for them to pick pocket.

Ellora caves was nice and in particular the temple cut out of rock (downwards!) was a marvel, but like hell would I go again. Because of the experience I decided to skip Ajunta caves and advance my itinerary by making my way North-West towards Udaipur. I purchased 20 bananas, some other food stuffs, and drove off.

50km north I found a superb spot for camping, away from the main road and complete with it's own little rock pool. Here I boiled eggs, chopped tomatoes and made a light tea. As soon as darkness fell, about 19:00hrs, my head was down and I was out for the count.

The following day I expected to wholly comprise of mundane driving. Garmin advised Udaipar to be 700km from my current destination, two days riding if the roads held up. To begin with the route comprised of a small mountain pass with thin squiggly roads and aggressively driven trucks that would launch into corners, horn on, hoping to subdue any oncoming vehicle into submission. Dropping off the side would be a terminal mistake. Once the pass ended the road became modern and near European standard. I devoured the miles.

412km from Ellora, a figure that I would imprint on my memory with vividness, a ratchet style sound began from the lower part of the scooter. I dropped the speed to 50mph and stuck my head down below the screen to try and determine where it was coming from and seconds later there was a large bang followed by silence. The scooter had lost all power and I coasted to the side of the road where I brought it to a stop. Flicking the side stand down, I said a quick prayer and then dismounted to inspect the damage. Engine oil was over the road and around the rear wheel. I tipped the scooter onto its side and located a significant hole in the crankcase. Excellent. While no expert on engine internals, I hazarded a guess the piston rod had snapped, rotated 180 degrees and punched its way through the bottom. This was a serious problem.

As usual several Indians have arrived, all very excited about the prospect of profiteering from the situation at hand. The only affirmative action I could think off was to load it onto a passing truck and transport it to the city of Indore. Here I was likely to find a Honda dealer, not that they stocked this engine, and I noted there was an airport if I need out. The best possibility to flag down a truck would be at a petrol station but the Indians who'd stopped said the closest was 3km ahead. Blustered, I began pushing the scooter to get away from the crowd while simultaneously pushing Garmin. It indicated a petrol station 1km back so I turned around and headed for that. The Indians had already phoned there friends 3km ahead and tried to entice me to continue going that way but I ignored them and continued on. By now I was incredible hot, but I wasn't pissed off. It was what it was and I had to deal with it.

On reaching the petrol station I contemplated how I'd flag down a truck, which seemed harder than I first realised as they were all full of material or not going to Indore at all. A young Indian said his mate would take it for 1,500 rupees. That was about $30 USD to cover 100km. I agreed, and one hour later the scooter was loaded on a very small van and on its way. Garmin located a Honda dealer but I suspected I'd have the same "unauthorised" crap I had from the last one, but that was not my main concern, my main concern was security – being able to park the scooter up for a few days while I explored the available options. I believed my best chance was at a dealership. Would Honda extend the warranty to India and help me out? How long would it take to fix? Could it even be fixed? Would the carnet people come after me if I had to scrap the scooter without exporting it out of

India?

The van was underpowered and it took over two hours to reach the city and by which time it was dark. It was extremely smoggy, utterly jam packed with people and shanty like Mumbai. The traffic was gridlocked and at the sides of the roads the hustle and bustle of street life was alive. People were even selling everything, even Santa outfits and red christmas hats.

My driver was agitated but spoke no English so communication was impossible. We reached an area in the northern part of the city, a part with a very plush hotel from the Sayaji chain and several other more realistic options. I was worried by the amount of people around, which would mean immediate and unrelenting hassle.

The dealership we'd pulled up at read Hero, and it was closed. The security guard there explained Honda until last year had ran a joint operation with this Indian company before going it alone.. It was too late to continue searching and by now my driver was mouthing off. I ordered the driver to stop and take the bike off. I knew what was coming, he wanted more rupees, but he was asking the wrong man. With the bike unloaded several passing locals became excited and a few teenagers began playing monkey. I pushed the bike into the dealership grounds and asked the security guy if I could leave it in the corner overnight. He said no. I asked to speak with his boss. He shrugged a 'no understanding'. Then out of the building came the last employee, a man working in finance, and I asked him if he could instruct the security man.

Accommodating, he did just that, and also advised where the actual Honda Service Station was located, some 3km from our current location. I removed the luggage and went in search of a cheap hotel. Along the road I came across Hotel Park, charging 800 rupees a night (about $ 16 USD). I checked in and went in search of an Internet cafe where I could write an email to my contact at Honda Thailand to plead for a replacement engine and the RAC carnets department in case I had to ditch it. Nothing in India was easy. I knew they'd be plenty of red tape and regulations to contend with.

In the morning I was apprehensive over what to do next but the day began at the Hero dealership where I'd left the scooter overnight. I commended their staff who were unbelievably helpful, the security guy had even gone about cleaning the scooter! Chai was served and after a discussion they decided it best to take the scooter to the Honda dealership 7km away. To do this an engineer freewheeled my scooter while another engineer on a separate bike stuck his foot out and pushed on the back of the right hand side pannier. Thrusted forward, horns aloud, we dodged roundabouts and auto rickshaws and made it unscathed. I was on the back of the second bike trying my best to warn traffic behind what was going on. Top marks then for Indore Hero's effort and courtesy. I couldn't thank them enough.

After the experience I had at the Honda dealership in Goa I was expecting much the same: they would refuse to do anything as the model wasn't a bona fide import. But I was wrong. On arrival the service manager came out, followed by several engineers. Chai was served and I was made to feel welcome from the start. They tipped the scooter over and several began whistling at the damage. As I understood it they believed the crank rod had snapped and punctured the crank casing. They also stated that the internal damage, that I could

150

not see, would be significant. If the timing had gone out then the piston would have hit the valves. The piston and walls were likely to be damaged. It would be a big repair and a a new engine was the safer bet. They began enquiries with Honda India which led to a parts estimate of two months, if I were lucky, but Indian law didn't permit unapproved vehicle part imports without certification, and my vehicle wasn't a certified type. I would have to lean on my contacts at Honda Asia and grovel a bit further. Meanwhile a large thread on Facebook offered suggestions including buying a cheap Royal Enfield Bullet or a bicycle. These were all credible and I had to consider them. I left the Honda dealership at 13:00hrs while they got to work on the scooter. For minimal cost they would take the engine out and to pieces to find out exactly what would be needed to get it fixed. It would take 4 hours, or so they believed. While they worked I crossed the road to a shopping mall with a MacDonald's. Comfort food! While eating a young girl, probably 16yrs old, approached my table and asked without any introduction whether I was married or single.

The next three days I spent communicating with Honda Asia on whether they'd be willing and able to sent a replacement engine. The cost of doing so by courier would be substantial. Honda India concluded bad fuel had upset the fuel ignition timing which in-turn bent the piston rod and eventually led to its failure. This was a credible theory as the engine ran at a high 1:11 compression ratio and the fuel injection was never designed or tested with Indian fuel. I was keen to put forward this explanation to Honda Asia as it would uphold their reputation for having built a robust engine. I neglected to mention the previous ford drownings.

The Honda India dealer was exceptionally courteous and

there'd been no mention of fees at this point, but this being India I was always expecting a slam in the face. A few regional Honda managers were passing the dealer every other day and also integrated themselves into the solution. The more the merrier. It looked like having contacts at Honda Asia made Honda India think I was sponsored, which I wasn't, but I was happy to play along while there was no mention of money. A manager made a Powerpoint presentation with a step by step pictorial and a parts list, then sent this onto the India head office. With so many people involved, all I could think of was, am I being billed for this?

Honda Asia were willing to help and I immensely appreciated their efforts. After their PR office discussed the damage with their R&D team (these being the people that build the engine in Thailand) they concluded it best to replace the entire engine. I received a slightly cryptic message saying they were looking "at how best to support you". I imagined someone up the food chain was analysing my website hits and Facebook likes and deciding if the substantial cost was worth it.

While the deliberations went on Honda India let the cat out the bag when they said the authorities required notification of an engine replacement and that there would be extra formalities due to it being a foreign vehicle. To permit any alteration they'd require a written letter from Indian Customs. This could take months.

Another option was to have the engine fitted illegally, but when exporting it out on the Indian/Nepal border if the authorities were to check the new engine number to the one registered in my Carnet de Passage the letter would be asked for, or the vehicle seized.

There was also a 50% tax on importing a new engine and I'd have continued problems using the carnet in following countries.

It was time to take a step back, to reflect, to summarise, to conclude. At the end of the day the scooter was a tool. It was a tool chosen because of it's low cost and simplicity, and right now it was neither.

The cost of flying the scooter after Nepal from Kathmandu to Thailand would be a little under the scooters worth. The cost of flying it to North or South America would be substantial. I was nearly spending more on flying the scooter than in the places I was visiting.

The carnet, the 'formalities', the paperwork, the breakdown, all I could eliminate in the future, if I eliminated the scooter, but how easy would it be to scrap the scooter in India and could I break my attachment to the ease of on-tap power? What were my alternatives; bus, train, bicycle?

I wanted to draw a line, yet I had no ruler. In a way I'd wanted Honda Asia to say no, it would have made the decision for me. If they said yes, who knew how long I'd spend in Indore.

While Honda pedalled the possibilities I did little during the day other than take the long walk to the Honda dealer to see if there were any update on the formality process or entering the expensive Hotel Salaji and defrauding my way onto the wifi network by lying about my non-existent room number. In the evening I happened upon a small backstreet restaurant where I began talking to a Nepalese man who'd worked with several famous journalists from the BBC back when Nepal's political stability was volatile. Named Manoj, he was hoping to entice a documentary team to visit the Nomadic people of Nepal and could facilitate such a group thanks to his contacts. Living in India for only his wife, he had no work and no money and wasn't eating so that his kids could. A genuine and charming guy that asked for nothing, my own peril was little compared to his own and I bought all his food and wrote an email which he could send to the appropriate organisations.

Dear Sir/Madam,

My name is Manoj Shehi, I'm a Nepalese resident who has led and facilitated journalists and broadcasters through Nepal's political transition and other topics. I am currently looking to facilitate a documentary team on the lives of the reclusive Nomadic people found in the mid-west district of Surkxet, Nepal.

These people are like nowhere else in the world and rarely allow foreigners access to their lives. Living entirely in the jungle, they won't grow food but instead catch and eat out of the area they currently live. Diets include jungle pig, monkeys and bats. A documentary team would be able to see the hunt and consumption of such delicacies!

With no outside connections, the 15-35 members in each community move approximately every two months in search of food. The Nomadic people don't build houses but make huts. Not all is well, as the jungles they live in are partly destroyed in their quest for food and shelter, and also by outsiders. Lack of any medical treatment is also placing strain on the numbers of these people.

Most interesting of all are the political and social workings.

One leader is recommended, not appointed, to lead the group, and has final say in all matters. Marriage is chosen by song, where a man and male friends compete with a group of similar numbered females in a folk duet festival. The male will sing a question and the female group must reply. Should they fail to outperform the males, the male leader can choose his bride. Even such small groups afford enormous discrimination among each other. Many brothers can marry one lady, and when a husband dies they believe the wife to be the cause. Afterwards they view the widow as completely useless, and her life turns into a pale existence of its former self as an outcast who has no option but to try and survive within the only domain she has known.

If your organisation has a small documentary team who would be willing and able to cover this fascinating group, please get in contact.

Yours sincerely,

Manoj Shehi

After writing up his references we walked to a bicycle shop to look at the possibilities. Most the bikes in India had strong rear racks and many of the newer bikes have a huge solid bar as an extension of the frame and a rack welded on top. One stated it could carry 30kg and looked robust, as so long as I could swap the flimsy looking wheels that came with it.

If it did come to scrapping the scooter I would need authorisation and a member of customs present when it was surrendered. How to go about this was anyone's guess but

Manoj took me to the RTA which was responsible for handling all vehicle licensing in the country. The RTA didn't have a clue and instead gave the location of the customs department for Indore, at which I'd have to speak to the commissioner. After travelling another 10km through heavy traffic, I found the commissioner was out of the city and would be back the day after, perhaps, and that the Indore customs wouldn't help with anything even when he returned. I'd have to go to Mumbai customs for that. I asked the Indian Automobile Association to confirm this and was told it was the case. To summarise, I'd have to pay to put the scooter on a truck and then pay whatever fees to surrender it to customs. Two further points; there was no method to scrap a vehicle in India – they simply didn't crush and recycle vehicles. On surrendering the scooter I would have to pay the import duty which the Carnet had covered, or stick the scooter on a flight out.

To top it off, the customs department at Indore said the authorisation Honda India required to fit the new engine would be denied. At that point I knew what had to be done. I had to dump the scooter and cut my losses. I'd forfeit the Carnet de Passage deposit of some £550 and move on.

Afterwards my Nepalese friend Manoj took me to another part of town where I found what looked like the perfect bicycle for mounting my gear and cracking on with the trip. At $180, the bike had twin disc brakes, a substantial carrier and appeared well built. Then again I knew nothing about bicycles. Later Honda replied to an email I'd sent asking about the expected time delivery of the replacement engine, answering 10-14 days thereabouts and another five or so to fit it. It must be said, Honda were doing an exceptional job with support. I had no contract with them and I'd subjected the scooter to untold abuse. They could have told me to get on my horse, as the saying goes, but by now my mind was already made up.

One evening I ate an unbelievably spicy vegetable biryani. The chef clearly tipped in every spice he had, and all of it. I felt the need to challenge myself, despite the first mouthful sending a conflagration down my throat, and I finished the plate in its entirety. On the first night stomach pain ensued, then increased until I spent the rest of my sleeping hours in torsional pain. At 03:00hrs I was doing sit-ups to try and release the wind. That failed, and I twisted, stretched and foetal postured until the sun came up. Two days later and I was almost over it.

On Saturday, 15th December 2012 I emailed Honda Asia my intention to surrender the scooter to customs and that morning wrote a letter to Indore Customs to clarify the hand over. Manoj drove me to the Honda service centre and I announced my intention, which went down better than I had expected. I and several employees the parts I wanted to retain for sticking on a bicycle and they retained bits they wanted for other bikes, such as the brakes and mirrors. I was sad to see my vehicle dissected and in such a sorry state, we'd done a lot together, but at the end of the day it was only a tool. Thankfully it was cheap enough to throw away.

A Honda employee used his scooter and leg to push on the back of my scooter to Indore Customs. The grounds were closed but a second entrance was open around the rear and we slipped in. There was only an inspector available and I had Manoj state my intentions in Indian. He wanted us to wait for his boss, fat chance, and I handed over the letter, the keys and waved a swift goodbye. I wasn't waiting to be told I had to

157

take it to Mumbai customs. No way. Using my camera I gathered photograph evidence to show I'd surrendered it and then we left, back to the Honda centre to pick up the steel panniers I'd removed from the scooter and then on to a shop to buy a bicycle.

I would continue on two wheels, less an engine.

The bicycle cost 11,000 rupees or about $203 dollars. It wasn't tremendous value, similar specification and quality cost the same in the U.K, but for a lack of choice I bought it. The shop owner agreed to chuck in spare disc brake pads, a multitool, spare tube, puncture repair kits and change the tyres to road going rubber. The wheels were relatively small at 26" and the front and rear suspension would need adjusting to work with the load. The cycle rack didn't have rods to the rear wheel as the suspension won't allow it. Instead the frame was oversized and hung over the rear wheel. I worried the weight on the rear rack would put too much pivotal moment about the suspension point and cause it to fail but by that point I hoped to be in a country where I could buy something better. Riding around, the bicycle was a head turner and I vowed to lessen it's attractiveness by removing all the colourful decals. The following day I sourced a shop selling stainless rod and a backyard outfit that could weld up a frame. Neither were easy to find, the Indian markets use mild steel or aluminium and I walked several kilometres in all directions to make it happen. There was a lack of ideas on how to attach the new frame to the rear rack, so I told them to just directly weld it. Following a quick trail I swapped the front mudguard for something more substantial and fitted an extra long seat post, plus the iPhone 4 holder from the scooter and a speed/trip computer. There was space in between the two panniers mounted on the sides for my mosquito shelter and roll-mat while the army cot bed I would donate to Manoj. Other than the helmet, PCX parts, biking coat, jerry can everything else I would keep.

Manoj received a couple responses to his email and I was pleased that I could help him in his quest. He asked me to proof read what he wrote in further emails and I arranged to meet his wife and young son at 18:00hrs a day before I was due to leave, but missed the time when the bicycle welding dragged on.

As I was eating with the locals in cheap back street cafe's I had almost persistent diarrhoea. I retained control but some nights awoke to sweating and chills. I remember one night in particular where I vomited so much into the bathroom sink I filled it. While simultaneously shitting my pants.

I was working to leave Indore as soon as possible. Christmas was 10 days away and for sure I'd miss being away from my family. I wanted to be on the road to take my mind off it and the sumptuous roast dinner my mother would be cooking back home.

While I assumed Indore would be a lonely place, devoid as it was of any tourists, I'd met other good people including an Indian working insurance at the Honda dealership who insisted I meet his family, go to his friends jamming session and then to an upcoming concert they had arranged for the wednesday. I hoped to have left by then, but the concert would be interesting.

Postal regulations stated the gear I'd boxed up to be sent back to the UK had to be cotton wrapped, then sealed with wax from a candle, I wasted another three hours of my life on silly rules. The post office cited no metal of any kind could be sent through the post. Who were they kidding!

Another Indian, a 20yr old from the local restaurant which was so frequently upsetting my bowels, would practice his English and invited me and Manoj to his house for evening supper. His young wife was pregnant with his first child. She was good looking and made exceptional nan bread. Afterwards I was given a tour of the city night markets. Later he drove to a hotel named Amanddeep which ran the slogan 'It's feel like my home'. This looked like a bar and I paid the 200 rupee entrance fee expecting a few beers but I was in for a shock. Inside were two main rooms, each with a stage area and a row of seats at the back on which young girls waited with faces of despair, like they were going to be raped. In front of them, girls stood and forced dancing, clearly not wanting to be chosen by the rampant meat-eating men which were flashing money and bartering with the pimps at the sides. As the only white man in the crowd I was quickly noticed by several pimps and awaited the inevitable. A worm of a man who I could've gladly snapped in half came over and tried to chat. I told him to fuck off then got up and left, wondering on my way out what I could do that would shut the place down. Manoj later explained the girls were from small villages, lured by the promise of a Bollywood role. Instead they were given a hotel room, fed and told who to fuck. The police were all paid off.

My Indian friend caught me as I walked back to the hotel and was upset in his failure to entertain and facilitate. He thought I'd be happy with the place! I said I was just tired.

Manoj was very happy that my email had drawn the attention of a large production house in New Zealand. They were very interested and arranged to call him on the Thursday. On the Wednesday I sorted further welding to the rear rack, added a front rack for my bag (a three year old could weld better) and swapped out further kit. On Thursday morning I hung around in the morning to assist Manoj with his call and afterwards departed Indore on my new wheels.

Chapter 14

Rajasthan, India

Heading north towards Ujjain I hoped the day after to make the state of Rajasthan and many days later Udaipur, but I'd no idea if the bike, it's equipment, or its rider, would hold up. I'd never cycled such distance or rode such a heavy bicycle. As the tyres needed further inflation and knowing my $1 USD pump was useless I stopped at a garage where I told the assistant 60 PSI and pressed the up arrow until it displayed that figure. The tyres said 45 PSI but that just wasn't good enough for all the luggage. He somehow made the front 96PSI and the back 72PSI. I took a little out the front and prayed neither would burst. Even at 72PSI the back looked a little flat, but it made a hell of a difference on the road. I made a note to up it to 90PSI which looking back was ridiculous for such cheap tubes and tyres. Meanwhile the rear suspension didn't snap, and the welding held up. I was impressed - finally my engineering decisions were improving! There was a noise from the back wheel, possibly a spoke or bad bearing, but I ignored it. While I rode drivers would honk and try to stop and chat (aka sell something) but I would reply in French and they'd give up. Similarly, stall sellers would shout "Oy! Oy! You Stop Mister!".

At the end of the first day I'd covered a respectable 90km. Having found great annoyance with every vehicle on the road, I was now partially deaf due to their incandescent urge to blast their air horns just before overtaking.

At 17:00hrs, just before sunset and what I expected would be a mosquito fest, I set up camp at a large swamp lake away the main road. Here I made an egg and tomato mix, which I ate with fried nan bread Manoj's wife had cooked as a leaving present. The swamp was beautiful with random palm trees, birds I couldn't identify and a seclusion I'd yet discovered in India.

The mosquitos never came but I slept badly, in no small part due to the lack of camp bed and the rough ground. At 09:00hrs the next morning I was back on the road, complete with very sore legs, and heading towards the town of Ratlam. Along the way I upped both tyres to 90PSI and at 14:00hrs the rear popped. Taking the tube out, it had a small tear most likely from the rim. The tube was Chinese while the replacements I carried were Indian. Unsure which was better, I stuck the Indian in and pressured to 60PSI, but not with the one I carried for mine had no pin in the nozzle and was useless. Someone at the Honda garage had nicked my decent pump I'd carried for the scooter. Luckily there were plenty of tyre compressor places in India.

I made 85km and thought I could have rode more. My legs didn't have the numbness of earlier in the day and I was enjoying the ride. Where did the hours go? The bicycle was holding together but the frame was creaking and I couldn't push much more than 20kph on the straight. I picked up a handful of tomatoes and a bag of pea pods and made a questionable dinner with left over pasta. At a turn off from the main road, which led to a dry riverbed and overhanging trees I set up camp and texted my mother, four days before Christmas. Cycling alone was proving to be a lonely experience.

On the third day of cycling I passed a 100km milestone. Passing through many villages full of Indians who'd never saw a tourist, their eyes locked on the moving ATM, me, and longed to make a withdrawal. The people missed nothing and I developed a cunning technique to subvert their efforts to make cash. Earlier in the day I'd bought some sort of egg pasty and in the afternoon stopped at a quiet part of the road on a cliff facing a dry river bed. There was little around but before stopping I rode to the other side of the road and faced the opposite direction to which I was travelling. I began to eat. 60 seconds into the pasty and a honking bus passed and someway up the road pulled over. Five blokes disembark and from a distance began the usual 'Hello, oy, what's your name?" chatter. Due of the way I'm facing they thought I'd have to ride to and through them. Instead I turned around and rode off.

I finished the day in Bangalore at the cheapest hotel yet, a mere 170 rupees or about $3 USD. In the corner sat a TV from the 70's, a mattress from a similar era and a wanting bathroom deficient of any kind of sanitation. Compare to camping it was perfect. I laid my tarp over the mattress, stuck the mosquito shelter on top and left to find an internet cafe. When I found one the guy ripped me off, charging double the going rate. I suspected it and double checked the price with another cafe around the corner. I revisited and told him but he kept to his lie. I talked to two shop owners across the road then satisfied I wasn't making a mistake revisited saying at 09:30hrs I'd be back with the police. This always works in

India, they are shit scared of the police. He relented and handed back half the amount I paid. I told him I'll be back at 09:30hrs anyway, for a free hours usage, and if he didn't like that he could talk to the police regardless. His face squirmed like he'd been hard done by. The little dishonest shit bag.

It took two more days to reach Udaipur. The second last day was pleasant enough, bar a mob of twenty young kids and adults trying to see inside my wallet when I was buying veg from a side stall. I wild camped on the side of a large hill where I had a little difficulty remaining unnoticed but eventually the sun set and my profile lowered enough that I could boil potatoes without somebody crawling along the road with their horn on.

Christmas Eve and the last on the road to Udaipur was strenuous and one I won't forget. By now the horns had already made me a bag of jumping nerves, but worse was a bad case of the shits. By 11.30hrs I'd had seven of them. Oh for the promise of a decent hotel and tourist orientated food! On Udaipur, The Lonely Planet guide spoke of cafes selling apple pie and cinnamon rolls, and restaurants serving real pasta dishes. Throw in a Skype call to my family back home and I would be happy. I would ride until there. I would not spend Christmas on this damned road. Unfortunately was a mixed bag with some badly broken up stone, potholes and other obstacles. My progress dwindled, but with determination and several bags of crap crisps, I rolled in just as the sun dipped below the horizon. My legs had burn't out. I had nothing left.

I found a hotel smack bang in the centre charging 1200 rupee, significant, but it was Christmas and the shower looked heavenly. I washed a layer of grime off my face and found a cafe up the road selling apple crumble: a dollar worth of shear beguiled pleasure.

I hate relatively low hopes for Christmas day in Udaipur. As a non Christian country I hadn't expected an influx of celebrating tourists and that is exactly what I got. Although a few tourist couples bustled through the cafes and streets for Hindu dominated India it was business as usual.

The main attraction for a new arrival like myself was the main palace overlooking the large lake. I couldn't help but be irritated by the four fold price increase since 2009, and the fact this buys access to little more than the car park and toilet. To visit the internal museum costs extra. To take a camera inside the museum costs extra. To leave a camera outside while you go in costs extra. Metal detectors and bag searches ensure the rules are adhered too. Further into the palace ground there was another museum, chargeable, and the rest of the palace was shut off to any non-resident of its plush hotel. I paid for a boat ride around the lake, which stopped at a quant hotel/garden in the middle. The entry to this hotel/garden was chargeable on top of the boat ride and a coffee here was four times more expensive than the normal rate. Royally milking it.

That was it for Udaipur. There was a sunset point, tourists could walk around the partially polluted lake and the back lanes offered some charm for those who hadn't experienced better, but I had and they were nonpareil to those found on the Greek Islands. The tourists kept to themselves and places serving beer closed early. I simply used the next two days to check out nearby cafes and restaurants selling delights I'd not seen since England, to fix my bike and source an inner-tube and to give my jaded legs time to recover. On December 27th

I departed for Pushkar.

The NH8 was a busy main highway serving the northern route while Pushkar, a religious and symbolic town for Hindus, wasn't far off it . Back on good tarmac it should've been easier going, however the route was still long and two days in Udaipur wasn't enough to allow my legs to recover. It took the whole morning before they'd loosened up.

I made 80km up the NH8, past an incredible amount of marble sellers before I spotted what looked like a run down fort or small castle high up on a mountainside. If it were disused it could potentially provide a great place to camp, so I turned off the road, passed through a village, and began the off-road climb. A young lad, probably around 15yrs and his small brother trailed behind. He couldn't speak much past yes and no, but more disconcerting was his stare and expression of deep coldness; his lips never parting from horizontal. I tried to get rid of him but he persisted, and he mentioned money. I took it that he wanted some. Knowing he spoke little English I just idle conversed as I made progress up the hill.

"Do I look like a mobile ATM?"
"Yes.", he replied.
"Look, what do you want?" I retorted.
"Is my home." he said, pointing to the castle.
"Full of shit." I mumbled, knowing he wouldn't understand.

I pushed on, the incline reached about 15% and the front tyre tried to slip sideways due the rear weight. I sweated protrusively. The last section was at least a 25% incline and decimated my energy reserves. It transpired the old fort was being used as a temple, and that's what the lad meant by it being his home. Oops.

The door was locked and a few Indians watched with interest to see what I was going to do next. I asked them how old it was, 1000yrs old if I heard them correctly, then I set-up camp just beneath it and boiled some potatoes. The night was warm but I urgently needed some sort of second form or air mat. Sleep seemed impossible without and I kept waking up to pain in my backside. The marble shale explosions from excavators working throughout the night didn't help either and consequently the morning arrived with a headache and my reluctance to get going.

But get going I did, and I made a further 120km, my best yet, before turning off the NH8 at 17:30hrs to find a spot to camp. For the second day in a row I overloaded on boiled potato. I would have loved to have added butter and cheese but finding such commodities was seemingly difficult out of the cities and I was not yet well versed in preparation for bicycle travelling. Although only two days ride from Udaipur it was hard to break the desire for comfort and good food. I'd had it too easy on the scooter. Before I slept I read up on Pushkar from the Lonely Planet, guide. My mouth watered from the simple words *Banana Pancake*. Pushkar it said was small, had a fabulous lake, cheap hotels and good western food. I could see myself staying there for an unnecessarily long time.

On the third and final day before reaching Pushkar I'd to cover only 80km. My legs were now getting into the swing of it, but the crap bicycle seat was awful and detrimental to riding with efficiency. More than not I ended up standing on the pedals rather than sitting down. The sun rose at around 07:00hrs but it was becoming colder each morning and my body ached from the lack of a decent camping mattress.

I forced myself to have a poor mans wash by filling an empty bottle at a nearby water pump, somewhat refreshing, and after picking out impressively long thorns that'd managed to go pierce the base of my mosquito shelter, I got under way.

The ride up the NH8 motorway was as boring as it sounds, but good food flashbacks helped to forget the pain in my backside and my stiff neck. The posture of the bicycle was all wrong.

Pushkar turned about to be 20km further than I'd originally assumed and all went smoothly until the final and steep hill from Ajmer. Exhausted, I dismounted and pushed the heavy cycle up the incline and nearly made a home run when two scooters carrying two people on each decided it would be fun to take the piss. One came alongside and tried to spark up a conversation. I ignored the broken English and usual questions on whether I needed a hotel. They were all very excited at this vulnerable looking travelling cash-point and the last scooter pulled in across my path so that I had to stop and go around. Pushing the loaded bicycle up a steep incline, this was far more annoying than you might believe, but I did it without displaying an obvious rise to my temper. I continued on up and again they came alongside and continued trying to sell and offer services, which I again ignored. Then the first pulled across my path. By now I was really sweating and panting. Outraged I lost it. "WILL YOU FUCK OFF!". I pushed the bicycle around the scooter and continued up the hill knowing that soon I'd reach the summit and be over it - a nice decline all the way to Pushkar central. Moments later the first scooter came to pass and the rear passenger tried a swing for my head but missed. Smarting, he looked back with a big grin on his face. The second scooter came to pass and the passenger took a swing which connected with the back of my head, not at all hard, but that was the end of my self-control. They drove on, but now I was at the summit, spitting fury and venting rage, and the bastards with their 50cc scooters were equal game downhill. They were 200m ahead and traffic had slowed them down.

Right.

I put the gear into highest and give it all I had. Police were manually controlling the traffic. Only one thing was going through my mind. I would catch up and put my fist into the arseholes face.

I traffic filtered, caught up and threw my bicycle down uncontrollably onto the road. I stepped along the passenger on the end scooter and punched him in the face as hard as I could.

I don't recall having hit anyone in my life, a remarkable 29yr offensive free period, but I did a sound job on my first go. Knocking him off the scooter, he fell off onto the ground out cold. Instantly police and the curious enveloped the scene. It was evident I was a tourist and the police didn't even heed an explanation. They simple stopped the traffic, picked my bicycle up and pointed the way. I was none the calmer, but with just several kilometres to the centre thoughts of a shower and apple crumble filled my head, and the rage melted away.

Chapter 15

Pushkar, Jaipur, Agra and Varanasi, India

In Pushkar, life was far too comfortable to leave quickly and I had no intention to leave until sometime after the new year. A hostel called the Milkman offered a near empty dorm for a mere 100 rupee, decent wifi, hot water and excellent food at very good prices, so I settled in until I'd completed one of my objectives.

The software I'd been producing for eternity and which was running my website needed a bit of polishing before I could use it as a demonstration of my programming abilities. When the money ran out, it was that or teaching English, and I no longer wished to teach.

During the three weeks at the hostel I did little other than consume a minimum of two banana custards and a tomato/cheese pasta every day, plus a lot more. The management were happy to have a long haul customer, though I spent relatively nothing. It seemed like I couldn't stop eating, but I had a grand time at being productive and comfortable.

I mostly ignored the coming and going tourists and must have came across as quite reclusive, but I was driven to get the software complete and spent twelve hours a day at it. On New Year Eve I had a few beers with some Australian tourists. A girl among them, from Queensland, had the most utterly beautiful and oddly British accent I've heard. She was well educated, good looking and head strung. Back home she did modelling and had written a book which was in the process of being published. I loved her drive. She was 19 years old, (too young for an oldie like me).

I visited little points of interest although I did carry scout around the small lake quite often. Usually this was only to collect another ton of boiled sweets from one of the many small outlets. I loved Pushkar, it was small enough not to overwhelm, and it's lake and ghats were always a pretty sight. I was tempted to do a short camel tour, but then I witnessed white folk and the gormless amentia of it. On two of the mornings I was up very early for the walk up to two high point temples. Monkeys would usually trail behind hoping to forage food and as the sun rose over the horizon the air was bitter cold.

Pushkar was also a chance to sort better kit, and especially to solve the sleeping discomfort from camping on hard ground. I spent a day at the nearby town of Ajmer but came back empty handed, thought I did source a better bicycle seat for a mere

172

90 rupee. The boss of the hostel, a helpful chap, was adamant he could find a mattress and the following day he returned with just that. I doubled it over and stitched it which gave three inch of form. It was hardly portable and a shame that most of my big black bag on the back of the bike was needed to carry it, but sleep was more important.

With my software complete leaving Pushkar and getting back on the bike was almost a challenge in itself. I'd reduced the weight of my equipment but I'd a backlog of banana custards to shift. On my way out I met a Canadian and Italian couple who were travelling to Australia by Vespa. We got on terrifically well and our twisted cursing and story swapping of the Indian mentality had us all laughing. We swapped details and hoped to meet sometime in the future.

I departed for Jaipur at 11:00hrs on the 22nd January and made 100km along the venerable NH8. As always I tried to source a secluded place to camp which for that night appeared in the form of the foot of a hill about 1km from the main road. As always it wasn't good enough. Seven kids arrived and stood around, and wouldn't bugger off. They finally took the hint and left but then returned five minutes later, and just stood around once more. Now wanting to erect my bivi tent I was irate, but what could I do. I couldn't smack them. When they bored of it they left I put the bivi up and crawled inside. At 21:30hrs I heard rustling outside, which was two wild dogs trying to get in one of my bags. Fifteen minutes later I heard quiet footsteps and on looking out of the bivi front I saw the outline of a child running off. Probably the same ones. I don't know how I heard any of this as I had headphones on and was now watching a film. At 22:15hrs though I was alerted by two Indian men standing outside my bivi. One ordered me to "get out". The way he said was infuriating, the fucking impolite cock, I thought to myself. I undid the flap and immediately one of them blinded me with his torch. I tried squinting to give him the hint, but he didn't care and kept pointing it into my eyes. Feeling disadvantaged, I stuck the diffuser on my head-torch on max and showed him some back. Now I could see who I was dealing with. The two of them made expressions, as their English wasn't good, that I was to leave. One was older, traditional dress and a large stick. The other looked like a trouble maker, probably related to one of the kids that I'd tried to get rid of, or possibly he was related to the hotel on the other side of the road I'd came off, as they both were keen to repeat the name of it. I wasn't intimidated. The torch of his continued to blind. I flipped up the diffuser on my own and the stuck the highest power it offered into his eyeballs, which was enough to make him turn away and partially stay that way. I told them to sit down while I called the police and the very mention of the word was enough. They mumbled and left. With their backs turned and walking away I shouted "good night!". I zipped the bivi front up and slept well on my new mattress.

I was up early just before the sun and managed a quick bottle shower (fill two empty water bottles with non-drinkable water in the evening, use them in the morning for a wash). At 07:00hrs I had another smatter of publicity including two women, one of which thought it quite acceptable to go through my black bag. The audacity of such an action I found unprecedented, yet there was no remorse when I caught her. In fact, they'd already spotted a bag of boiled sweets and wanted to share them between themselves. Amazing! I had a fleeting thought on how racist I was becoming, and how righteous I was to be it. Why won't the f**kers just leave me alone and treat others with respect? I already despised a lot of India, but I was beginning to dislike the population with it.

The following day I stopped to eat a sandwich behind a gate in a disused field and an old hag tried to shoe me off. It was literally just of the main road and I'd done it to prevent being seen. It was happening too often.

I arrived at Jaipur and planned to head straight to Amber, avoiding the city entirely. However, I had an unexpected tour of the city when I followed the incorrect map from the Lonely Planet and then followed the incorrect map from my Garmin GPS. It took three hours to undo that mess and head in the right direction. Just north of Jaipur centre a bicycle rim tape wrapped itself around my front spindle. Twenty meters further my front tube popped. I was in a busy side-street and knew that fixing it would be much easier without attention so I pulled onto someones drive-way and politely asked if I could use it for 15 minutes. The family were fairly well off and the 20yr old, a public school educated lad, spoke good English and ran his own suit firm. Thanks to his support I swapped the tube quickly and before it became dark. Curiously, the tube blew because the rim tape had 'gone'. The valve of the tube had come away from the rubber and was still sticking through the rim hole. How on earth the rim tape had come out I couldn't work out.

As the light began to fade I found a patch of trees just off the side of the road and pushed my bicycle well into them. I made camp, watched the remainder of the film from the night before and fell asleep. At 05:00hrs I was awaken by wild warthogs scavenging for food, but they were easily shoed away. I hadn't slept well due to lack of water for a bottle shower, which in turn meant I was sweat sticky all night. At 06:00hrs I noticed a figure standing on a ridge watching my camp for a good five minutes.

"Can I help you?" I asked.
"This is forrest. You not stay here." he replied.
"Says who, and this is no forrest, it's a few trees." I replied.
"You need permission." here we go again.
"Perhaps I have it. Anything else?" I asked bluntly.
"Where are you from?"
"None of your fucking business.", and I ended the conversation there.

At 07:00hrs I was packed and ready to go. As I pushed the bicycle out a one inch thorn went through the front tube. I sighed, fixed it and rode the remaining distance to Amber. It's palace had better be worth the page space allocated in the Lonely Planet guide.

Amber Palace was, and there's no more appropriate way to word this, quite crap. All the walls had had their original décor plastered over, which was now failed in many areas. The rooms were drab and basic. In the 19th century one had been converted to a billiards room, a fact I found bemusing. The thing about palaces is they are built by very rich people and are nothing more than large homes designed to impression wealth and aplomb. But what I really hated wasn't the palace itself but the installation of the toilets. The first were the 'free toilets', and were manned by an Indian issuing a sheet of toilet roll and demanding tips on the way out. These toilets couldn't be flushed and one didn't dare sit, squat or hover above any of them. They were repulsive. Given that all the hundreds of tourists per day are paying to get into this palace, what gives with charging to urinate in squalid conditions? Where's the money going? On the up, in the palace itself there's a labyrinth of small rooms and passageways which can lead up to fantastic views over the lake and landscape. Looking down I could view the meathead tourists riding the poor enslaved elephants up and down the embankment.

The original toilet of the palace, now part of the feature-set, comprised of simple system of large grooves cut into the floor. Strangely the room still smelt strongly of urine, which made me curious as to whether the public or the staff were accustomed to keeping the room functional.

It was now the January 25th and I was running out of time to make the trekking season in Nepal. I still had Agra and Varanessi to go. As one Facebook user put it, I needed to hurry up unless I liked rain and leeches. I left the palace at mid-day, rode back to Jaipur and took the road to Agra. 227km. A two day ride.

On the way to Agra I made impressive speed thanks in no small part to a substantial crap I left under a bridge and a refreshing shower at a toll-road toilet facility. I really wasn't expecting such a facility to pop out as it did. While showering from the rusting pipe above my head, I nearly jumped for high heaven when looking down just inches from my feet was a brown recluse spider fending its way from the splashing water. It was the first time I'd seen any dangerous wildlife. By 18:00hrs and with the light fading I'd still 150km to ride before reaching Agra, but by now I'd passed potential wild-camp sites and had entered a stretch busy marble sellers and wheat fields.

After another half hour of searching for a remote spot I relented and pulled off the motorway, travelled over broken dirt track and then towards what appeared in the distance to be a mansion. It wasn't, but a farm house with several people that could speak moderate English. I explained my position and trying to be utterly polite and sincere to secure somewhere I could doss for the night. Luckily it worked, and the man of the house offered the use of a bed inside one of the rooms. None of the kids could speak any English, so I taught them a few basics (I was astonished at how quickly they picked things up). They brought chai and some overly spicy food, then watched in delight as my eyes watered and my nose ran.

At 21:32hrs it was dark and everyone in the rural area was in bed. The silence was broken by an explosion, a large BOOM that echo'd in the night. Disconcerting to others of my house as well as myself, they checked on their cattle and dismissed it. Not long afterwards a shotgun unloaded. For comfort, I pulled my blanket closer and shivered in the dropping temperature. Then, the unmistakable sound of a rifle, the sharp crack echoing off the nearby buildings, and either a strange animal or a human impersonating an owl like creature emitting a howl. A man would follow this up with another strange noise. What on earth was going on out there? At 21:56hrs another shotgun fired off. By 22:00hrs I'd accustomed to it and fell asleep.

The morning was brisk, temperature not much higher than freezing and I had breakfast and chai with the family. A motorcycle with two large aluminium barrels turned up and milk from the cows was tipped in. While this was going on the elder explained there was a crazy farmer on the other side of the village, ex-army, who set traps to keep his cattle safe. Presumably the traps were meant for predators not people, but you never know.

I rode 100km before arriving at a medium sized town called Bharatpur. My right knee had ostensibly given up and the pain being what it was I checked into a budget hotel to let it rest.

About 50-80km remained and the following day my sore knee, which hadn't improved at all, cut my speed in half. The choice of bicycle was wrong and had done me no favours. I really shouldn't have gone with suspension either as it was soaking up my energy.

Following the signs to the Taj Mahal, I was led to believe there was several kilometres between the three gates, but this was only the case for motorised transport. Pollution had been causing the Taj's marble to tint a shade of yellow, and the authorities had established a traffic free zone to try and thwart this. The walking distance between the gates was short, ten minutes at the most. Around the gates there wasn't a shortage of hotels or touts willing to provide full tours of Agra for the right price. This part of Agra didn't feel setup for budget travelling, but I did find a hotel that had converted one of its rooms into a dorm and was offering it out at a reasonable price. I rode into the entrance lopsided to ease the pain from my right knee while the rear suspension or a part linked to it sounded worn and creaked loudly.

With an intention of being among the first to enter the Taj Mahal the next morning, I was up before the sun, around 05:00hrs and joined a queue of people with the same idea. Everyone was there to witness the colour change as the sun rises and refracts its rays upon the marble. By the time the entrance opened, 07:00hrs, the sun was ready to rise above the horizon and I had to literally run to get to the central viewing area.

Sadly the Taj didn't change colour nor look anything as nice

179

as in the photographs. With too much haze brought on by pollution taking good photographs through it was difficult, however setting a side the problem the Taj was and is a magnificent, stupendously impossibility feat of work and highly impressive. There was a limited amount to see and it took only an hour to walk around it all. The Taj Mahal, an expression of amour propre perhaps, is a fake tomb for the wife of a very rich husband, but thank goodness people with far too money to realise the daftness of such a project go ahead and do it anyway.

There was little point in staying in Agra. I could have visited Agra Fort but more than not I felt 'done' with India. With my knee healing but still hopeless for riding on I decided instead to experience the Indian rail network by taking a ride to a town close to Nepal called Gorakhpur. As there wasn't a direct ticket I had to go via the capital of Uttar Pradesh province called Lucknew. It was an even earlier start as the train left at 06:00hrs and on the train I met an interesting German who was backpacking through rural India. He was on the way to Varanasi, which I had opted to miss to Nepal quicker, but the more he spoke of it, and the more I read, the more I thought it could be a version of Pushkar. If so, and given I'd no plans to return to India, I felt obliged to fit it in. At Lucknew the German went to find the reserved ticket office and I went to release my bicycle from the luggage department. We never met again.

Lucknew was immediate and unrelenting hassle. There was no parking for the bicycle, a measure clearly took by the authorities, but several companies charged to store bicycles, scooters and the like. The reserved ticket office was disconnected from the station and awkward to find. Impressively difficult steps ensured I had no choice but to pay

180

to park the bicycle, something I always tried to avoid. With few if any reasonable places to stay in Lucknew I queried about a ticket on the overnight train to Varanasi departing in the late evening. The Indian railway had several ticket classifications complements of the British class system, the cheapest being second class, and you just turn up and pay. Tickets are, I believe, unrestricted and thus space for you and luggage can be lacking or even unavailable. There were multiple air con options and sleeper class, which came with a small two foot form mattress suspended in bunk bed format. I opted for this. The train would depart at 21:45hrs.

I made a slight mistake with the train, which I read as being delayed by a couple hours. At 00:30hrs I boarded what I thought was the right train, but instead of getting on the train to Varanasi, I boarded the train coming from Varanasi. I located my quaint bed with the same allocated number and slept throughout the night, without knowing I was heading back to Agra. At 06:00hrs I awoke to a newly boarded passenger wondering what I was doing in his bed mistake. I felt rather silly, but at the same time sleeping on the train was great! At Agra I sorted another train ticket in the evening which would be another two part journey, the first a one and a half train ride to Gwalior, approximately 150km south of Agra, and then a twelve hour sleeper on the second train to Varanasi. The bicycle would already be there.

The one and a half hour train ride was on a 2nd class unreserved ticket and by god was it packed. My body and legs were contorted into impossible positions while my big 70 litre bag perched high on a shelf ready to fall onto frail old ladies sitting beneath it. Five minutes into the journey the train applied its emergency brakes and everyone became a single entity. Swiftly there was a smell of burning, like a clutch on a car, and then the train hit something. The impact was unusual and interesting, like something had separated into a million pieces and gone under the wheels. The carriage shuddered and jostled. After the train came to a stop the passengers, suspecting children had put small stones on the track, jumped down from the carriages to find out what was going on. The cause was, and I emphasis on was, a large cow, that had stood on the track while the intercity hurtled towards it. I was told, and I have no evidence to argue the contrary, that the front of the train was quite a mess. The driver was given a full minute to pull himself together, then the demand of his passengers had the train on it's way. In the "bogie" as they call it, I met a similar aged lad who spoke excellent English. In the "carriage" as I call it, and with around a hundred Indians (that number is not exaggerated it was that packed) listening in, we discussed at his request whether British influence and practice still affected Indian life sixty years on. He was very keen to point out the richest person in England was Indian. I told him we were happy to have Indians selling the minerals and resources of India for huge profit and spending that profit in England. To this he laughed. Nothing much has changed.

Thankfully I arrived in Varanasi to find my bicycle awaiting and rode slowly to avoid stressing my knew over to the river and ghats late morning. The pedal, crank, or whatever it was called, had a lot of play in it and on inspecting the rear suspension I noticed the rod was bent. I'd have to fix both sooner than later and I didn't do much looking around at where to stay to begin with, sorting a guest house with a tout for 250 rupee, which was about right for Varanasi. With so many to choose from, the best are barely mentioned in guide books or on the internet. I found a popular cafe called the Monalisa German Bakery where the cakes in particularly

182

were cheap compared to Udaipur, the last place I'd found a cafe selling the delight that is apple crumble.

In the evening I joined other tourists, holy men and touts at the Manikarnika temple where bodies were burning on piles of wooden log. The burning was carried out on four levels based on India's controversial caste system. Although abolished in theory, the practice of 'knowing your place' based on which family you're born into, is well and truly alive in India. It's a hilariously discriminately system that limits a persons success based on what their father did. If your father worked in Government, you could expect to end up doing the same, no more, no less.

"At the top are priests and holy figures, followed by Government and social workers, followed by businessmen and then road sweepers.", explained a guide hoping to collect donations to pay for the wood being used to burn the bodies.

As I don't support discrimination, I donated nothing.

The following morning I checked into a new guest house, one with a large dormitory and monkeys that stole clothes from the drying line on the roof. It was here that I met Jesus, but more on that later. Early, at 06:00hrs I was up and walking to the Ganges riverside where I and two Koreans I'd got talking to in the Bakery took a one and a half hour boat up and down the river Ganges. Like the Taj Mahal, the sunrise was ruined by hazy pollution. The highlight of the boat ride was probably seeing another boat of tourists being attacked by hundreds of pigeons and listening to the anguish of several Koreans as they were hit by fresh droppings. Later a floating corpse, minus most of the arms and legs brushed alongside our boat, which satisfied my expectations for that morning in full.

Afterwards, hungry, I ate a hearty breakfast.

Varanasi was busier than usual due to it's close proximity to the city of Allahabad which for 2013 was hosting the Purna Kumbha Mela, a Hindu event occurring every twelve years and the biggest amass gathering of people on earth. I can't fathom how busy Allahabad must have been, but Varanasi was jam packed. The roads were exceptionally dangerous with too many people on them to heed traffic regulations. Lights were ignored by all, rickshaws drove around roundabouts both ways, then against oncoming traffic, and everyone ignored the incumbent police who'd been drafted in to restore order. The rickshaw drivers continued their exceptional arrogance of stopping in the middle of the road to tout passengers, and everyone, without hesitation, was undercutting, pulling out without looking, and using their horn without let up.

To fix my bicycle, which I felt was already on its last legs, I had to find a shop selling metal of either stainless box section type or aluminium bar, and someone to drill the holes into the metal and fit it. In the chaos what I thought would be a relatively simple task took five hours to complete. I attempted to count the amount of impacts with my bicycle, the ones I noticed anyway, but stopped counting at 14.

A German girl, a seasoned traveller who'd spent five months travelling throughout India, joined me for the first hour but became visually stressed by the chaos and turned back. Varanassi wasn't for everyone.

With my bicycle fixed I reverted to the guest house to unwind and chill out and I began talking to Jesus. Jesus was Spanish and had travelled around the world staying and preaching the word of Christ as a missionary throughout India. He looked to be around 60 and had a 'well travelled' look, the sort easily confused with being unwashed and tramp like. He was the picture of every Jesus mockup, and his straggled long grey hair, his age and his drab grey clothing set him a world apart from every other keen young face in the dorm, and I listened with polite recourse as he recited religious gobbledegook with an unexpected energy and passion.

With Varanasi done and dusted it was time to make my way out of India and into Nepal. Eager, and untrusting of my knee, I decided the fastest way to do this would be by taking an overnight sleeper train to Gorakhpur and then to cycle to the border in the early morning. I was informed at the train station luggage handling department that there was no bogie wagon for the cycle and that it would follow on another express train fifteen minutes after my own. At Gorakhpur I found it wasn't on that train, nor the following 11:00hrs service, and so I wouldn't make the Nepal border that day and had to check into a basic hotel. This was a blessing as India had left me with a leaving present in the form of yet another dose of insanely horrible trots. At 17:00hrs I was just leaving my room for the train station and unexpectedly shat myself. After switching pants, my knees wobbling from the fever, and a throbbing headache, I made my way to the station to be told the cycle wasn't on the third train either. I was quite mad and after causing a stir was given assurance it would be on the following mornings 07:00hr service. I went back to my room and vomited. That night I alternated between shivering and sweating, all the signs of Malaria and with my lack of medication I was prepared to get tested in the morning if signs didn't improve.

By good fortune my cycle arrived as promised and in one

185

piece. As for the delay, the guy tried a fake 20 rupee handling charge. The audacious mother fucker!

I felt good enough to leave and did exactly that. Making a quick dash north with the thought of Nepal and it's trekking possibilities, I forgot about my knee injury and pedalled too hard. The pain began and reduced my speed in half.

It was 90km to the border but I made only 70km before the evening came and it began to pour down. I spotted a nice field with large trees and made my way to a small house there to ask permission to camp in the grounds. An hour later my bivi tent was erected and the tarp hung from the trees for additional cover. The owners were helpful and generous; laying out hay to offset the rocky ground and bringing a superb creamy chai. On my last full through India I felt a little guilt at my critique of the people living there. They're not all bad.

In the morning I packed up and rode the cycle back onto the main road. Here several well dressed children were waiting with their hands out. They spoke only the words "I am poor", clearly taught from their elders.

I was so close to the border. I'd spent three months in India and hadn't even touched the south, such as its vastness made so difficult to cover by the lack of an engine. I was however utterly delighted to be leaving. For me, Nepal was the start of something new and fresh, a country geared for action and adventure. I'd visions of trekking to the Everest base camp, rafting and throwing myself from the ledge of a bungee jump. I only hoped the people there would be consistently more honest and helpful.

Chapter 16

Nepal

I was so excited to leave India I missed the Indian exit office and the Nepal entry office. A few minutes after riding into Nepal I realised the visa office wasn't coming up and backtracked to pickup the various exit and entry stamps. The border crossing was entirely open, like passing between many E.U country borders, and Indian/Nepalese travel freely between the two. That made me wonder if getting the scooter into Nepal would have been just as easy, but there wasn't any point dwelling on it now.

Back in Varanasi I'd been advised by fellow travellers that Kathmandu was comparatively a small Delhi, with filth and pollution. Pokhara on the other hand attracted only positivity and was described as clean, relatively small and having a Switzerland feel about it. Nepal's roads were vertically challenging and that would present a problem for my still aching knee. Plus the visa had a 30 day limitation. Instead of cycling I chose to cheat one final time by catching bus to Pokhara. The bicycle went on the roof and I joined another 70 people on a vehicle designed to carry 40. Never again. The eight hour ride was extended due to a flat tyre and the money collector insisted on overfilling the bus beyond reasonability

187

before he would instruct the driver to depart the bus stops, of which there were many. It was late when I reached Pokhara, but my spirits were higher than almost all the time I was in India. Even in the darkness of that late evening (another power cut), and with everything closed or closing, I'd high hopes for the place. Things were clean and organised. No horns blasted. It was tranquil.

The next day I came to better understand the difference between Nepalese and Indian people, although in doing so I'm generalising and for which I apologise. Nepalese are extremely helpful and don't rip you off, or 'cheat you' as they say about their Indian neighbours. I was still in Indian mode and subsequently defensive on any offer of help or guidance, but slowly I began to to remove the barriers I'd erected and to accept the Nepalese for who they were; great people.

I fell in love with Nepal on my first full day. Pokhara is Gods playground, an area full of action adventure activities including rafting, paragliding, trekking and more. It was cheap compared to say Australia, but it wasn't free and as I was unemployed and finances were on the decline I was limited to cheaper activities. From a little boat I rented on the lake I watched dozens of tandem tourists paragliding the thermals. Someday I would come back to Pokhara with a lump sum and blow it.

Back to my reality, I made a plan to trek part of the Annapurna Himalayan circuit to a viewpoint named Punn Hill and then east and north to the base camp.

The hotel room within which I resided was classed as a dorm, a last minute decision by management to create one save customers go elsewhere. The room with its twin single beds was charged at half rate but I was told if another person were to turn up I would have to share. Being that it was low season it looked unlikely, however the following day someone did. Martin Turk was Croatian, the same age as myself and had thrown away his life of an excellent job, car and money to travel on a similar shoe-string budget to myself. The similarities were uncanny. His Eastern Balkan accent, which slighted every English word, would take some getting used to, but we agreed to trek the Annapurna route together since we had similar plans anyway. Martin was a keen photographer, easy going and had a sense of humour. It was probably going to work. A lovely Argentinian girl called Maria in an adjacent room joined us for a few beers across the street and that evening I learned more about Martin. I conjectured he'd smoked one too many joints, but he'd left a girlfriend madly in love with him and was looking for that feeling money can't buy. With only a month on the road he had yet to find it, as indeed had I, but his travels through India made me aware of similarities in our approach. He was quirky and looking for a story; scenes for his large DSLR camera and web blog to capture. Comparison let to a sycophantic feeling, but I felt, as a team, hilarity would ensue. After Nepal I agreed he could buy a bicycle and ride with me. Why not!

That same day we went shopping, twice around each shop selling fake North Face gear (Pokhara is a hub for this) as we bartered on price. I wasn't prepared to spend £30 on fake trainers and chose instead to trek in my big, heavy and inappropriate Goretex army boots. The drawback of these boots was nothing when compared to the rest of my preparation, which included no waterproofs, no coat, one pair of underwear (which I was wearing) and thirty bananas. Martin, feeling the need to match my unsuitable provision, wore cheap £5 trainers, packed a sleeping bag rated to only

10c and wore his heavy DSLR and L glass lens around his neck.

Ready for Annapurna, we left the next day but late and managed only two hours of walking before darkness fell and we had to check-in at a lodge, of which there are many. Camping, while possible, was actively discouraged by a clever scheme operated by the Annapurna Conservation society. The organisation has fixed all the prices for food, which they pre-determine by distance and height to the base camp. It was a cartel and prices at the beginning stages were significantly more than the Nepalese average, so we could imagine how they would rise as we trekked further into the sanctuary. Bringing your own food to eat would result in a 400% lodging price hike, so staying at a lodge required an agreement to eat a meal in the evening and to take breakfast in the morning. For a tourist with a swag to blow this is all well, but for those expecting a cheap trek, the cost mount up. Still, as I was to learn over the next week, it's worth every penny.

The next day we powered to the top of Punn Hill, 3200 meters, and in excellent time. In fact, it was too fast and another part of my leg as well as the bad knee from cycling became troublesome. Resting was impractical, so I didn't. In the morning we rose to watch the sunrise and the startling view of the Himalayas come into sight.

On the route east the terrain became icy and dangerous and in front of us an older Australian slipped and broke his leg. For him it was game over, and his guide went on to find a horse. A helicopter wasn't possible here and we doubted even a horse could get up the ice. Despite being chilly, the energy we expended traversing up and down the valleys and gorges was such that comfort came best when dressed in shorts and t-shirt. Even then I still sweated. The impracticality of my boots meant I switched to my backup, sandals, and hooked my heavy boots to my backpack. Taking a five minute nutrition bar break in my t-shirt and shorts I would quickly freeze, necessitating the need to keep moving.

The decorous trek on day three was one of the highlights of my life. I now understood the mindset of those who felt the need to set records mountaineering. On that day tourists were few and far between and the compendious clarity of natures voice this far away from the drum and dross of main life made a lasting impression. I was immeasurably happy here.

Passing a lonely wild cow and the odd building works on the pebbled path we made a village called Chomrong and continued on, however the route down to a wooden bridge crossing its adjacent valley and the climb back up the other side finished us off for the night. After ten hours of solid trekking I was exhausted and my body ached.

On day five we made the Annapurna Base Camp, abbreviated as 'ABC', where the British established a base on an expedition in 1970. At 4200 meters the day was cold, but the evening was colder, and a bunch of us huddled together in the main cabin appreciating and revering the unusual place we now found ourselves in.

The night was colder and the temperature dropped to -22c. The paths iced over and with no electricity walking between our hut for the night and the singular toilet had to be done with care. The battery in my DSLR, full an hour before reaching ABC, now registered empty. My iPhone which was at full charge and turned off to save the power would no longer turn on. Martin, being cognisant, had stuffed his camera batteries near warmer crevices of his body so could still take pictures. The water in my flask froze so I couldn't brush my teeth.

During the night I had a massive faecal release into the lodge's squat toilet before realising that the water in the flushing bucket was frozen solid. The rooms had no insulation so there was no heating. The walls separating the rooms comprised 1mm plywood and flexed when bumped into and that night I shivered in my -30 extreme rated sleeping bag. Through the thin wall a Chinese women argued with another, possibly over the stupid hair-drier they'd had their porter carry all the way up. Martin with his +10c sleeping bag opted to drink a few bottles of a local liquor called Roxy and in the morning I found him face down in the wrong room.

The reversal down from the peak was a little depressing, like the end of a great holiday, and my leg offered significant pain with every step I took. It needed a lot more rest than the one cold night I'd bestowed it and as the hours passed I limped down the steps in near tears with pain. I told Martin to go ahead, hobbled on, then rested an hour to try to try and make continuing bearable, but I gave up after an hour and checked into a lodge early. The following day, an hour after walking, the pain was back. I continued on regardless and tried my best to block out the pain.

In the evening I made an area with hot springs and joined several other tourists in the hot water, candles flickering in the darkness and the outline of bats swooping over the pool water. The hot water neutralised the pain in my leg and softened my aching knees, taking what seemed like ten years

192

off them. Martin wasn't to be found, presumptuously I thought the lure of wifi to upload his endless picture taking would have enticed him to push on back to Pokhara.

In the morning I set off early and again the pain from my leg hindered progress. I finally made the first stage of the trek which was accessible by jeep and negotiated a taxi to take me back to the start point. From there I found a packed bus going back to Pokhara. As I waited for it to depart it began to rain. Monsoon season was on it's way to Nepal, and I was lucky to have been dry all the way through the trek.

As I'd expected Martin was in the hotel when I arrived and we celebrated our reunion by visiting an excellent sandwich shop around the corner. This cafe was crazy good with mouth watering choices.

In the morning I made an assertive decision to sell my crap bicycle. My knees deserved better. Of the $222 spent on the bicycle and the $150 worth of stainless panniers, I hoped for a paltry $100 return. I spent half a day going around the rental and trekking shops of touristy Pokhara and shouting into all the doorways "bicycle for sale!" I received, and had to accept, a best offer of $67.

The following morning we packed for Kathmandu. Martin's nationality required a visa prior to arrival in Thailand so we had to be in the city five days before flying out. I now carried two fake waterproof Northface bags, potentially waterproof anyway, two smaller fake waterproof Northface bags, definitely not waterproof, a fake Northface bumbag, and fake Northface trousers and a fleece. Martin had even less idea than I had and still had his enormous backpack and way too much underwear. He'd learn the same way I did; by getting on the road and throwing it all away!

Having taken a mini bus to Kathmandu we stayed at a popular but overrated hostel that walking the fine line between extracting much out of its many tourists while not damaging its reputation, which included fancying up it's common room and having the staff announce free cups of tea to prospect enquirers, who would later find they were consistently unavailable. The common showers didn't work and the toilets were so small it proved impossible to shut the American western style doors once I managed to squeeze into one. The twenty to thirty dormitory tourists found themselves trying to use the one quality shower provided in the adjacent hotel. Owned by the same management, this featured porous glass through which other tourists could and would peer through to gauge if the shower was vacant. To nail the coffin shut, the beer was too expensive.

Thamel in Kathmandu featured copious shops selling the same fake Northface gear at Pokhara and all flavours of crap like bracelets and beads; popular favourites for the brain-dead. Thamel was undoubtedly expensive, the cause and affect of the high rental prices in the area. A common dish of Momo's, chicken wrapped in pastry and then steam cooked, would cost anywhere between 120-220 rupees in Thamel. but further afield backstreet restaurants would do the same for just 40 rupees.

Martin and I switched to a hotel just outside the centre, but still two minutes walking distance into it, and paid less for a room than we had in the previous dorm. A fellow electrical nut, he wouldn't shut up about whether to buy a new Canon 6D camera. It was always going to happen and I stuck the $2000 cost on my credit card, as his Croatian cards wouldn't do the entire amount and we were flying out the next day. While we scoured the camera shops I treated myself to a new super wide lens for my own Canon in the hope of better pictures and video.

We spent a day at Monkey Temple. The entry price of 200 rupees seemed steep, but we went around the back and cheekily entered through the monk entrance instead. The hassle inside was remarked and there was little worth seeing. If I had any desires to stay or dine at one of the many hotels/cafe/restaurants that have been built inside the complex perhaps I'd have enjoyed it more. Oddly there were many more monkeys on the steps leaving up to the temple than in Monkey Temple itself, so even they must have become sick of the hassle. With my guard down, one of the monkeys snatched my coke bottle out of my hand and ran into the bushes where, fascinated, I watched it try to open the bottle. Using my new super-wide lens (which required being super close to the object to fill the frame) I attempted to get a close up of another monkey's face. Thinking that it would be fairly domesticated and used to people, and that it would sit still and comply, it instead threw a left hook! Monkeys then are thieving, uncooperative and cunning. I like them a lot.

The following day myself and Martin left Nepal on a flight to Bangkok via Delhi. As I was flying with Air India, the curry served on the plane quickly ran out my rear in an almost identical form to it's ingested state. You'll have to imagine my frantic attempt to reach the toilet at the rear of the plane, which involved an impossible squeeze by a stewart and his meal serving trolley. The passenger on my left was a young guy in his 20's. Covered with tattoos, he appeared to be in the recovery stages of an acid trip in that every so often he would violently jerk.

Chapter 17

Thailand

So that I'd have no pretences on what awaited in South East Asia I'd watched no Youtube videos or read any blogs or books. I thought Thailand would be underdeveloped compared to Europe, so the reality of the place was quite a surprise. I hadn't expecting such modernness, nor the vibe that began soon after setting down at Bangkok airport. Other backpackers shared the taxi with myself and Martin and we were then on our way to the Khaosan Road area.

The party life where 18yr old spunks come to get wasted and laid, Khoasan Road made me feel like an old man, and a dirty old man at that because I couldn't keep my eyes off the unbelievable talent that was parading among the white people and their dollar converted baht. I was not alone. Lingering between the gorgeous Thai girls and the loud booming nightlife were other dirty old men, many of them British. Alongside them Australians partied obstreperously, while transexuals touted for an overly drunk tourist who'd believe he was bagging a catch. Macdonalds and Burger King were doing a roaring trade while the streets were littered with the usual throw away mess of kebab wrappers. This was party land, yet, and I was partially dismayed to believe it, I held little interest to join in. It no longer floated my boat.

I was there not to drink myself into a ditch or to fuck a whore but to source another bicycle and to get on with it. And so I began searching.

Away from the tourists 5km from Khaosan Road I found a street littered with cycle shops. Still having no real idea what I was doing, but with an intention to spend as little as possible, I spent 9,000 baht, about 300 US dollars, to kit out an aluminium framed hybrid bicycle with 700c wheels. Compared to the previous bicycle, this one was lighter with better Shimano equipment, but it came with shoddy brakes and wheels that weren't as strong. Whether it would take all my kit was again questionable, but feeling an urgency to get back on the road, I added a metal child seat and took a hacksaw to it to transform it into a luggage carrier. Martin did much the same.

With the bicycles sorted we visited the huge MBK shopping mall. This had a staggering amount of shops selling exactly the same stuff at exactly the same price. The forth floor was mostly made up of phone accessory shops. My macbook charger had died the day before and trying to find a new charger here was difficult. Of course I just wanted a fake copy, something much cheaper than the £60 Apple wanted, but after three hours all I could find was an original for 2,000 baht, a saving of 25%.

The day after, and the day before I was determined to leave, Martin threw a wobbler. What set it off was unclear, but I think the enormity of what he was about to undertake, the things that could go wrong, the rain and heat during monsoon season, his lack of suitable luggage and the speed factor made him change his mind. Well, cycling isn't for everyone. He made his choice and it was better to make it then and there than a few hundred km down the road. He lost 3,000 baht reselling his bicycle the next day.

I left Bangkok at 12:00hrs the following day, just four days before my 30th birthday. On the motorway towards Kanchanaburi the traffic was a quarter of the Indian intensity which made cycling pleasant and stress free. It rained and for the first time I knew what it was to ride in a monsoon downpour. The bicycle with its terrible brakes glided along the motorway at high speed and as I left Bangkok, the scenery changed into pastures of green. All was well, but then was a 'pop' and I was snaking left and right screaming 'SHIIIIIIIIT! SHIIITTT! SHIIIIIIT!', and trying my best to steer left away from the trucks in the right lane. At that moment working brakes would have been useful. Somehow I stayed upright.

I'd only rode about 50km and an inspection of the bicycle offered no real clue as to why the tyre had came off rim but I was lucky to have not had an accident. From what I could tell the rim was unmarred and a replacement tube I fitted stayed inflated. I tightened several nuts that were now loose and tried to improve the useless brakes, but failed. It was only as I was to pull away that I worked out the tyre issue, bending over as I did to read the digits on the tyre. 'Max 50 psi'. I was running 100! It didn't make sense, how was just 50 psi possible on a 700c road bike? Most mountain bikes tyres could do that. I then saw a stretch mark on the left side of the rubber. I would need new tyres pronto.

Further up the road I reached a small town called Ban Pong where a Thailand cyclist advised of a bicycle shop which sold better tyres. An hour later, relieved of further money, but

198

happier to have higher endurance rubber fitted to the wheels, I decided to call it a day and look for somewhere to camp. The cyclist who'd assisted me to the bicycle shop showed me to a grassed area with a free park and gym which he said would be safe to camp at and then left, intending to meet back up later on.

The grassed area ran adjacent to a railway line and crossing over that led back to the bicycle shop and several cheap restaurants. I shifted my cycle and bivi over to that side so I could watch over it and eat. From the bicycle shop a young Thai who introduced himself as "Beer", with long hair and a wide grin, crossed the road with his girlfriend, who introduced herself as "Halloween". They asked if I wanted to stay at his house for the night. With names like that I sure did. As I began to pack the bivi away I felt the smattering of light rain. Lucky again.

The evening became more surreal and brilliant. Beer didn't speak so much English but had enough to get by. Aged 20, and a music teacher, he lived with his grandma in a large rustic house with deer and crocodile heads hanging on the wall. There was so much uniqueness to the place I felt overwhelmed by it, and I'd never seen so much dust in my life. Once I'd inspected one of the first Thailand radio sets to be invented, I was shown around the 'fish farm'. I should have guessed. Never one to shy away from enterprise, the young Beer was also dealing fish to the Chinese. His hundred or more fish tanks were full of a type with an extremely large brain and what looked like Chinese hieroglyphics running along its width. I wasn't sure why there was only one fish per tank, perhaps it attacked others. I also wondered if the Chinese ate it or used it for medicinal purposes.

The grandma brought me a potato mint soup, steamed rice and an unknown dish. Within the unknown dish was a mushroom of a sort I wasn't familiar and which my brain automatically labeled hostile. Mushrooms are the only food stuff I do this with, as I've read too much on the succulent but deadly difference between the types found in Scotland. People die every year picking the wrong types and so I can't help but think it. Grandma raised her arms into a Popeye posture to indicate eating it would make me strong. I thought eating it would make me die.

In the late evening I sat outside with Beer and wrote. He practiced Hendrix on his guitar for an upcoming lesson and I was transfixed at his talent to play what he heard. Grandma had fallen asleep in the lounge and I knew I wasn't long behind. Before that I was bitten by several mosquitos, then their friends, and wondered if the area had Malaria. Beer offered a perfumed powder that he said the mosquitos didn't like and I donned a thin polyester long sleeved top. The mosquitos bit through it and ignored the perfumed powder. I applied my cancer-inducing 100% deet spray and wondered how I'd cope when it ran out.

Beer produced a bottle of Procodyl and explained the story behind the fish. The Chinese were buying them to make an antihistamine. As I drifted off my mind raced on how I had only £2,000 left in the bank, how easy it would be to sell my house back home, how much I missed my family, whether Australia would check the $5,000 bank requirement if I applied for a working holiday visa, and how lucky I was to be experiencing a random Thai's house at that moment.

I found out the following day how good my new tyres were, which is to say they weren't. My average speed dropped from

28 to 20kph and a noticeable drone came from both. Cursing the seller and myself for yet another ill-informed purchase, I also discovered the new brake callipers I'd had fitted were too short and in the case of the front brake, it applied itself to the tyre rather than the rim. This was noticeable later on in the day when an etch was grooved into the front tyre, a time bomb advancing each time I touched the lever. I'd need to source another cycle shop, but being outside of major cities the ones I happened upon sold very cheap Chinese mountain bike parts, or the same tyres as I'd had fitted the day before. The final shop in six was ran by an old Thai who spoke no English. He tried to rip me off on some used tyres and then kept his composure and arrogance as I flamboyantly told him I wasn't stupid and attempted therefore to secure a reasonable price. He wouldn't budge.

In the evening, hot and sticky from a days sweat, I came upon a closed restaurant with the entrance gate ajar. I entered and went looking for the owner to ask if I could use the toilet, which I presumed would have a bucket shower in it. Despite knocking hard on the door there was no answer, but the bonnet of the car outside was red-hot, so the owner was either asleep or too afraid to answer. I parked the cycle around the side of the building and had a wash. To the left of the restaurant I found a large football field with trees surrounding the perimeter and set back away from the village it served. It was a good spot to camp for the night and I quickly erected the bivi and made tuna sandwiches with bits I'd picked up at markets along the way that day. Mosquitos moved in just as the sun sank, and they came in droves, even biting through my socks to get at my ankles. Ever afraid of catching Dengue, I slipped into the bivi, zipped the mesh up, ran my torch around to see what had also slipped in, killed what I found, and attempted to watch a film. As I did a mosquito landed on the screen, and I went berserk trying to kill it, which in a tent resembling a suffocating condom must have looked unusual to the casual onlooker.

In the morning I noticed the wind had picked up, a good thing as I'd sweated greatly in the night and needed refreshing, but bad as I was the engine riding against it. My calorie intake was rising and I was drinking about a litre of water an hour, plus numerous cokes. I would yearn for sugar.

My mind was set on the rolling resistance offered by the dreadful tyres now fitted to the bicycle. On reaching Suchen Berg I found a small shop ran by a fantastic Thai and he went out of his way to find compatible tyres offering less resistance. What he turned up was better but well used and the rubber had cracked from where they'd sat in sunlight for too long. I swapped them anyway, confirmed there was no chance to fix the useless brakes, and after numerous photos with all of his family, rode on.

By 10:00hrs I reached an upmarket bicycle shop selling a range of high quality bicycles of the sort I should have purchased in the first place. I was gradually learning about parts, compatibility between different technologies, and becoming able to distinguish between the models offered by the various brands. I was thus able to understand that my brakes were designed for a light weight road bike carrying no weight and that my chain-set was just one notch up from the crappiest offered by Shimano. Plus the seat, the frame, the pedals, the handlebars were all wrong for touring. Although my money was dropping I intended to keep an eye out for something better, but in the meanwhile I rode out of the bicycle shop with two new tyres made by Panasonic, at a whopping $30 USD each. The amazing employees working there tried to swap the rear dérailleur but found no newer model to be compatible. The brake issue they partially resolved by dremmeling the frame to make both wheels to sit marginally higher. I worried strength would be compromised but deemed it a risk worth taking to be able to stop. As I rode off my average speed rose by 10kph and I was back in business.

As the evening closed and the sun dipped below the horizon I began looking for a place to wild camp. I'd heard a place called 'Home Stay' but a Thai rang them for me and they wanted 1200 baht per night, out of my budget by a long way. I was inclined to turn up and play poor for a discount, especially as I'd have preferred to have woken up on the day after, my 30th birthday, in a comfortable bed and my newest like; the ice coffee. This was working on the element of chance, so I was still on the lookout for an alternative. As I rode I spotted a shanty restaurant with a large table area and sockets near the tables. I rode around the rear and found a spot under a metal roof which looked perfect for my tent. The owners were cautious, spoke little English but mentioned the word hotel every so often. I played poor and innocent and after eating and a rough Q&A they said it was ok to stay around the back. When the pattering of rain began on the roof they said I could sleep inside, plus there was a shower. Communication was poor but one of them, I think, asked for 100-150 baht, which was fine, for these were Thai's in the middle of nowhere who for which tourism had yet to reach. Alternatively they may have been talking about buying beers down the local market, I couldn't understand either way. They went out there way to ensure my comfort, bringing in two fans, ensuring the mosquito net around my area was sealed and bringing water and ice before I dosed off at around 22:00hrs.

I awoke perhaps an hour or two later to find one of them had slipped my shorts down and had my penis in his mouth. I froze for what seemed an eternity as I came to terms with what was happening. Fuck! Then I bolted for the door leading to the room with my bicycle, picking up both my bags as I rose, thinking that on reaching it I'd go for the knife in the front basket. On reaching it everything was ready to go and it was much easier to diffuse the situation instead to ride off into the dark of the night. In the speed of the moment I left my sandals and rode off bare footed before realising someway down the pitch black road that I'd left them. I wasn't going back.

I rode for another five minutes and succumbing to a compelling urge to wash my genitalia using the water bottle on my bicycle. I then rode for another half an hour before finding an acceptable area to pitch my bivi. I can't remember the time but it was early hours of the morning and I'd turned 30. Happy birthday Andrew. Exhausted, sweating, profaned and partially raped, I tried as best I could to sleep.

The same morning, some hours later, I was up for blocking out what had happened and my new age by setting a new personal best on the mileage registrar. During the day I squeezed in a visit to an aquarium and a zoo, neither anything special, but thrillingly at the zoo I found the giraffe feeder had left a maintenance door open. Once he disappeared around the side I slipped in and got up and close with two of the tall necked animals. I'd no idea how aggressive or dangerous they were, only that I had to take a few pictures as it was a rare chance to do so from behind the metal bars. They acted like like scared horses. In total I rode 150km, nearly making the town of Phitsanulok, but my knees began to give and I slept outdoors in a large field behind a service station.

The following day was an easier 90km ride to the popular town of Sukhothai, known for its Buddhist ruins, and by now the daily routine of riding was helping to forget the incident two days before. As I turned onto the final road leading to the town I happened upon another Brit on a bicycle, only his had a large house alarm battery and a massive subwoofer mounted on the back. Reggae D.J Jay Pete was riding from Bangkok to Chiang Mai for BBC Comic Relief. A fellow cheapskate, we lifted the bicycles over the metal fencing around the rear of the grounds to avoid paying the ticket charge.

I deliberated on whether to write about what had happened in the last week on Facebook and my website blog. If I did I knew some would say just move on, and some would say it was my fault for being so trusting, and most would take the piss. While I decided I wrote a teaser stating I'd stayed over at a random place and something unexpected had happened. Later I decided it was important to tell the truth about the journey, warts and all. In twenty four hours thousands of people read about what happened and thirty eight left comments on Facebook.

"You need to be careful what you order in those restaurants", wrote my Greek friend Kostas.

"Which eye opened first?", friend Gillian (who was at Paul's wedding) wrote.

"Thanks for sharing son, I'll let you know who won the sweep stake when I've stopped laughing", wrote my dad.

Jah, the D.J with the sound system on his bicycle, wasn't

carrying video gear and I thought it charitable to create a video for submission to Comic Relief for him. Whether it would make any airtime was an unknown, but I would use everything I'd learned so far to try and put together something short and interesting. We'd four days to the show and had three days riding remaining to Chiang Mai, leaving about a day to edit the footage and submit it. I wasn't worried about the latter, it was the ride which was going to be the issue. Pete had rode all his life and was in better shape. He had the slower of the bikes but carried less equipment and could outdo my mileage.

Sukhothai to Uttaradit was a paltry 80km which left plenty of time during the day to stop and video capture along the way. Having time to look for points of interest, I found a railway crossing to capture Jay going over, captured front, back and sideways roll bys and persuaded a policeman to make a false arrest. We talked the principle of a school into making kids dance as he passed between them. The day gave up around sixty seconds of useable footage, once I trimmed the clips. Jah thought he had a food freebie and possible accommodation sorted at Uttaradit but I was skeptical, which seemed to annoy him. I was right, the guy who owned the large resort in question served us a glass of water and a $1 fried rice. Dessert was a business card and a brochure. His rooms were of course full. I was annoyed at how far from the centre the place was. We rode another 5km to a hotel recommended by the resort owner, but I was left unimpressed by the tiny room and high price, plus I wanted something in the centre where I could grab a beer and decent food. It took another 5km to find what I was looking for; a cheap and solid hotel for half the price, but Jah was weird on how clean it was and kept dithering. Perhaps he was dehydrated, it had been a long hot day after all. To me it was clean and functional, but then I'd suffered India and accepted lesser standards. I left him to do whatever he wanted and booked a room for myself.

The second day of riding to Lampang nearly broke my resolve to carry on pedalling. Having lost Pete, I could ride at my own pace, but the lengthy 174km of road was by far the greatest I'd attempted yet. The last 30km bore an incline up a mountainous range and by then it was dark. My legs ready to collapse, I grabbed the back of a dual wagoned truck and with only my head-torch and the red lights on the back clung on as it dragged the bicycle and I up the incline. With the weight of my luggage this put considerable strain on my arm, while the other tried to counterbalance the tendency for the cycle to pull inwards towards the truck. After a few minutes I was actively trying to block the pain from my arm but then the battery in my head-torch died and my attention shifted to bracing pothole impacts instead. Right to the top I didn't let go. I couldn't. The remaining kilometres downhill to Lampang were blissful. I made a note to never do such distance again. Ever.

The final day to Chiang Mai was approximately 100km and relatively flat. It was accomplished with ease and I checked into a hostel where I was quickly unimpressed by the pricing strategy that included advertising breakfast as included and asking donations for it, and charging two times the going rate for water. The place felt fabricated, staff were abrupt and the tourists, many American, could only communicate at volume while conversing over the most dull of topics. At least the girl in the bunk below had a fantastic pair of boobs.

I switched the following day to a more centrally located hostel at a third of the price and with an authentic backpackers feel to it. I tried to secure seven days at the place but only one was available. In Thailand's more popular hostels this was quite a frequent technique and translated meant 'we'll see if you're the right fit and offer you more time if we like you.' I bought something from the menu and chilled out.

It was now several months since I left England and I'd no idea what the date or day was. I was transitioning between life at home and life on the road, such that life on the road was becoming home. I'd previously read such travellers later experienced difficulty reverting back and had talked to others about it. One such gentleman, Geoff Thomas, who'd rode a Triumph Tiger around the world, told me his 'fix' was to work for six months in the U.S and spend the money he saved in Thailand.

My money was forever a worrying issue, because it was forever reducing in denomination. Sadly the tenant in my house was playing funny buggers and had dropped two months into arrears, so I served him a Section 8 eviction notice. My intention once he was out was to sell the house cheap, but other options at supporting myself included teaching in Thailand, which would earn about 35,000 baht ($1,200 USD) or South Korea which would pay double that. I believed working a farm in Australia would beat both those options. I couldn't see any way to make money by programming while I was in Asia.

Chiang Mai met some of my expectations and failed others. I appreciated the inner city design built around a square block and the range of services, but once I'd excluded visiting temples there wasn't much else to do. Tourism was at the forefront of everything and it lacked atmosphere and vibe because of it. While Bangkok was known as a resolute tourist trap Chiang Mai had a reputation for being laid back and cool, but with its growing popularity came corporations and higher cost. The Night Bazaar area featured the usual fast food outlets, shopping outlets, high end hotels and American coffee shops among with seedy bars and prostitution. Eating on the street was the best way to live and live cheap in Chiang Mai.

The bicycle was a money pit. At a bicycle shop in Chiang Mai the brake blocks were swapped for an improved design, new panniers were fitted to the rear and I had stickers created to promote my website and to hide the flaking paintwork.

The next morning I met back up with Jah Pete to put together the video and outside a rather snooty and soulless area of Chiang Mai. Full of pre-fab doll house buildings and businesses selling high markup items like coffee, auto water levelling ponds, immaculately measured grass and little bridges interconnected exclusive shops while a toy-town colour scheme complemented ghastly architectural decisions. The plaza was dominated by DSLR photographers with Canon white L lens glass. Some of the photographers had rented out young models to pose among the fake ponds, and I disliked them even more than the backdrops they thought would make for great pictures. I began using my own DSLR to take close-up shots of the photographers enjoying their discomfort.

One of Jah's sponsors had asked him to put on a little reggae gig outside the shop using his bicycle and the speaker system on the back. Unfortunately they hadn't thought about running it by the other shops and a booking conflict appeared around the corner, in the form of a 10,000 watt speaker rig and a live band. Jah didn't stand a chance, but he did it anyway. One local fruitcake got up and began dancing but that was exactly what I needed to end the video submission. I Final Cut'd everything together then submitted the final to Comic Relief. Jah handed the stage over to two transvestite comedians and it was all over.

Both I and Jah left for Pai, Thailand's hippy going chill-out town. Undiscovered by corporations and big business and yet to be exploited, it sounded like an ideal place to get lost at. Jah left early morning and I set off a bit later at around mid-day. The route was pleasant but became hilly which drained my energy and reduced my speed. I was having a bad time of it, and was pushing and cursing on yet another never-ending incline when a Hilux 4x4 shot by at high speed, then braked sharply and began to reverse. A very pleasant family inside, with a policeman at the wheel, offered to stick the bicycle in the back and give me a lift to the higher ground.

After an hour the policeman, his wife, young son and I, disembarked for a quick fried rice at a small village restaurant. Just as soon as we'd sat down, immersed in the tranquillity of peaceful bird song, a young Thai and his girlfriend pulled up in a 4x4, left the windows down, exited, and cracked open cans of beer from the restaurants fridge. With significant amplification in play and horrendous booming coming from the vehicles subwoofers, people began to become upset. My policeman driver, a seemingly passive guy, went utterly apeshit.

The remaining 10km to Pai I had to ride myself. I'd half expected to pass Jah along the way, glimmering in hope that I could give a friendly two fingers as I flew by at 100kph, but when I rode into town he was already there drinking beer with a random South African couple. How he'd done it so quickly was beyond my comprehension, so I told him he'd clearly cheated. He said he hadn't. Grinning, I said he had. He bought a third beer and I bought a first. "Cheers!" we said enthusiastically, both happily sharing the moment.

Before festivities began, we had to find suitable quarters at which to reside. I did a bit of poking around and thought the description of a place called Tropical Resort sounded positive. Because it was outside of the centre Jah was negative and grumbled like a small child all the way there. His face lit like it was Christmas when he saw it, and I was similarly delighted. The basic setup included a patch of grass on which people danced with circus equipment, an open hut with hammocks overlooking the valley and bamboo sleeping huts with roofs of laced leaf. It ticked our eco box, and the laid back staff, made up of tourists who didn't want to leave Pai, made the place a joy to stay at. Dumping our gear, we rejoined the South African couple back in the main town and drank a few too many bottles of Chang beer.

The morning should've began with a headache but the fresh air rustling through my hut must have helped. During the night my bicycle had fallen over and the handlebar now stuck through the lower roof. My mosquito net kept the bugs out and with the hut being open to all I was glad of it. The floor bounced like I was walking on twigs, which I probably was, but a thin laminate cover hid whatever lay beneath. The leaves on the roof flexed enough to allow a little wind to pass through and the hut was surprisingly cool even when the sun began cooking.

Jah had a whole month booked at a type of Jujitsu training centre and we spent two days chilling out in Pai before that. Pai had a staggering amount of hostel and hut options, which was only matched by the amount of places serving food. Despite what may sound like a nightmare, Pai was exceptionally chilled and laid back with no beefcake tourists or need of an agenda or plan. If you were to ask someone what they'd done that day they'll likely reply nothing. That was the beauty of the place.

Leaving Pai was a moment of sadness, but my 30 day visa demanded it. There were few places on the trip where I genuinely could stay for a long time. On the morning before I left Jah, we enjoyed final multiple fruit smoothies and honey and cinnamon pancakes at a small restaurant run by an Israeli couple. Then I packed the bicycle up and left on what I imagined would be a long slog to Chiang Rai, a northern city close to the Laos border.

Reaching Chiang Rai I predicted would take two and a half days. It proved troublesome from the start, where the first 30km was uphill. On the road, I met a Thai touring cyclist and admired his expensive bicycle and queried the capacious amount of water he carried. I couldn't understand why he wanted to carry several litres of water uphill, being that little shops were so frequent and numerous. At the end of the day I wild camped on a grassed extension of a winding corner.

The following day Garmin plotted a route through what looked to be a valley and instead of riding up and around on the fast motorway used by the buses going from Chiang Mai to Chiang Rai I went along with it. To get to the first road I had to leave the motorway and in essence travel behind it and use little backroads to join onto another that would eventually lead to the motorway on the other side of Thailand. Almost immediately Garmin took me to a bridge that did not exist, but then I was riding among paddy fields and enjoying the ride.

Everything went well until I reached the so called valley area. Roughly between two small towns called Phrao and Wiang, it began with a gentle incline and I neither worried about my lack of water capacity or the insane heat, but it kept getting higher and harder. I kept up my resilience, but then so did the heat, and I soon ran out of water. This was a mountain pass with no villages or shops. I resorted to flagging any pickup truck that passed hoping they'd have a large 15 litre bottle I could refill from. My mouth was dry and parched and exhausted I made little progress. To add to my woes my bicycle began refusing to downshift on an incline. Up, up and up it went.

My legs became so knackered I eventually couldn't make them ride up any degree of incline no matter what the gradient and I found myself only just able to cycle on a flat straight. Sweat would run down my arms and off my fingers and down my arms and drip from my elbows on an incline. Not being one for giving up, I pushed, literally, into the dark hoping to find the summit. As I traversed higher the air became smoggy from forest fires and the repugnant air made breathing more difficult. Around 23:00hrs and on thinking I'd reached the summit, I set up camp just off the mountain pass in a partially cleared area still with much jungle foliage. I was in close need of a wheelchair, for it was by far the hardest cycling I'd done to date.

I fell asleep almost immediately but awoke an hour later to rummaging in the nearby undergrowth. I couldn't determine the cause and tried to ignore it, but I couldn't ignore a large leaf bouncing up and down on a palm tree above me while all the rest on it remained still. Then a bat dropped from it on to

213

the ground, opened its wings and flew off.

The final leg to Chiang Rai was only 110km and would be straight forward once I reached the motorway. To begin with my legs were sore and unresponsive but they eased as the day progressed. To get to the motorway I had to descend the mountain, and now more than ever my shoddy brakes demonstrated an inability to function. There were times when I was pulling as hard as I could and still accelerating, but somehow I made it, and with a renewed hatred for my wheels.

Entering Chiang Rai I spotted three white females and with an enthusiastic "hello tourists!" enquired where they were staying. These young work volunteers took me to their cheap enough hotel and later at 19:00hrs to eat at the night bizarre they knew so well. The food here was good. I stayed away from the seedy one lane of bars and prostitution pickups. Chiang Rai was less touristy then the other places I'd visited and being en-route to Burma and Laos was frequented by those doing border runs. I found the city laid back and underwhelming in size, which suited me down to the ground as I could easily locate everything I needed. And what I needed most was a change of bicycle.

I knew I had to have it the moment I laid eyes on it. A bicycle shop not far from the towns centre clock sported a collection of new and used bicycles and a few for rent. It was a one for rent that caught my eye. A few general usage marks, but with little use and well maintained, the bicycle was made by Specialized and featured a large alloy trail frame, oversized and granny cogs, hard front suspension, v-brakes, 700c wheels and decent Shimano shifters. The cost was 10,000 baht, about $333 USD, while the new price in the U.S was over $600. The lady owner offered just 3,000 baht in exchange for my bicycle (it'd now cost 9,000 in the three weeks of ownership since Bangkok). I managed to get this up to 5,000 baht then relented, and while they swapped over parts I wished to keep, I set off to find a fee-less Aeon cash point to pay for it. Finally I would be riding something decent.

Back at the hotel I saw an opportunity to jumble sale some of the gear I wasn't using to some of the happy-go flush tourists. On a table I left a price list, the items for sale and asked for cash to be left at the reception if I wasn't around. On my return from the night bizarre I'd sold a bag, tripod stand, speakers and a solar charger. Someone nicked two Sanyo Eneloop batteries, the first thieving in eight months of travel, and a tourist no less.

With my newly gained terror of ascents, I enquired on putting the bicycle on the top of a bus to the Laos border, but then at the bicycle shop I bumped into a 74yr old American riding a recumbent bicycle around the world, and he told me there was no need. It was under 100km and flat most the way. The next day I set off on my new steed, found a sticker shop to plaster my name and website on the frame, and enjoyed a trouble free ride to the border. As northern Thailand came to a close, my bicycle glided with unkempt quietness, the better riding position meaning my neck no longer ached, and the brakes worked. Things were looking up.

Chapter 18

Laos

Chiang Khong is a small border town connecting Thailand and Laos and as so often happens on the road, I arrived later than I'd expected too. Immigration closed at 18:00hrs and with no alternative but to wait till the morning I went in search of a guest house cheap enough to set aside wild camping. As I ventured up the main road I came upon three very good looking girls drinking beers at a table outside a supermarket and they asked if I'd like to join them. This sounded like a very good idea, but famished I first needed to find food. By now I was thoroughly sick of rice, noodles, and all the Thai derivatives and was adamant someone, somewhere, had to stock bread or potatoes. Unsuccessful, I gave up and rejoined the girls, ordering a big bottle of Chiang. A drunken Thai came over and sat outside our little circle, occasionally trying to pour a little of our beer into his plastic beaker. The most polite drunk I've seen yet, when we said no he simply went back to his original position and reattempted five minutes later. After half an hour we tired of him and asked the shop keepers if they knew him, which they didn't, or if they knew how we could get rid of him. Such was the generosity of Thai's, they gave him a free iced tea from the fridge, some cigarettes and pointed him along the road.

Entering Laos required passage over the Mekong river to the small town of Huay Xai by way of a thin and long wooden boat roughly two foot wide. I questioned whether the bicycle would still be in it at the other side but it took no more than two minutes and cost only 40 baht for myself and the bicycle. The visa-on-arrival process was straight forward and cost $35 USD, and while filling in beloved paperwork, I bumped into a cycling Scottish and German couple called Esther and Warren. They'd been travelling the world for two and a half years, picking and choosing places at leisure. With much in common, we chatted and swapped detail, but whereas they planned to find a guesthouse in Huay Xai and chill before making a route towards China, I planned to travel south towards the small village of Pakbeng.

I dismissed the idea of taking a slow boat down the Mekong river instead wishing to find a backroad trail I'd heard about and to cycle that instead. The backpackers could have the river for themselves, while I took the lonely road. But where was it?

Laos was quite a communication shock compared to neighbouring Thailand, as nobody I spoke to spoke English. There were little in the way of road signs and nobody knew the place names of anything outside of a 50m radius where they lived. When asking for directions to the road I was determined to find if I pointed one way I'd receive a nod. Then if I pointed the other way I'd receive the same nod. Laos exposed my lack of planning and my ignorance for travelling without a map, and I was now frustrated. The road I contested to be the one I first required confirmation off. I went back and forth between little shops and guesthouses trying to find anyone who could speak English, but in the later part of the afternoon, with the sun at its peak, I relented and made my way back to Huay Xai to find a guest house for the night. I'd try again in the morning.

On my return Warren spotted my bicycle and called me over to the restaurant they were eating at. Explaining my lack of success, to which they found hilarious, they pulled out an extremely good map of Laos. On it was the confirmation I had eagerly sought. Requiring a copy, I took out my DSLR and captured a shot. The remainder of the evening we passed away with a cheeky beer and travelling stories.

Education wasn't the only immediate difference I noticed between Laos and Thailand, the latter being agriculturally more efficient and thriving with crops and plantations. Despite the short distance to Thailand, this part of Laos was surprisingly dusty and dirt trodden.

The shanty road to Pakbeng only began after 100 metres of tarmac which ended abruptly at a corner where the construction of immigration facilities was underway. Here a bridge which could to take motorised traffic was being built to enhance the Laos economy. I found the little side road of rough stone, dirt and ditches to Pak Beng and left it behind. My bicycle despite its skinny road going 700c tyres performed brilliantly on the rough and I passed through quaint little hamlet villages cheeringly responding to anyone waving or greeting. It was utterly beautiful and completely rustic. Everything was a wood hut. Some had satellite, at least to begin with, but there were no buildings made of brick, nor any slate or tile roofing. This was nature and people in harmony and a rarity to behold.

Eating in Laos proved identical to rural Thailand cuisine, thus noodles and rice were the menu, but prices I found to be almost universally higher. Packaged foods were all imported from Thailand and attributed to this, and I found bartering to be possible only when ordering multiple items at once. Initially shops tried to charge in Thai baht, but I'd purposely exchanged all mine to ensure I didn't get ripped off. One shop tried to short change and another tried to cheat, but otherwise sellers were honest and forthright. Since language was a problem I would hand over my iPhone with the calculator app open for them to type prices onto. Living cheap would of course mean living like a local, and I quickly became accustomed to a sticky rice and fried egg combination.

My first day heading towards Pak Beng ended just before sunset in what I thought was the remains of an open cast quarry. During the day I'd collected bits of wood and stored them on the bicycle. Now I lit a fire and began boiling eggs. While the fire gained traction and darkness set in I found three large branches and used a rubber band from my inflatable mat to create a wigwam style structure from which I could hang my mosquito net. It was too hot to use the bivi, and I draped and tucked the mosquito net under the inflatable mat to secure a barrier between me and whatever was outside. I was sitting inside writing on my mac and munching on the poorly boiled eggs when my shelter was breached by some sort of wasp-cricket-cockroach death insect. Despite my frantic efforts to kill it before it killed me, the four inch monster lived on and I ended up outside trying to spot it with my torch.

The sun was up early, before me, and as I began packing I was found by several young girls. They surrounded my pitch without attempting dialogue but were pleasant enough and talked among themselves. They all took turns to squeeze the tyres on my bicycle, something that had occurred the day before as well. The people of Laos were fascinated by tyre pressure.

Setting off, I was now in rural Laos and the rocky road I was travelling along was only used by the occasional pickup or scooter. The land here was fecund, odd given the proximity of the river, and every so often I'd spot an abandoned hut with a fallen roof, like a scene from a Vietnam war flick.

The road took a bend, leaving the river to go south, and an ascent began. I passed through numerous hamlets with bamboo and straw hut dwellings, and so many little children running between them. I adored the feeling of being in the heart of rural Laos, but battling the now constant incline was sapped my energy. It was so unbelievably hot, and the occasional vehicle that passed by had covered me and everything I carried in a bath of red dirt. In the dust I would cough, and I would pick my nose every half hour to remove the captured particles.

I was dismayed by the level of tree felling and slash and burning. As Laos population increased the need to cut and burn trees would intensify. Ultimately, much damage was being done to the planet right here.

Despite the sparsity many of the hamlet villages I passed through still featured a little shop selling bottled orange juice, my new hydration favourite. Sweating protrusively, sometimes I'd run out of water and find no shop, and on one such occasion I went begging at a hut whereon an old lady appeared at the door with her saggy boobs hanging out. Young children united around the hut and my water bottle was refilled from an old yellow container, which in another life had probably contained motor oil.

With the sun almighty and powerful I stopped at a hut and looked inside for a means to take cover. At the front hung a chalkboard while little wooden desks lined to the rear. Sheets of paper, some with crayon drawings on, were strewed around the natural dirt floor. The hut was a school, but today it would serve to lower my body temperature. From my pannier I took out a chocolate bar I'd purchased earlier in the day, only to find the chocolate had run off it and out of the packaging and down to the bottom of the pannier I'd stored it in. It was now a wafer. Walls have eyes in Laos and several young children came over to satisfy their curiosity. By now I'd picked up a few local words including the general greeting "Sabadi". The children wore small hand made bows and draped a quiver complete with twenty hand made arrows. I'd have liked to have been able to ask them in their own language if they were out to catch a meaty tourist for the evening roast.

As I progressed the road became very difficult, climbing from about 100m to 1650m and with endless inclines and declines. I managed a mere 65km in 10 hours of riding. On on the final decline, which was brutal, I only made it down in one piece thanks to the new brakes. I lost a quarter of the pad surface on just that stretch. On the old bicycle I would've certainly crashed.

Towards the end of the day, soaked in sweat and with no energy remaining, I overshot the road to Pak Beng. It was actually situated down from the main road and lacked a sign post indicating the turn off. On arrival I found it to be less of a town and more of a single street. The slow boat from Huay Xai, which took two days in total, mitigated a stay over at Pak Beng. By the time I arrived it had disembarked its passengers many hours before and so I was at liberty to haggle over the remaining guest house rooms. I did that and then ate an ungodly amount of food. As I'd anticipated, the place had plenty of rip-offs going on, plus hash and opium sellers trying their hand.

Pak Beng had built itself long before it became a stopover for tourists, and poverty was visible when I moved away from the ferry end of the village. Believing I needed a days rest, I wished to see how the little town ran during the daytime and found a second guest house at half the price towards the shanty end of the village. My new quarters was a comparative dump, but I could sit upstairs and steal the wifi from the restaurant opposite, and that would allow me to clear a backlog of work. That was the plan, but the following day I discovered the village lost electricity with the tourists leaving in the morning and only came back on in the evening when the next boat arrived.

During the day I witnessed a transformation as the main street became a community. The pushy sellers and the opium dealers had disappeared. A restaurant hosted a wedding celebration, kids played on push toys in the street, and locals strolled leisurely. In the squalid area at the top of the hill I ate a plain fried noodles while watching a guy living out of a pickup truck behind an unambiguously placed ATM machine.

Back at the hotel, with the electricity now on, it began to thunder. This was followed by rain, but not as I'd experienced prior, for this was omnipotent in magnitude. The lights in the village flickered and the electricity went off. As I finished a bit of work using the battery on my mac, large and fast moving mosquitos flew across my screen. I applied even more deet and hoped for the best. Later I tried for a shower but found the water was off. I asked the girl downstairs, who had for some curious reason had dressed up like a whore. She grunted and disappeared outside. A moment later I heard gushing from all three bathrooms down the hallway, if you could call them that. The reason the water was off was that every bit of pipework in the place leaked.

Pak Beng was a dislikeable place, with locals hooked on easy money and too lack a respect for those providing it. I was glad to leave.

From Pak Beng slow boat continued along the Mekong towards the large town of Luang Prabang. I too would head for this, but again I'd be taking a back road. Zooming in on the snapshot map I'd acquired the days earlier, the first road I'd take was yellow in colour, indicating a smaller tarmac road, and the second much longer road a red, indicating a motorway. Sounded easy. I left Pak Beng early and after a 10km ride the road dipped towards the Mekong and there it ended. Here the first signs of a bridge development were underway, but the crossing was currently possible only by small ferry. This took 30 seconds.

After another 10km, I was surprised to find myself close to the Thailand border. Looking left, I baulked at hilly terrain mountain range I'd have to cross if I were to head to Luang Prabang. Looking right, I could re-enter Thailand and have an easier life. I chose left.

I struck gold when outside a small shop buying some confectionary a couple offered to stick my bicycle in the back of their pickup all the way to Hongsa, a small town on my route. I sat in the rear with several boxes of the orange juice I so often bought, mirthful at the inclines I was missing out.

Sadly at Hongsa the couple tried to charge 100,000 kip for the lift, which was disappointing, and I returned the disappointment by rejecting their request outright.

Hongsa was an interesting little town, for its entire workings were dominated by the building of a new power station, which when complete would be the largest in Laos. Most the vehicles in and around the town displayed a 'Hongsa Power' logo on the rear, and the company had taken over entire streets for its employees and contractors. Riding past the centre of town, a sign advertised a guest house with wifi and I duly went to check it out, only to find it rebranded 'Hongsa House #12'. The front door was wide open and there wasn't a reception, but the rear offered a toilet and shower. Not knowing if I'd be wild camping that night, I discretely used both and then left to source alternative accommodation. At a restaurant I asked if I could camp on the grass around the rear but they said no. Although I'd only done 60km that day the sun had baked my head and I treated myself to an overly expensive hotel room for the night. I would refresh and put in a better performance the following day.

I awoke the following morning and made a coffee using a 3-in-1 satchel I found at the bottom of one of my bicycle panniers. Not long after setting off I ate yet another sticky rice and fried egg combination, then mentally prepared myself for the serious exercise that lay ahead, for ahead lay yet another mountain range.

I found the motorway turning to be closed. A large board with Lao wording was accompanied by signs indicating I should turn left towards a small village, but instead navigated around the barricade and continued on the original course. A steep incline followed and the road, still tarmac at this stage, had large chunks missing out of it where rocks from the left cliff had fallen down into it. Even if in a good state of repair this was no motorway. Soon the broken tarmac was replaced by dirt and the road began tom climb. It didn't end all day and by 15:00hrs I was ruined.

I came upon a remarkable little village with a wooden water wheel and children happily jumping into water pools. Initially I thought I was at a place marked on my map called Houayngang, but speaking to a local in broken dialogue contradicted that. An unmarked village before it? I had no idea. The local also mentioned a cyclist a few month back had tried to go past this very point but had given up and made his way back to Hongsa. Before he'd said that I only felt downright knackered. Now I felt downright depressed.

The local was employed by Hongsa Power and responsible for supplying all the units assembling pylons between Hongsa and Luang Prabang with necessary logistics. Each pylon had to be carefully positioned and a new road had to be made to that location for it's assemble and then wiring. The steel wire, wrapped in huge round wheels, was fitted by a special machine that used a lot of gasoline. Each day he'd send a pickup up the road with barrels of the stuff in the back, but today would be different, for he offered to send me and my bicycle as well. I agreed immediately!

The driver of the 4x4 fancied himself as a rally driver and took corners at insane speed. I sat in the back of the pickup with the bicycle and seven drums of diesel which despite there considerable weight shifted like pool table balls during an earthquake. At a pylon 'camp' the driver noticed that I was now soiled in diesel and ushered me into the passenger seat. The free ride ended high up the mountain, perhaps close to or even at the peak, with, I was told, 65km of road remaining to Luang Prabang.

Most of what was left now had to be downhill, and my spirit lifted in knowing it but there was still much inclination to do, and I spent three hours eating into it. It was dark when exhausted I turned off the road, set up my bivi on a dirt verge, and crawled in, along with the sweat, mud and oil I was covered in.

I awoke in the early hours of the morning to the noise of heavy rain on my bivi. Without delay I sourced the tarp I was carrying, moved the bicycle closer and covered all the bags and the front of the bivi with it. Although I could zip the bivi up completely and the gas permeable membrane would probably ensure I'd not suffocate, in the heat it would be hugely uncomfortable. A distant thunder echoed around the hills and the rain intensified, but knowing everything would stay dry I fell back asleep.

An hour later I awoke a second time, but not because of the impious downpour but the immediate and deafening crack of thunder. Both light and sound were synchronised above my head, and at 1,500 meters above sea level, it was loud!

After packing up and hitting the road that morning I stopped at a small shop with a table. A week earlier I'd tripped on a flight of stairs and somehow took a chunk out of a big toe. I'd bandaged it but it wouldn't heal and in my ignorance it'd became infected. Now I was walking odd. I took out my knife and cut away the dead skin and infection, cleaned the area with an iodine pad, applied antiseptic cream, and then a fresh bandage. The wife of the shop owner, impressed at my first aid kit, donated ten small and beautifully tasting bananas.

Having ate nothing for 24hrs, I also bought four packets of crisps and watched with curiosity as a dozen wild dogs and ducks fought it out for the scraps. Stinking of sweat and diesel, I rode the remaining distance to Luang Prabang.

I spent three nights at Luang Prabang, doing exactly what I'm not sure, but I did spend half a day visiting the spectacular Kuang Si waterfalls 30km south of the city. These were unparalleled in natural beauty, and in pool lounging opportunities. I became pally with a guy called Christopher from California, some small northern town within, and his girlfriend. They'd been travelling for a little while and had what I would call the right approach in that they didn't drink to get drunk, believed they could do whatever they wanted to do, and rather despised the common backpacker. Christopher was full of interesting facts that I wanted to remember and research later on, and he give a rundown on the weed growing that goes on back home. Apparently, if I wanted to make some money chopping and drying the stuff, all I had to do was stick a billboard around my neck with a drawing of a pair of scissors on it then wait on a street corner in his town. Memories of the 1920's American depression came to mind, in particular a picture I recalled seeing of a man doing the same but with the words 'will work for food'.

Luang Prabang had all sorts of tourists. I, of course, was in the cheapest quarters at the equivalent of $9 USD a night, cheap compared to what another American couple I ran into were paying, an eye watering $200 USD a night. The man commented that the hotel was 'really nice', and I'm sure it was. While they dined at some rather excellent restaurants, I mostly ate at a little place facing the Mekong river. I don't think they could be bothered with a name for it, but scrawny writing on a white board 'cheepest prices' (sic) indicated their target audience. My relationship with the place went sour when they charged 4,000 kip (just over half a dollar) to butter a baguette. Later, when eating a cheese baguette two cheese triangles were supplied, but when ordering the same to take-away they only used one. That was the sort of thing I had to watch for in Lao. They'll rarely short change, but they would short on the quantity or hammer on extras.

The night market was full of the usual useless crap nobody with a brain would buy, however those in the know knew there was a mobile food court on a corner which did superb food of all varieties at very good prices. The cheaper tourists waited all day for it to open and then pigged out there.

When the day came to leave I'd had solid rest and thought I'd be firing on all cylinders, yet mounting the bicycle and actually riding at a decent pace seemed difficult. I succumbed to the reality of having dodgy knees, both acting like they were arthritic. It was only when warmed up that they offered flexibility and stopped acting triple there age. They needed a couple weeks rest to allow the swelling to go down and the torn muscle to repair properly.

The target for that day was only 80km, as I'd factored in the incline I'd be doing for most of it. Good fortune shone down, because the sun didn't, and the temperature nose dived to the low 30's. A possible reason the sun stayed away might have been to do with the thick grey artificial clouds that had formed from tree burning. On one stretch of the road, I experienced an aural 5.1 surround effect when the snap, crackle and pop emanated from all four directions. While the locals burned trees for crop plantation, the resulting pollution was alarming and sad. I couldn't even take my sunglasses off, for the particles in the air acted as an abrasive on my eyeballs.

I couldn't breath properly either, and wheezed like an asthma attack was imminent.

Hours went by and towards the end of the day I made a grab for a slow moving lorry for a pull. The driver was unhappy and attempted to shake me off by veering closer to the side of the road. To get around this I would pull on my fingers to allow my arm to arch and go over the handlebars, allowing me to move directly behind the lorry rather than to the side. At what I thought was the the top of the incline I let go and cycled over to a flat area large enough to take my bivi. After checking it out, I made camp before dark, watched a movie and fell asleep.

I'd about 140km of riding left to reach my next stop, Vang Vieng, and attempting to reach the place in one day I thought likely to be difficult. After a 20km climb I was more hopeful when the road descended downwards and a pleasant breeze took care of my sweat. Decent made me happy and I celebrated by overloading on bottled green tea mixed with honey and lemon. On the road I met a cyclist from Belgium who'd been travelling for a few years. His bicycle was an ultimate weapon, both in technical components and price tag, and he rode using an artificial leg from the knee down, a product of an old motorcycle accident. I told him about the significant incline he had to tackle and ventured that he might like to grab onto the back of a passing truck.

About 25km from Vang Vieng my legs began to loose power yet again. The heat probably had something to do with it, but I had to make Vang Vieng else I'd suffer another sweaty night in the bivi. When I stopped at a little shop I tried to heighten my moral by necking a big bottle of beer. Never before had a beer hit so hard and so quickly. I nearly keeled over!

Back on the bicycle it took more effort to stay upright then to hit the ground, evidently I was dehydrated. I forced two litres of water down and the alcohol quickly wore off. Suddenly I spun into an insane overdrive, my legs forgetting their woes and firing like the pistons of an engine. I stuck the bicycle in the highest gear, lowered my cadence and hammered it. Slightly downhill for the remaining 20km, my average speed rose to 45kph, with regular 50kph sections. Whenever the road flattened out I tried even harder to maintain the speed until I reached the next decline. I flew through the little villages towards Vang Vieng at warp and as the sun disappeared and flying insects came out, I breathed hard and ate many.

Arrival. The speedometer bestowed a fabulous 147km for that day and I settled for the first cheap guesthouse I came upon. My legs buckled into a seat, and I called over to the shop next door to make a tuna baguette. Four of them. And two lemon honey teas. The maker muttered something in Lao and then left. I ate the baguettes and fell into a reverberant sleep.

When I awoke in the morning I began scouting the main streets for a decent sized breakfast. I hadn't expected the amount of guest houses for such a small town, nor the ceiling mounted flat TV's they featured, playing re-runs of Family Guy or Friends. The tourists were lapping it up; lounging around on the sofa-seats all day and ordering westernised food. At selected restaurants one could find happy menus. A lace of light hearted drugs, normally decided by the chef, included mushrooms, hash and even opium.

Vang Vieng had once been a full on party and drug town, but alas it was no more, curbed by the authorities when things went too far. Once upon a time tourists would float down the Mekong river in a tractor inner tube, drugged and drunk, while locals would meet them in the middle with further stash. It took a few tripping tourists to go overboard during the monsoon season, and subsequently the drownings of, for the Government to step in and pull the plug.

I found tubing to still be an enjoyable experience. There was only the one river hut offering beer, but they were doing so at high cost and I didn't really care for it anyway. As I slowly floated along I remembered I hadn't applied suncream and tried to cool my body with the colder water, but I burn't and my head cooked like an egg. An Australian ahead of us had dropped his waterproof camera in and hadn't backed up the memory card inside it. He'd issued an award of 2,000,000 kip to anyone that found it (a can of coke cost 5,000 kip) and beside him in the water several locals had donned diving masks. Outside monsoon season the river was slow and easy going, and for much of it I could easily stand up, just as well, as my tube had a hole in it and over the four hours it and I slowly sank.

Vang Vieng was quiet with only a smattering of small bars. The buzz of the place had dwindled and the main club where everyone ended up in the late evening was popular only for a lack of an alternative. In it I stuck to the floor and continuously thought how crap it was. Some went on to a 'Jungle Party' but remarked in the morning that it was no good. Vang Vieng was no Thailand Pai, it didn't have the hip, the atmosphere or the coolness.

On studying a Canadian girl digest a magic mushroom pizza, trip out to Family Guy and continuously remark on being "very hot" I reaffirmed drugs were never going to be my forte. Meanwhile a 23yr old lad I'd met on tubing had ordered a happy strawberry shake. Sipping on my Beer Lao, I curiously watched it take hold and half an hour in he wore a permanent grin and a fixed stare into space. The Canadian girl then developed a compassionate desire to eat bananas. At that point I decided against mushrooms.

I knew my desire to stay was limited, but I'd set up a pre-interview for a programming role in Amsterdam. I was unsure if I wanted it, and for sure I didn't want to live in Amsterdam, but with my finances dwindling I knew it was time to begin looking at options.

I held the pre-interview over Skype and fifteen minutes in everything was going well with only a few wifi failures. Then the restaurant's router broke, and I couldn't find my sandals, so I took somebody else's and legged it down the road where I could pick up another connection in hope of keeping the interview alive. Towards the end the lady asked about my salary expectation, and I was openly frank that I couldn't command a top salary due to my lack of corporate experience. The boundaries for the role on offer were 40-60k euros plus benefits. I said I'd take 40k and we could mutually reassess once I've proved my abilities. Perhaps I'd just done myself out of 20k, or perhaps my non greedy approach would go down well. She advised about the bonuses and perks then set up a technical interview booking for the following Tuesday. That one would be much harder, but in the (admittedly unlikely) event I passed that, they'd fly me to Amsterdam for a final interview.

Another reason for budget was draining faster than expected was the house I'd left in the UK. A noose around my neck,, the tenant had lost his job and had defaulted on two monthly payments, leaving the mortgage to come out of my budget. I sent my dad and some mates around to find out what was going on. They reported back that the house was 'roasting hot', which probably meant he was growing weed. I served him a Section 8 notice, giving him two weeks to cough up otherwise I'd file a procession claim with county court. Magically the tenant spoke to the council housing benefits office and wrote an email to let me know they'd back date the rent. I couldn't trust him and told him I'd need confirmation from the council directly. It was much more difficult trying to sort this outside of the UK.

I left Vang Vieng for the Vientiane, the capital of Laos, on what was a glorious ride. Nearly all of it slightly down hill I easily managed the 155km distance in two days. Along the way I bumped into a Spanish couple riding Asia for six months and had a good chat about Malaysia and Indonesia. At Vientiane I found an adequate, if lacking, hostel doing a special 25,000 kip per night rate ($3.5 USD) and booked in until the Wednesday. A scrappily written sign on the door requested customers refrained from bringing lady boys back to the hostel.

Bordering Thailand, Vientiane was surprisingly sublime with quiet streets and not much going on. Thailand imports were cheaper and so hence were all the prices. Passing a bicycle shop I purchased a second pair of panniers for the front of the bicycle, some bungie cord from a market stall and one afternoon fitted and spread the weight. It was a Friday and the Thailand embassy where I'd apply for a two month visa (entering by land offers on 15 days on arrival) was closed for the new year. Preparations for Songkran were already under way and the whole place had a buzz about it. Back at my hostel I met a newly arriving Chinese lad called Whitley and went out with him for cheap food and a beer. He was looking for work in the Chinese district of Lao, enjoyed traveling and hoped to do more if it in the future. I doubted he'd make much financial headway in Lao, but the country offered a better lifestyle than Europe, in particular Amsterdam, so who was I to judge.

The following day Songkran began. Booming music came from every stall, cafeteria and pickup truck while outside everyone ensured they had the means to throw water. Refilling from anywhere and everywhere, dry people and scooter drivers trying to make it home dry were a particular target. The place went mental.

That night the hostel became a magnet for travelling cyclists. The first to turn up was German, slightly older than myself, and sporting a four year track record. He was fine, if a little strange, and hoarded anything he could get his hands on. For example he'd cable tied strings of ripening bananas around the frame of his bicycle. As he had a dose of the shits I gave him a packet of special antibiotics I'd bought in India, but of course I had to ask for the unused ones back.

The following morning my bicycle, kept under the stairs inside the hostel, became inaccessible due to the arrival of three more laden bicycles. Two belonged to a pair of British friends called Chris and Richie in their mid twenties, who'd left the UK for pastures new. They were heading down to Australia with a working visa. I was greatly impressed with their £3,000 budget and alarmed that they had just £300 left to reach Singapore. In an instance my financial woes were put into context. Meeting these two supported the argument the more money you have the more you worry about needing more of it. The other bicycle belonged to a Spanish lad who was a bit crazy, probably because he was originally Argentinian and had that unusual energy about him. In jest the Brits asked him to recite the story on how he'd woken up with a lady boy. He just smiled and shrugged.

On the second day of Songkran Vientiane locals and tourists roamed the streets armed with buckets, super-soakers, water bombs and hose pipes. Old, young, unemployed, business people, teachers, policemen, everyone was at it. Teams of several people, sometimes more, sat in the back of pickup trucks while they drove the streets looking for a good target. Once found they'd fir a barrage of water in their direction.. Joining in, I and the Chris and Richie spotted two older British tourist who'd exited an expensive hotel and were doing an admirable job at evading the locals. We ran after and managed to separate them, then targeted and drenched one.

Lady boys, of which I can assure you there were many, didn't stay indoors. On the streets this led to remarkable scenes of semi-naked and provocative dancing. Previously I held a belief that the distinction between a man and a women was clear, but here in Laos I learned otherwise. Some had boobs women would pay good money for, and covetous bodies and legs that would grab even a blind mans attention. In some cases it was only the beginning of a tash, or a deeper voice that forced a double take.Wet tourists like myself were of particular interest to them, and they frequently tried to grab, stroke or smack my and other tourists manhood.

That day was like being inside a video game. Adults became kids, and took a lesson in being young. Everyone was equal. It didn't matter what people did, it was just a case of being wet and wetting other people. Here there was equality.

The following day, a Tuesday, celebrations continued and brought with them the throwing of talcing powder and what I suspected was egg mixed with flour or noodles. The two British cyclists had left for another hostel while in the evening I had the technical interview to do. I spent the day doing rapid revision, which I knew was pretty pointless, and spent time sourcing a quiet hotel with good wifi. 19:00hrs arrived fast arrived and the technical team, who'd be holding the interview over Skype, were late. It commenced ten minutes late and then my suffering began. For thirty minutes I was asked a series of questions to which I gained a good understanding in my ineptitude at explaining what it was I so often had used.

"Can you tell us what map does?"

"Well, erm, urm, sure, it sort of, well." Fuck.

My brain was going mad, saying to itself "You use that command! Talk you stupid fuckup! If you can't then pull a fucking example! Move!"

"Could I pull an example from some of my code to better explain it?" I asked.

"Sure", the interviewer replied, most probably presuming I was Googling it.

"So, it takes an array, iterates through it and sort of,.. erm, does something to the value then passes it back. Optionally passes this back. Passes back the values together." Fuck. At least my answer hadn't sounded like it it had come from a script.

"Ok. Can you tell us what indexing on a database does?", the interviewer fired.

"It allows queries to execute much faster, although I don't understand the inner workings of it." Another lame answer which would translate as 'Not Really'.. I would drink myself insane for that.

"So, do you put indexes on all columns"?

"No, only primary, perhaps foreign keys."

"WHY DID YOU JUST SAY THAT!" my brain screamed. "You use foreign keys to provide relevance matching on software YOU wrote. Retract that answer!"

Too late, the next question had already arrived. Thirty minutes later I shut the lid on my mac. The interview was over, and so was I. It was time to forget.

A few hours later I was drunk from a few too many bottles of Beer Lao and riding a clapped out Honda scooter with no front brake and a buckled rear wheel to a dance club at the edge of town. Riding pillion was Whitley from my hostel, who became ridiculously funny once he'd had a beer. A really hot female friend of his drove another scooter and I followed closely behind. Inside the bar I bought a large beer and tried my best to ignore the god damn awful music being played at volume. Everyone else seemed sober and danced too liberally for not being drunk. Confused at why I wasn't dancing, or why I'd not yet pulled a lady boy, I found others being far more than generous at refilling my glass with beer then they needed to be. It was the first bar I'd been too where the other attendees were trying to refill my glass, and that made me

237

both confused and alert of an agenda I wasn't aware off. Two Thai girls tested the water but I sent them packing. The toilet included its very own tuck shop which among its items for sale included a variety of chewing gum (probably 100 types!) and a guy who automatically gave shoulder massages while people urinated. On one visit I attracted two blatant homosexuals who then occupied the urinals on either side and without any attempt to hide what they were doing, starred at my penis. This was possible because the urinal basins and walls were positioned at a height so low that even a man with no legs could take a leak. I doubted it to be a design flaw.

I awoke in the morning a bit worse for wear but pleased that I'd had the sense to come back before things had became unbearably weird. Whitley woke me up early to ask if I knew why the steering lock was jammed on the scooter. I tried the key, which freely rotated in the ignition, sighed at the problem I might have had a hand in, and then went back to bed.

My time at Vientiane felt like it was coming to an end. Chris and Richie felt the same and commonality was realised; we all needed to apply for a two month tourist visa and we would all be heading to Bangkok and south after that. After applying for the visas we agreed to ride a little North and camp, perhaps near a lake at which Whitley had secured a job. Being the end of Songkran the embassy was packed which delayed our exit in the evening. Instead we rode and found an incredibly beautiful and non-inhabited area at which we erected out tents and began a camp fire. Chris tried to capture some small fish using a mino trap, basically a two litre bottle with a flap cut down which confuses the fish. Whatever he caught would go onto a makeshift real I made, complete with hooks and weights I still had left over from Iran. After a few hours he'd caught two tiny fish, which couldn't really be cut up effectively to stick on the hook, so we politely asked him to eat them without chewing. Afterwards he found a shellfish, which I gutted, sliced and stuck on the five hooks. I cast the line out and it immediately caught on something, then snapped as I tried to play it free. That put an end to our little fishing expedition.

That night was my worst yet. The heat, in the high 30's, perhaps touching 40c, made life inside my bivi unsustainable. At first I tried to hack it and in doing so sweated so much a pool of it gathered at the side of the ground plastic. At 03:00hrs I began to panic with a feeling of suffocation. Perhaps that was what it was. I exited the bivi, moved my inflatable mat to the side and stuck my mosquito net under and around it as best I could. Feeling liberated, I managed a few hours of sleep before sunrise.

Chapter 19

Thailand (Part 2)

After riding back to Vientiane and picking up our visas from the Thai embassy we took the Friendship Bridge to exit Lao. Not long afterwards my rear wheel became caught in a train track and the sidewards motion as I counteracted it with a hard right turn, buckled the rim. I disabled the rear brake to stop the rubbing of the brake pads against the sidewall and carried on.

For several days the three of us rode steadily south towards Bangkok, covering about 120km each day. In the evening we'd stay at a Buddhist temple and on most of our visits monks would offer free water, the occasional bit of food and occasionally an excellent supper; truly generous of them. On the road I began following some of Chris and Richie's money saving tactics including the refill of 1.5 litre bottles on the cheap by sourcing big 15 litre containers used by the locals. As the temperature continued to climb towards the high I'd last experienced in Lao, reaching 40.5c on one day, rehydration became ever important.

Chris and Richey had an acute ability to spot fruit trees,

something related to stealing it from peoples gardens in Georgia they said, and occasionally we'd stop to whack mangos down from tree branches. Usually the trees had vicious biting ants that would come down with the fruit and cause surprisingly painful nips. I implored the way they lived off the basics, the fact they cooked most nights and reused what they could. It gave me recourse to stop being so lazy in the future.

Days passed by and were unproblematic, other than my continuously aching backside, but 150km from Bangkok on a fast declining road Richie veered sharply out the way leaving me with no choice but to hit a big rock at about 40kph. My rims buckled, the lips folding in entirely at the point of impact, the front tyre shredded, both tubes blew out and the rear spindle bent. One step short of soiling myself, I wobbled to a stop on the very busy motorway. After counting my blessings on the verge I used pliers to bend the front rim back into a reasonable straight line and then replaced the tube. The rear proved more difficult and required the use of a screwdriver and a rock to force the rim to bend back, and on my effort it fractured instead. The replacement tube blew as soon as I mounted the bicycle. I'd no other option but to stick the bicycle on a bus. Ten minutes later I was at a bus stop. Ten minutes after that I was making my way into Bangkok. Engines made life so much easier.

My return to Thailand's capital brought with it a recollection of how much I disliked Khoasan Road, but it was the cheapest and easiest place to source accommodation. My top priority was to fix the bicycle and using my previously gained knowledge on where the shops were the next day I found a suitable place that could do the work. The cost was quite substantial but at that point I still didn't understand the difference between the old and new technology. The shop owner tried to explain but I wasn't convinced and felt it would be better to keep the original equipment where possible rather than to change to something with arguably little benefit. I thought of bicycle technology like the bits in a computer. Every few year processor manufacturers would change the processor socket forcing a purchase of a new motherboard and probably new memory and so on. Based on my previous experience I felt I'd either make further bad purchasing decisions or get fleeced. I opted instead to only lace up new rims and spokes and to replace only the front hub.

On the evening I took a bed in a dormitory in agreement I could keep my bicycle inside. I emailed Chris and Richie about it. In the evening I was told it would have to move outside and I demanded my money back. They said no and I went off to get the police. When I returned Chris and Richie had arrived and were wondering why the owner was being so tetchy with them.. The police said I couldn't have my money back because I'd already checked in. When they left we talked outside the entrance for a while, stirring trouble for the owner. With bystanders looking he threw a bottle of water at Richie who stormed "Come on then fat gay boy!". The owner and his associates picked up glass bottles and chairs in what looked like the beginning of an American wrestling showdown. The owner needed a fist in his face and having been cheated out of a whole £5 I was very ready to provide it, but just as tensions had flared, tensions then subsided. The moment passed and we rode off.

The next guest house only had a double room and I didn't think much of the owner or the windowless options they were pushing. They took it and I headed off in search of a single. I found a place with no other occupants, unsurprising really as it was unkempt and in a state of disrepair. The mattress appeared lice free, plus it had wifi and a window so the fan could circulate my sweat. The lack of guests meant it was sublimely quiet, another positive. I took it.

In the evening we all had a few beers and things began to get out of hand. At 6.5% the beer here was stronger than Europe and none of us had any great tolerance to it. To begin with we sat and drank from a local seven-eleven across from a bar playing live jazz music. Here we chatted to a Korean lady and an Aussie doing the same. The Korean was a bit drunk, a bit old at 41, but somehow looked 30, whereas I was 30 and felt I looked about 41. At 02:00hrs I called it a night while the other two kept going. Chris awoke the next day at 10:00hrs face down in the sidewalk of a random street. He said he'd "ate a bag of drugs" and visited a whore house where oddly the girls decided who they wanted to fuck. I learned this at 14:00hrs the next day when I awoke him at his hotel. Richard hadn't come back, but turned up at 18:00hrs having walked for "hours". He could vaguely remember sleeping with a woman that he described as being "very old". No quantitive figure could be extracted.

An email back in from my tenant back in England. The backdate claim for the two month default was ongoing and the benefits department had agreed to pay two thirds of the original rent. It was enough to cover the mortgage but the house had now turned from an asset into a liability. I spent the following hour arranging to put it on the market with an online estate agent.

While Chris and Richie recovered I spent time on the internet researching about bicycle technology and putting it together with information Chris and Richie had imparted for long distance touring. I'd already made up my mind to continue without a combustion engine for I was fitter than ever, it was cheaper, and it was less hassle and so I hoped further purchases would be better informed. I learned about the difference between the older freewheel hub I was running and the modern free-hub design (which explained why my rear spindle had bent twice). I compared modern group-sets (3x10) and discovered why my older 3x7 speed continuously needed adjustment and always sounded rough. I read arguments for and against v-brake and disc brakes for touring, about good touring seat design, and good quality rack and pannier systems.

Realising that a front handlebar bag would be very useful I went shopping some 10km from Khoasan Road where I bought an Ortlieb similar design by a Thailand company called Vincita but at half the price. Unfortunately once I got back I found the bracket wouldn't fit the oversized handlebar on my bicycle.

For the following day I'd arranged an interview for a job teaching English in South Korea. Unlike the interview for the role in Amsterdam this one I knew would be a walk in the park. The problem was I really didn't want to go back into teaching, but with just £1,000 remaining and no programming job prospects the wise decision was to take an interlude and to tackle the rest of the journey a year on. But doing so would mean I had failed.

After two days of Bangkok I had to get out. I went to find the other two but they'd already left to meet a friend at Bangkok airport. Without phones I was unable to communicate, and Thailand's south and it's picture perfect islands were calling. Before heading in that general direction I made a detour to the head office of Vincita to pick up a replacement bracket to allow the fitting of the handlebar bag. I got talking to the manager there and to my delight persuaded him to donate four touring bags and a better front rack. These were the real deal; fully waterproof, welded seams for strength, and tear proof. I was closer to becoming a serious cyclist and I hadn't paid a penny.

The road south west out of Bangkok was slow and tedious and came with an element of self imposed danger. Because bicycles aren't permitted on motorways I wasn't permitted to drive over the two bridges leading out of the inner Bangkok traffic. This I ignored. Traffic was full-on and I had to take regular breaks to cool down. Occasionally road going cycling groups would power past, offering their enthusiasm as they did so. The traffic thinned, the light began to diminish and I began looking for a complementary temple. The one I found offered a semi-enclosed concreted floor and monks who brought a generous amount of food stuffs; apples, orange juice, bottled water and soya milk.

The following day was much the same, it was about eating into the distance and enjoying the remaining weeks of the two month visa in places where I could kick back and enjoy. In the evening I stayed at another temple where a monk called Noi offered use of the wifi connection there. I was fairly stunned. Wifi?! He took me upstairs to a room tourists can't venture, made from top to bottom in stained and lacquered hardwood. No expense had been spared, and yet ornaments and artefacts were few and far between. The lack of material items reenforced the beautifully simplistic design that it was. Monk Noi could speak very little English but so we conversed using our laptops and Google Translate. He supported Arsenal, had been engaged prior to becoming a Monk (oh dear!) and had a Facebook account. Having a monk 'like' my fan page was bewildering and a moment to remember. I then thought back to the German girl I'd met in Goa, who by now was probably a converted Nun. Staying at temples had bestowed upon me a great respect for the beliefs and values of Buddhism. My only problem with it was if people give up a want to desire, as Buddhism teaches, then surely we stop pushing ourselves to develop and better ourselves. I'd have to ask the next monk that spoke good English.

I had other questions. I asked myself how I could repay their imparted kindness. Did I offer money? Freeloading I thought of as sin like when those offering had little. How little did they have? Some of the monks were so thin they looked weak. Was this a lifestyle choice? I had to further my knowledge.

I didn't bump into my British friends who had surely left Bangkok with their friend (who was riding from the Bangkok to Singapore with them) and couldn't be sure if they'd be behind or in front. I presumed the latter, but I had no desire to catch up in the current heat.

When I reached the small coastal town of Cha-am the gloriousness of the sea and the sound of it's waves lessened my worries, however there were way too many fat white tourists walking the promenade, so I cycled a few kilometres further until the touts and deck chairs thinned out. I found a tree with good shade and from where I could hide from the enduring sun. It was a touch over 40c and I'd no intention to ride on until the rays diminished. I propped my roll mat up against a tree and dosed off.

Not one to easily siesta, I awoke an hour later feeling out of sorts. It was still too hot to move and the scene was good for work, so I looked around for my pen and notepad, forgetting that I'd ran out all the way back in Nepal. I walked to a Seven Eleven and picked up set. While there I drank an ice coffee from their self-service machine, tremendous value when filling the 1ltr container with coffee and minimal ice. Boom I was awake!

In the late afternoon I rode another 25km from Cha-am to the next town. I found wifi Here I read into the contract I was going to sign for working at the school in South Korea. A statement in it said I couldn't work for any other institution, which seemed unfair as they were only buying a block of my time, not all of it. My agent stated in an email that the visa rules had changed in 2011 and that it was possible if the school allowed it. I sent an email to the current teacher at the school to see if it were possible and left it at that.

My worrying restarted and I realised on this, the last day of April, that I was wasn't about me but my mother. My brother Adam, the favourite one, was venturing out to America and then had a wish to visit Australia. I knew once he'd left the UK, like me, he'd not want to return. My brother give my mother purpose, she'd be lost not looking after him. Then there was the matter of the 15k credit card debt and her having no job. I received an email from her saying she wouldn't sell my house for me and I was overloading her. I responded quite harshly then, outside of wifi, regretted what I'd wrote. Essentially I told her that selling my house was key to solving all our problems, so she should try to be more proactive with the help. With the equity I could pay off her debt and solve my own woes. To save face she wouldn't allow me to pay of the debt, but I'd enforce that later on.

It was dark and I continued to worry the entire night. My addiction to ice coffee was growing, and I found myself inside another Seven Eleven at the vending machine filling another extra large container. Boom! How funny, looking back at my University years when I chastised my Greek friend Kostas for drinking the stuff.

The next temple was slightly up hill and in a beautiful location. I was assigned to the storage area packed with ergodic items. In one corner my eye caught crystal encrusted jewels, which was probably why they locked me in, however these were of no comparison to a magnificent grandfather clock standing bold and tall in the opposite corner of the room. Engineering and craftsmanship perfect, it's hourly chime was beautifully harmonic, every bit as good as Big Ben, and I sorely wished I could compact it into something I could carry.

I tossed all night, probably there were flees on the floor, and by 02:30hrs I'd had enough. I wasn't going to get any sleep here so I'd ride. Given the front doors were locked I had to find another way out. The toilets were in a side building with a door made from metal bars and two hinges screwed on the inside. Using the screwdriver carried for my bicycle I had these off and then rode off into the night. Before leaving the temples ground I was attacked by fifteen or so cowardly wild dogs.

After an hours riding I decided to have another go sleeping and found a small patch of grass. It didn't go well, but I got an hour in four sleep and then had the usual breakfast of rice and eggs.

I was staring ahead preparing myself to set off again when

unexpectedly the Brits cycled past, plus an addition called Jimmy who'd flown into Bangkok. Jimmy was riding an economic special purchased from Tesco. His hat was missing the top and his clothes were soiled, as was how they were when he put them on. He was definitely one of them. I rejoined them for the ride to Chumphon, from which we'd catch a ferry to the diving island Kao Tao.

We rode for two days. On the first day the bearings in my rear hub collapsed, but since I was using the old style hub it was easy to source replacements at a local car mechanic. The spindle had bent yet again and was placing a side load on the bearings, so the replacements I'd had fitted were on a timer. Longer term I'd have to upgrade to the newer style hub.

On arrival at Chumphon we found the ferry left at 23:00hrs and would take five hours. Waiting at the port, beers were purchased from a small shop down the road and then all topics of banter were brought up. The first was the recent death of Margaret Thatcher and a rant ensued over her merit. Then Chris tried to justify why he'd once stuck his finger up his arse, which was followed by deliberations on what was the best way to utilise toilet paper; fold or scrunch, under or around, and lastly reminiscence back to a time when Richard was so drunk he washed his hair in the basin of a pub toilet.

I was happy with the beer alone but they'd a supplementary bottle of rum for afterwards. When boarding began I headed straight to the air conditioned dorm room to grab as much sleep as I could. The trip was peaceful, even if there we're thirty or so bed bunks.

At 05:00hrs the ferry docked at Kao Tao. Still dark the blend of dim artificial and moonlight offered an impressive ambience up the hillside. The bay was scattered with small boats and little roads while further inland looked luscious and green with tall coconut trees and dense foliage. The road we followed left out of the port led first to touristy accommodation and then along the beach front. Needing to wear off the rum, the three Brits retired under the first trees they could find and conked out, but I was up, had more steam and wanted to begin the day early. So I left them and in the darkness came upon a small beach front with a rocky front. Mosquitos were out in force so I donned my diving googles and hit the sea. The water was warm and relatively clear and despite last diving at the Greek islands the cycling had maintained my stamina. I was immensely pleased at not being out of breath. As the sunrise began the islands colours blossomed and a few locals began to stir. A refuge collection service trundled along the road. The day had began.

I hadn't a clue about the islands layout and rather than finding a map I opted to explore without, hoping to discover niche places in doing so. Riding into town I was confronted by several diving institutions, overpriced restaurants, drinking bars and accommodation to suit all budgets. I knew this sort of place well, it had a partial Khaosan Road feel, and thus I knew I'd prefer being away from it. I continued riding north past all of it where at the extremities found more reasonable priced hotels, but then the road ended at an expensive resort. I found a diving flyer lying at the roadside and used a terrible map drawn on the rear to try and gain a bearing. From it I realised there were just a few roads leading to just a few bays and all were relatively short in distance. I made a rough plan to check out all the bays, starting with Mango Bay, top dead north of the island.

Reaching Mango Bay proved more troublesome than I had

expected, complements to the islands high middle and steep passes to overcome it. The peak of the pass going north had what appeared to be an abandoned resort at the top. A monkey sat high in a tall tree, a rope around its neck anchoring it to the ground and restricting its movement. I watched in fascination as it manoeuvred the rope over branches and other obstacles to move around as best it could, then with no one around I retrieved my knife and cut the poor thing loose. I watched again as it pulled the rope up, now confused by the lack of tension on it. Two stupid dogs barked throughout and I threw stones at them until they cowered and ran. Continuing on I came upon a side road which according to my crap map led to a viewpoint over the west coast. The locals had obstructed the entrance using two chairs and a section of drainage pipe. A liquor hut had been built on one of the rocks and a 20 baht fee was demanded for entrance. I pushed the pipe aside and told the thin Thai to bugger off. The viewpoint wasn't up to much.

Back on the main track the sun had me in sweats. The fair concrete road was replaced by dirt trodden rock while the yearly monsoon had gorged deep drainage patterns that snaked like small river networks and which ultimately made riding forward difficult. The road began an ascent so steep in parts that my brakes couldn't keep the bicycle stable. I prayed I wouldn't have to try getting back up it. I reached a small shrine and the sea was now visible in the distance. I had to make a decision whether to go down some serious looking steps and to hope for an alternative way out at the bay, or to turn back. I wasn't turning back, so down I went, the pedals and wheels noisily connecting on the steps and walls. It took forever. At the bottom I found a drinks-only restaurant featuring a stunning view over the Gulf and a small hotel on the beach front where a few private yacht owners had beached their transport. This bay had nothing here. A chartered diving boats dropped a pair of masked tourists into the clear water. I stuck my bicycle against a wall, donned the diving googles and joined them. The sea was deep with several corals. An interesting blue sponge, found on several rocks would periodically scrunch up into half its original size and then return to its normal state. I chilled out for an hour before swimming over to one of the diving boats to ask if there were any chance of a lift. The owners didn't understand English and I made my way back to the only restaurant where I downed an expensive can of coke. Querying the waiter, I learned I could charter a taxi boat for 700 baht to the main port. That was expensive and being a stubborn git I chose instead to push the bicycle out of the trap I now found myself in.

It took four hours and the combination of 40c heat and extreme inclines, of which I could barely push my laden bicycle up, resulted in the expiration of my new sandals and the removal of skin from most of my toes. Another fine mess I'd gotten myself into, I was a member of the walking dead when it was over.

Before sunset I rode slowly and painfully to the south of the Island in the hope of finding a cheap guest house for the night. I was in desperate need of a shower and to give my feet a rest, but like much of the island, commercialisation from diving tourists had ruined it. Little of the beach remained public while dive houses and restaurants had done a resounding job making walking along any of it difficult. One had even dismembered a tree so that it remained alive but cut the beach off completely, forcing walkers to re-route through its restaurant or through the water.

I was happy to be alone for a while having spent so long with the Brits and I was wary when a young Argentinian lad going in the opposite direction began a conversation. Thin, with long raster hair and a backpacker weathered look, Guam as he was called carried a large backpack of which half the room inside was taken up by a saxophone. With some reservation I agreed to look for cheap accommodation for the night. We found a place offering a room for 250 baht, and he skilfully reduced it to 225 baht. It had only one large bed though, and a double room was 600 baht, to which he remarked "no problem – we'll share!". A brief flashback of 'that night' went through my mind, but no, this was different. I went with the flow.

Before I collapsed from the days exertion, my arm and leg muscles tight and my feet in tatters, we ate sticky rice and eggs at a cheap restaurant.

I awoke in the morning, for the record without my meat and veg in his mouth, and we began the day with what would be a long walk over the eastern side of the island. We opted for a central route in the hope of better scenery but my toes and the lack of skin on them, plus my broken sandals, made my life difficult. I tried to repair the sandals by cutting up a motorcycle inner-tube I found by the road side. This didn't work and by the time we reached Tanote Bay my feet were an even greater mess and I was hobbling forward as if drunk. Setting that aside, the bay was chilled out and like nothing else I'd seen on the island. Ignoring the lacerations on my feet and the initial salt water burn, I free dived down to find small reefs and beautiful fish. A thin, tall and wide type, yellow in colour and always swimming in a pair was a highlight. Afterwards we ate pot noodles that I'd brought over from the mainland thanks to a restaurant being generous with hot water. The sun began to dip and I knew the long walk back would be painful even though we'd decided to take the southern route instead of our earlier track. Mosquitos came out in hunting packs. Large and fast, only movement would stave off a blood sucking attack, so we began the ascent. Luckily Guam managed to secure us a lift almost 2/3rds the way and back to the main road. After that he insisted I wore his sandals to ease my pain while he walked barefooted. His manners and kindness was quite humbling, a genuinely nice person who had little and did not want more. Part of me wanted that happiness. In a few month he'd be back on an Italian island playing gigs with his saxophone and then making more travels.

Before reaching our room Guam bought fruit, or to be specific, he was given a few out of date mangos for free. Beyond ripe, the first was uneditable but with my low standards I ate most of the second. After washing up we went out for a beer. An hour later the mango had liquidated my innards and I found myself with stomach cramp then a desperate need to find a restaurant that hadn't put a lock on their toilet door. Guam was again helpful, going off to buy water and insisting we flagged a taxi back to our accommodation, I meanwhile knowing that he'd not the budget for taxis. I told him he was kinder than Jesus but the taxi wasn't necessary. I'd done India and could take this milder form of the trots in my stride, even if my feet where shagged.

In the morning I was a walking wreck, something akin to an arthritic eighty year old, and the looks from curious locals went from my posture and then down to my dunlop sponsored sandal repair. Talking to Guam, we both agreed that the islands beauty was diminished by the awful tourists, most being Australian, and uncontrolled commercialism which had restricted anything and everything unless one got their wallet out. In that respect Kao Toa was a disappointment and I chose not to experience more the same by aborting my plan to travel to the next two and returning to the mainland and continue riding South. I'm sure the other British cyclists would have already left, it wouldn't have been their scene either. Guam was intending to do the same but would head North.

We'd purchased tickets back to Chumphon for 23:00hrs and intended to kill the hours leading up to it in a bar holding a buskers night. I was quite eager to hear Guam play his sax, but we arrived too early and had to go back and sit on the nearby beach instead. There we talked travelling, and it was obvious Guam was happy and content with life in general, even if, in my opinion, there didn't seem much behind it. Perhaps I was jealous at the simplicity. I began asking myself whether age had brought on cynicism, since all the travellers I met in their early twenties came across as more positive than I was. Maybe they were, or maybe it was bullshit and I was the only honest bugger out there, but by now quite a few people I'd met had commented that I could come across as gloomy or negative. I didn't feel I was, it was just my approach to reality of it all; telling it as it was without prejudice or bias. Those travelling long-term will, like me, find the picture postcard isn't all it seems. It's all to easy to generate the missing bits in your head and to forget the bad parts so as not to feel let down. Kao Tao then, twenty years ago, was probably a paradise. Now it was its fair share of idiotic tourists and opportunists.

Having walked back to the bar we found again we'd arrived too early, but it was only an hour to go. Unexpectedly we found ourselves in the monthly island meeting, a conglomeration of local government and business owners, of which were mostly diving instructors. Statistics floating around included a $1,000 USD per day fund for a clean-up operation; the tourists bringing additional overheads which the island had to counteract if it were not to damage the islands reputation. Sitting quietly in the corner I noticed the diving instructors were typically steroid pumped, older and completely bald.

Afterwards Guam played his sax, and was utterly fantastic at it. With a keen ear, he jammed with anything being played with the other buskers. I was genuinely impressed.

In the early hours of the morning the boat docked back at Chumphon and from there I said my goodbyes to Guam. From there I chose to ride over to the west coast where I knew it would be less touristy and then on to a small town called Ranong. My plan was to take on a slow ferry to the island of Koh Phayam. Said to be the last island to be saved from over-development, this was exactly the reason it had caught my attention, but it took a solid day to ride from Ranong and I missed the daily ferry. Earlier I'd found and bought a hammock with an integrated mosquito net and now, having found a Buddhist temple for the night, I had an opportunity to try it out. It was the first night in a long time of sleeping outdoors where I didn't sweat my backside off, for suspended in air, the floor become another vent. In the morning I knew the bivi tent had to be retired.

The following morning I arrived back at the jetty where after a short stay a small and old wooden boat pulled up along the dock. The skipper insisted I lifted the bicycle onto the top deck, an impossible feat, save it drop onto my head or into the water, and in no uncertain terms I told him just that.

Eventually common sense prevailed and it went in the lower deck with all the other luggage. The ferry departed and as it slowly made its way down the river I could make out the Burmese on the docks sorting fish into huge trays and pallets. While the jetty I had departed from served only Koh Phayam the main jetty further along at Ranong served Burmese islands forbidden to tourists. Not all were forbidden and a trade agreement allowed Thais to transit for business. As I looked on from my own ferry it was clear what this meant in reality. Burmese were what the Indians were to Dumai. They were cheap labour.

A hour or so later the ferry docked and right away I noticed Koh Phayam, during what was the first week of low season, was eerily quiet. From a distance it looked rudimentary and unexploited. Departing the ferry I cycled over wooden slats, through a welcome banner and into the southern bay. Exploring, I found a little bay of sorts named Aow Ku-Kyu which featured a closed restaurant and an abandoned beach. It was beautiful in its own right and I'd probably have stayed had the bay not featured dreaded steps on the final decent. I simply couldn't get the bicycle down, or if I did I certainly wasn't getting it back up. Afterwards I explored the west of the island, a stretch made up of approximately 3km of golden sand and murky water. Aow Yai beach showed the first signs of the island going to the wall, with bungalow huts from one end to the other and little if any breaks in-between. On the beach I tested out an alcohol burning stove I'd made from a coke can. Either the 70% alcohol I'd earlier bought from a chemist or my production skills weren't up to it, and instead I ended up gathering drift wood from the beach and using the alcohol to make a small fire. To use up all of a can of condensed milk in one go, I made far too much rice pudding and was nearly sick eating it.

Only a few huts were still open and the the best of the bunch, and the one with any human presence, about five in total, was called Lazy Huts. Residing here was a Finnish man who was either drunk, drugged, mental or a combination. The other guests kept a wide birth but I couldn't be bothered to move away from him. I could rarely understand anything he said and instead entered negotiations with the guest house owner on whether I could hammock in his grounds for free. Negotiations fell in my favour. Not only would it be free, but I'd sleep a damn side better in my hammock than in one of the bungalow huts on offer. The food and drink prices were reasonable, he had wifi, and the later the bar rose ten fold when they lit a large beach fire to mark the end of the season. The fire licked across the sand, casting shadows and throwing embers higher than the palm trees behind us. As if the visual fest couldn't become any better, far out over the sea a lightening show began. The clouds would momentarily flash and for the briefest of moments there were contrasting colours from the fire, the sea and the sky. It was simply incredible.

The following day I explored the remaining parts of the island but found to my dismay that all were unsuitable for free diving. The murky water rendered any opportunities useless and in addition the water was said to be full of nasty jellyfish. A sign on the beach informed of the various types, not that I'd be able to see them when in the water, and an arrow pointed to a bottle of neutraliser hanging of the side.

Later I came upon a special place called Hippy Bar, special because it was made entirely from drift wood, even having a replica ships bow built from the stuff. The place was artistic and brilliant, but this being the slow season, it was also dead. Not even the owner had bothered to turn up. I found a stash of coke cans around the back and left a note and some money on the bench.

The few roads on the island, all unable to take four wheeled traffic, typically resolved into thin dirt tracks and would terminate at a bungalow complex. During the daytime the sun was too much to bare and taking cover brought boredom that I could relieve only be doing some web work or programming. The island however had few wifi connections and these rarely ran during the daytime since electricity was only available in the evening. I found myself on a perfect island, unable to dive, unable to swim, unable to venture out during the daytime, and unable to work. A conundrum developed over what to actually do.

In the afternoon another cyclist arrived on the island and introduced himself while I cowered from the sun in an overpriced tourist cafe. A bit old, and a bit German, Francis travelled the Philippines and Thailand every year and had done so since the beginning of time. That made him a knowledge bank of information and thanks to a good level of English he was able to describe how Koh Phayam had transformed since his first visit back in 2003. The answer was a lot. The roads had been widened since the previous year indicating dreaded four wheels would soon follow; tractors, heavy machinery, doom. It was through talking with Francis that I realised how much I preferred the company of mature travellers to those who were younger or around my age. Less egotistical, they always displayed a keenness to listen, even though they had the most to say. Francis had a love for the outdoors and always slept on a mat without a tent whenever the weather allowed for it. He joined me at Lazy Huts on Aow Yai beach and on the moderate surf waves demonstrated an acute ability to catch the surf at just the right moment then turn his body into a surfboard. Despite my best attempts to copy him, I couldn't replicate his talent.

The prospect of rain was high and in what was seemingly becoming a trend, I agreed to share a bungalow with Francis, as like myself he was travelling on a minimal budget. Finding out the hut contained only a single king size bed caused apprehension. Play with fire and prepare to be burnt and all that, hadn't I learned already? Francis thought nothing of it and I went with my gut rather than my memory. Still, during the night I awoke sweating and asking myself over and over if he was moving closer. As the electricity had stopped, and so had the fan, I opened the front and rear door to the hut to better the circulation of air. While outside and at the rear I spotted a fantastic spider and at the requisite distance ogled at it using my head-torch. It was another moment where I regretted giving my SAS survival book to an Indian child. I went back to bed.

I awoke at about 06:00hrs, as did Francis, and after an early breakfast we departed company. He was staying for four or five nights, while I, not knowing what to do with myself, had decided to return to the mainland and to ride on. Koh Phayam was an enjoyable place, far more so than Kao Tao, but its soul wouldn't last forever. I'm glad I got to experience it when I did.

My tenant, now on the dole, had requested housing benefit a few month back but Durham council hadn't actioned the request. Meanwhile the mortgage kept coming out of my travel budget and although I was being incredible thrifty with my money, for the first time the bank balance dipped under £1,000. I'd always said this was the cut off point, one at which I'd abort travelling and plan to make money, by whatever means. Although I'd tried to pre-empt finding work by looking into teaching English in South Korea, I'd received an email back from the agent I was dealing with telling me I'd been removed from his list, lost the position and that I shouldn't try to illegally manoeuvre around visa regulations. I wasn't remotely bothered. Racking my brain for other possibilities, I emailed the Malaysian company I'd had contact with back in India, which was more plausible now I was closer and had a better idea of my availability, and this time offering to work for two weeks at no charge in return for free accommodation. This would give both I and the company a chance to see if a match was viable, and since I was going by their office in Kuala Lumpur anyway it made sense. If it didn't work out, I'd continue to Australia and work a farm or whatever else was going.

After returning back to the mainland I made my way back to the road known only as '4' for the long ride towards the tourist island of Phuket, with an intention of riding straight past it, towards the non-touristic island Koh Jam. This island had been recommended by the two cyclists Warran & Esther I'd met back on the Lao border, and the last email I'd received from them recommended a cheap place at west of the island near a sea gypsy graveyard. I felt obliged to try the island out given only Koh Jam, Koh Payam and nearby Koh Chang (solomon side, not the east coast) were now recommended for a lack of development. Francis had also been to and recommended it, but with caution. "Vatch Zee Snakes!"

Snakes, I'd never liked them, and thankfully I hadn't seen any up close and personal. Having travelled through Asia this seemed wrong, but travelling through south Thailand dead ones were becoming more frequent, always found at the side of the road, flattened like a pancake. These were very much unlike the snake I mistook for a branch, and which was very much alive. Only when I was passing it a couple feet away away did I see its body flex and it raise it's front off the ground. I was doing enough speed at the time, but my heart rate still doubled. I turned around and took a photo of its relatively thin yellow and green body. I'd identify it later.

Travelling on the "4", buddhist temples were replaced by mosques as I entered the first muslim communities of Thailand's south. I pulled over at a shop for a drink which unusually had wifi. In the heat, I decided to spend a little longer than first anticipated to identify the snake. My fingers sweated so much the iPhones touch screen was unable to recognise any commands and I pulled the mac out instead. Five minutes later a Muslim, importantly dressed, and a friend of his who sported a dyed red goaty, appeared and said hello in Arabic. I muttered the same and focused on identification the snake hoping they'd bore and leave, but instead he stuck his head right next to mine, then asked in broken English if I were Pakistani. What give him that impression I do not know, but his face beamed as if it must be true. I wiped that off by telling him I was English, but then having digested this information the beaming face returned.

"Muslim?".

"Christian," I replied.

Not only did his beaming face sullen, it went outright cold, he just couldn't hide his disgust from his face. I'd not had this in Turkey, Iran or the UAE and my dislike for the man grew to a loathing, of which I knew the feeling was mutual. Of course he was too important to leave me alone.

"Who do you think made the sky?" he began.

"Dunno",was all I could muster, still trying to identify the snake.

"And why, Inshallah, does night come before day?"

"Some might say day comes before night", I almost said with laughter, but holding back. I couldn't tell where this was going but it felt like a sales pitch. Bored of him, I gave up with finding the snake and closed the mac.

"Sorry, I must leave before dark." I politely responded. As I began to push the bicycle I hesitated, deciding to end the conversation subjectively. Fuck him. "Tell me, why do you dislike Christians?". His silently sitting friend smirked. I was expecting him to be taken aback but instead he recited a prepared answer about us all being children of God. I rode off.

10km down the road I came across a Buddhist temple and being late in the evening I called it a day. A monk confirmed the region was 100% Muslim. As I'd moved south through Thailand I'd noticed the temples, "wats", were further holding reservation on whether to allow sleeping inside the grounds. Once I'd befriended them things went alright, but hesitance was apparent none the less. I erected my hammock from the rafters of an open building and while inside it writing up notes on my pad the rope on one side failed and my backside hit the deck with a resounding thud. Ouch. A monk heard the noise and helpfully fetched some better rope to hang around the rafters. While fixing it I realised just how intense the mosquitos were becoming. I'd since bought mosquito coils but these and what was left of the 100% deet spray weren't keeping them at bay. There were at least three types now, the most recent of which had a zebra styled body and an excellent ability to avoid swatting. Francis had told me he'd caught a milder form of Dengue back in January. The blighters tended to live and replicate around toilets and showers in close proximity to humans, which had me query why mesh covers on fresh water containers and effective drainage which did not pool water was not mandatory.

For the next two days I punched out 135km and 90km respectively. For both I stayed at temples, the second featuring a whaling monk on the loudspeaker throughout the early hours of the morning.

Reaching Krabi, I became aware of frequent services launching tourists to the island of Ko Phi Phi, but unlike every tourist I spoke to, I was leaving for the nearby pier at Laem Krod and then onto Ko Jam. It took quite a bit longer than I'd expected to reach the pier, which in fact was well outside of Krabi's town centre. My boat was a thin and long wooden vessel, aptly named a 'long boat', with a diesel engine from a car mounted at the rear and a propeller welded onto the prop shaft. The driver pivoted the engine for steerage and angled the prop shaft into the water for propulsion. We were underway. For what it was it went pretty darn fast, and it was incredibly noisy.

Ko Jam, a fellow passenger on the ferry explained, was only a part of the island, the other segment being Ko Po. Strangely then the island didn't have an official name and people were calling it either. Taking a long boat to another segment simply meant being dropped off at another pier. It sounded large and I began picturing large amounts of terrain that would take days to tackle. When the little wooden plank dropped ashore, scraping against the concrete and dirt and I rolled onto solid ground once more, I was surprised by the lack of, well, anything. A few huts and a dirt track and that was it. From a passenger inventory of ten, I was the only tourist to arrive, and none were returning to go back to the mainland.

I rode the dirt track, cutting through trees and with no visible life on either side, and soon hit a thin and broken concrete road. I turned left towards the main village towards the Ko Jam side of the island. A few km more and I was there. The village school looked shabby compared to the modern types on mainland while rusting Thai signboards hawked back to the days bygone. Along the road, a mixture of modern bungalows and older wooden huts offered the usual services but generally they were few and far between. The village was just a single lane, neither long or dense. I found a tourist information building but could find no personnel there. Pushing the unlocked door ajar, I found a hand drawn map of the island on the front desk and snapped a picture of it. I left the way I'd came.

Travelling west and northwards I eventually found the sea gypsy graveyard mentioned by Esther and Warren and the bungalow huts beside it. I was reluctant to take one, feeling that in the present heat my hammock would offer greater comfort. The owner said that was fine, and I settled in with a superb value banana smoothy, followed by a second. The sea gypsy graveyard next door had everything I needed; a roof and running water, but this complex would be better for socialising. When I say socialising, there was, as best I could see it, only myself and one other tourist on the island. Another bungalow complex was still open one kilometre down the beach front, but it was entirely empty. I didn't really talk to the other tourist. He looked like a loner and best avoided. I probably looked much the same.

Intending to pass the time slowly and sweetly, I got stuck into some programming and later a few locals turned up. Two appeared female, but deep voices gave the game away. Repeatedly they attempted to entice me over to their table. A tactical beer arrived, which I raised to them, drank, and then I didn't move. What they were after was in their body language, and I had no meat sausage sandwiches for them. That night I slept close to a small boat, damaged during the Tsunami disaster all the years before, and did so well.

The lady who owned the complex was every bit as characteristic as Warren and Esther had described, and I don't think I've met anyone quite like her. Plump, short and round, she was the most untroubled soul I've ever came upon. Her purpose, as she saw it, was to live her life by making others happy, and she went about her business doing exactly that. One day she'd organise a group together to gather rubbish that had washed ashore from Ko Phi Phi. The next day she was liaising with the Government for funding to concrete sections of the road where dust was posing a hazard to the health of elderly locals. She lived by her single rule and had in the process became a product of it. Happiness didn't just beam from her, it poured like a waterfall, and meeting her I solved a long standing riddle of the trip. The route to happiness wasn't to be found in giving up all desires at all (as I'd discussed with the two young ladies back in Goa, India), nor was it to be found in faith. It was by experiencing the happiness of others through your own efforts to make them happy.

With that marvellous insight in mind, I knew how to go about the rest of my life. But first I had to ride my bicycle, and make money, and see things. Happiness would have to wait.

Doesn't it always?

I spent most of the following morning doing nothing much, a conscious decision to try and learn how to relax after riding every day, but by mid-day I'd given up and packed my hammock away. The boat back to the pier was at 16:00hrs and unbelievably I felt like I had to be one it. The perfect island with its astonishing white beaches was not so perfect after all. I was bored after just a day. To kill time before the return ferry I travelled north to the other side of the island, Ko Pu, which was a separate community with its own school and community services. I couldn't see why such a small island with few people had generated two separate communities and wondered if Buddhist and Muslim faiths had fractured the land into two. I never found out.

I missed the boat, but then perhaps I meant too. Rushing from one place to the next was insane, so said logic. By now I'd taken several good pictures with my camera to stick on Facebook. I knew people would see a paradise and comment that I was a lucky man. They'd fail to see the heat, the sweat, the loneliness and the lack of ice cold refreshments. They'd assume semi-naked massage services were just out of shot. They'd fail to see because it wasn't there, yet omission invokes imagination which in turn clouds reality. They'd wish, and imagine they could be here for weeks.

Having now rode the roads and tracks offered by the smaller than expected island my opinion was that it were a pleasant place and I was being an idiot by trying to leave so soon. To cool down in the sea breeze, I opted to walk along the west beach and to push the bicycle over the wetter and harder part of the sand. I came upon the other tourist on the island and began talking to him. I'd thought he was staying at the same bungalow patch as I, but in fact he'd arranged a large bungalow for a mere 100 baht at another resort and had only visited mine to socialise. The owners of his resort had closed up for low season and moved back to Bangkok so he had the place to himself. Looking around it the showers were fantastic and I decided to sling my hammock in the reception area here instead. He disappeared to the village for something to eat and I discovered a window open around the back which on climbing through led to a kitchen complete with gas cookers and a basket full of all the keys to the bungalows. I made myself a hot lemon tea then mulled over whether squatting was morally acceptable. I found the key to a treehouse hut overlooking the gulf, the sand beginning at the trees truck and the sea washing out just 10 metres further. It should have been exceptional, but thin and steep steps leading to the top were awkward to climb. Ants of the worst kind, stinging swines, furiously defended their right to live without a primate next-door, and dropped from the leaves and branches to bite. The hut had no running water and a trap-door that made carrying up my gear enervating. I locked up and reverted back to the hammock.

In the morning I took the early boat back to the mainland. The day didn't begin well and while loading the bicycle I slipped on the boat's muddy ramp and went down on my backside and into the water. The bicycle crashed down but didn't follow. The spectacle was enjoyed by a complement of local fishermen, who'd keeled over with laughter. Beetroot red, I quickly hid inside the boat and tried to wipe down my soiled clothes.

Back on the mainland I began to shortcut my way from the pier to rejoin the motorway leading south. Sometimes this involved taking the smallest of dirt tracks through thick

268

foliage and I frequently had reservations on where I'd end up. Incredulously, I ended up inside the security perimeter of Krabi's electricity generating plant. To get to the motorway I then had to go through security without entry clearance, which drew dumb founded expressions all round.

I slept that night at another temple however this time it rained and then some. I'd slung the hammock within a large open-sided building, but foolproof it wasn't, and driving wind carried the downpour horizontally. For the first time I had to deployed my tarp for protection from the immense rain. Had this of been outside between two trees I'd have been very wet. The downpour brought with it a welcome temperature drop and I slept well.

By now the replacement bearing I'd had fitted to the rear hub was becoming noisy mitigating a need to replace the hub as soon as possible. Triang, a town where I could hopefully sort my bicycle, was only 60km away and after a hurried breakfast I packed up and began eating into the distance. On arrival I found Triang had two decent bicycle shops but both were largely a front for new sales and didn't carry much in the way of parts. Neither stocked the type of hub I required. To cheer myself up I spent a whole 200 baht on a hotel room. Basic and a bit of a dive, the bathroom had more spiders than tiles on the walls. On the street I set off to find wifi, ice-coffee and perhaps even some cake. I was spotted by a young Thai who helpfully took me to a good place and then insisted I joined a group ride at 16:00hrs. Delighted for the accompaniment, but worried how the bearing in my rear hub would hold up, I was fortunate in a way that they never turned up.

I fired out of Triang the next morning, south towards Malaysia, which I estimated would take two days. I'd little

269

desire to follow the coast and to try Ko Liang, another Thailand island. That night I slept at another temple, whereupon I was surrounded by hyperactive young children. At least half were disrespectful and I felt an urge to slap a few into a state of normality. I wasn't sure how this would go down with the parents who were at the festivities going on at the other side of the temple. Finally they left, but another menace arrived and proved just as troublesome. Having untapped fresh water from the recent rains, mosquitos had completed a gestation cycle and were out for blood. The children left to take cover and only my hammock and its built in net stood any chance of providing relief. I found myself cowering away, my ears listening to the high pitched whine from their wings as they unsuccessfully tried to pierce the hammocks bottom.

Chapter 20

Malaysia

Although still plenty to do between Triang, Thailand, and Malaysia's border I was keen to move on. This agenda resulted in a relatively boring but straight ride to the lesser used crossing North of Kangar and Perlis. Dumber tourists took the more expensive option of a ferry crossing to the south, dumber still, cyclists like myself would forget to check the terrain and altitude. The border formalities were the quickest yet, in all about 45 seconds to exit Thailand and enter Malaysia, leaving me to climb a hilly area and to make my way south. A good amount of time later I'd climbed about half of the incline and had stopped outside a toilet attached to the entrance of a national park. Exasperated, I'd doused all my clothes in water to try and cool off and I was lounging around thinking how I didn't want to climb an intense incline to my left. It was then that I heard the rumble of a slow moving truck, and as it crawled by I launched out of the toilet, grabbed my bicycle and rode as quick as I could to grab the back of it. Five minutes later and half way up the incline I realised something was wrong. I'd left my sunglasses next to the toilet sink. Fuck. These were special sunglasses, a whole three dollars worth of fake Ray Bans, but they were strong and were holding up where others had broken. Besides, the sun being what it was, I was guaranteed to need new eyeballs without them. I let go of the truck and miserably returned back to the toilet.

Malaysia was strikingly different, a contrast to the organisation of Thailand. Here the grass wasn't cut to a legal minimum. Rusting signboards pointed the way and road verges decayed, many having been damaged by small landslides. The people here were still friendly and nodded and smiled as I rode by. Widely varying religious beliefs were visually evident with women wearing either no, partial or full burkas and men being dressing conservatively with trousers, despite the damning heat. Unexpectedly I found myself momentarily homesick. Malaysia had so much Britishness in it. Setting aside the difference in trees, here were British roads, lots of British style food (I even found a place selling quiche!), tile roofs, British electrical sockets, and unlike Thailand, most spoke some or a good level of English. As I had no Malaysian money I found an ATM and did a small withdraw. There were a lack of money changers around, but then I wasn't on the tourist route and expected it. Clueless about the currency, I bought a kilo of mangos for three times the going rate and further up the road read a sign displaying the real price. I berated myself all the way to the town of Kangar for having wasted a whole £3.

Kangar was to be another attempt to sort the bicycle hub but the only suitable shop in what was a surprisingly small town didn't stock the 36 hole hub I needed, and besides which they charged a small fortune to fit one. No camaraderie between cyclists here, I was left to decide whether move on or stop for the night. With no Buddhist temples I'd found a lack of places to wild camp and the heat would make the night uncomfortable. Across the road was a cheap hotel, run by a Chinese family and I dodged the traffic to take a look. The price I'd been told was 30RH, about $10 USD, but the check-in guy wanted 40RH and wouldn't budge. There was no price list on the wall and I didn't put up too much resistance, so having reluctantly agreed I carried the bicycle upstairs and to my room on the first floor. For the extra 10RH I paid I took my bicycle into the shared showers and give it a thorough clean. Walking around town I found a wifi connection and received an email confirming a two week placement in Cyberjaya near Kuala Lumpur. The head of the company also enquired if I was passing by Alor Star and if I'd like to stay with his family for a couple days. I couldn't decide if employment wise this was a good or bad idea but I was passing the town and said yes anyway. As it so happened, Alor Star was the next stop, just 50km away. I'd have two days to kill before heading to his family home, and thought I could surely have the hub fixed in that time. I rode the distance the following morning and arrived early afternoon.

Alor Star was even more spread out than Kangar, with no obvious centre of town. I didn't worry about where I would be staying that night so early on in the day and set about visiting bicycle shops I'd marked on a map. Each had about 15km of road between them which would make the process time consuming. The closest was a Specialized importer, the same manufacturer as my own bicycle. They were closed on a Tuesday, and being a Tuesday, I was out of luck. I rode towards another situated at the east of town. The vehicles here were old, most looking like they dated from the 1990's. The most popular brand was Proton while the gleaming new Toyota Hilux's I'd became so accustomed to seeing in Thailand were no where to be seen. The next cycle shop, like those before it proved inept at carrying a decent amount of parts, however good fortune struck, for inside were two parents browsing for a bicycle for their daughter. Conversing in English, they were unbelievably helpful and began phoning every shop in Alor Star for the part. Afterwards they offering to drive me to them to double check if it were the right one.

Three couch-surfing requests I'd put out had been rejected (they all wanted to meet up for a drink, typical couchsurfing lark, it's not warmshowers) and none of the shops visited stocked the part. Now later in the day, the family offered me to stay at their home for the night. Later I met their son Adam and his younger sister. At just 19yrs old Adam was running his own office supply business. His parents ran a construction business, but the M.D (the wife) was on long term sick leave, which you might imagine would upset the company's president, but in this case not, for it was the husband. I don't think either were too fussed about working much and had left the construction of part of a mosque to their other workers. They seemed more eager to help me with my little problem. Their friendship and generosity was overwhelming; I tried but couldn't pay for anything, and their efforts extended into the evening whereon I was given a guided tour around Alor Star's different areas and different types of beverage and delicacies on offer. One I will remember well was made from fresh milk and called Dadih. Dadih I was told was difficult to find, especially fresh, and by God it was delicious. Sort of like a thin dessert, like a drinkable blancmange, its simplicity and that it was served just above freezing made it a resounding treat. I had four in one go.

On the morning, after playing Cat Stevens *Father and Son* badly on the family piano, the family drove me 18km to the outskirts of town to a factory outlet, which some had told them was in fact a Shimano wholesaler. It was my best chance at having the hub fixed, else I'd be riding to Kuala Lumpur and probably breaking down along the way.

The owner of the factory was a bit of an eccentric, riding around the warehouse floor on a small white bicycle. The walls of the very large building flouted old British bicycles, most rusting, but probably still worth a few pennies to collectors. When the family told him about my touring efforts the price of anything I wanted dropped, however no matter how much I scoured the boxes and shelves I could not find a 36 hole hub that would accept a seven or eight speed cassette.

I'd had enough skimping, it was time to spend. I rated my chances at being kept on at the company in Cyberjaya highly, and even so I had enough to make Australia without it. If cycling was to be my thing, I needed to buy decent and modern equipment. The owner was offering parts below the price offered by any other shop in the world. It was time to upgrade. The family hung around while an employee swapped the front and rear dérailleurs, gear shifters, front crank, rear hub (a 36 hole 10 speed was in stock!), a 10 sprocket cassette and a new chain. I'd been told repeatedly Deore was the best balance of features, strength and minimum weight for long distance touring, and now I had it. Thirty gears, better efficiency and stronger hubs that could take the weight. I was now a professional touring cyclist.

Spending money on my bicycle made me happy, while spending money on myself did the opposite.

Saying goodbye to the Malaysian family that had been so utterly helpful over the past two days, I set off for the company bosses family retreat some 35km east. Would it be the start of a new long career in programming or would I balls it up before even getting to the office in Cyberjaya?, or would I find sitting in front of a screen programming unbearable? The challenge was afoot.

As I rode backroads that cut through paddy fields workers used petrol engined backpacks to throw rice seed, while my mind raced over how many things could go wrong over the next two days. I had an impression the owner wasn't overly wealthy, and that he was Thai, and probably in his 50's. Garmin took me most the way then I had a Google Satellite image with a paint style red ring around the pixels that represented the house. Turning onto the road I began counting the buildings and looking out for a rental car, for I knew he's flown into Alor Star airport. The houses along the road weren't at all flash, merely reasonable, but I knew when I'd arrived.

The house was impressive and suitably expensive with multiple brick facias, long windows, column supports for an overhanging outdoor reception and a marble foyer, the house belittled the new BMW sat on the driveway while down-lights lit the perimeter. The design was of a modern architecture, the sort found in fancy magazines, and several of those were in a rack to the left of the main entrance. Children that had been playing outside ran inside and a few moments later the boss walked out. Thin, definitely not Thai, definitely not in his 50's.

I spent two days at the house, time split between driving to places, playing with his fantastic children and demonstrating the programming I'd previously done. He wasn't the sort to give much away, but I think he liked what he saw, and I was glad I'd invested the three weeks back in Pushkar to make the demonstration go smoothly. Transitioning from a teaching to programming profession would be a steep learning curve to begin with and I was acutely aware of my skill deficiencies, but I appreciated the opportunity I was being given. For two weeks I'd just have to give it my best. I was sure I'd learn a lot either way.

All was not well back home. My tenant, who'd already racked up a £2,000 arrear, was receiving housing benefit of £300 a week, shy of the £440 required per the contract. When it was cut to £240 due to an overpayment I asked him to leave. We agreed a mutual date of October 18th, but I had reservations it would turn messy. That week my mother sold her house, however she hadn't a clue what she was doing after moving out. Once she'd paid of her ridiculous £20k credit card debt she wouldn't have enough for a decent house outright, which would mean another mortgage, but then she could have done that with her current house if she really wanted to. Instead she was toying over buying somewhere in Spain and using my house as a temporary base once my tenant had left. Presuming the tenant left as agreed, I could at least rest easy knowing the house would be occupied while I attempted to sell it. I stuck it on the market once again but this time at a firm £55k for a quick sale, and unbelievably, a week later I sold it. Undecided on whether I'd sold it too cheap. I backed out when I could see the stress it would put my mother. She'd already made up her mind on using it for a short period of time and if I sold it now she'd be forced to rent and that would mean throwing away good money and signing a contract for six months.

After leaving Alor Star I cycled up and over the Cameron Highlands. It was a fair ride to reach the top and the scenery along the way was both breathtaking and in many ways similar to that of Scotland. As the altitude rose the air cooled.

I refilled my water bottles at a pipe sticking out of a rock face which was labelled safe-to-drink. As my progress on the incline was so poor I'd do my old trick of grabbing the side or back of a truck at any given opportunity. Usually that meant waiting just after a sharp bend before the vehicle had a chance to accelerate. but I could rarely hang on for long as the road would occasionally narrow necessitating a release.

Cameron Highlands turned out to be so completely over-commercialised, and thus so ruined, that I took no pictures or notes. I'd expected peace and tranquility overlooking huge swathes of untouched green land, but instead all the land had been turned into strawberry farms, deforested, landscaped or had a hotel plonked on it. It might have looked like Scotland on the way up but it didn't look with the Scottish Highlands now.

At one of the two hostels there I met a really nice Canadian girl there called Danielle. Just a little younger than myself, we talked like we'd known each other for years. There were a few interesting tourists including one from Libya who couldn't fly back for fear of his safety and another who'd been in charge of building super yachts for wealthy princes in Dhabi. Danielle called him the BFG. He really was tall. Some were more annoying, like an elderly Australian man who'd always slot ' yeah, yeah, y..yy.. yeah' into every sentence.

Danielle and I had a couple cans on a hill overlooking the complex and then she left on a bus heading south. It was reassuring to know there were fellow minded travellers out there. This far into the trip I was resolute that I'd not end up with one, even if that was what I really desired. I'd always thought doing the trip I'd meet someone along the way and have to abort the idea in the name of love, yet if I managed to actually get talking to a possibility after a long days ride, it was assured they'd be leaving the day after and would be heading in the opposite direction. Two single individuals changing their plans to be together after a few hours to a few days of each others company? Highly unlikely.

I left, destination Cyberjaya, which initially began with a pleasant decent. The road was clear of traffic, quiet and twisty in nature. With no distractions I began trying to comprehend where my life was presently at and what lay ahead for the future. The fact was I believed I'd rather be working than travelling. It wasn't about the money, that merely caused a bit of worry and I knew it had no bearing on happiness. No, I'd actually be happy to be working again. The question I asked myself, as I applied weight left and right on the handlebars to steer around the declining bends, was why. I could only put it down to purpose, and feeling like I had one. If this were indeed the reason then I'd be unable to travel without one and to do so without for an undermined amount of time might lead to some sort of self-destruction. Some call this "drifting". Perfection then I could formulate as being to travel in order to change environment, working on the road to feel purpose, and doing it in the company of another or others. Had I then been travelling all this time without happiness? I couldn't say so. I'd had great times, times I wouldn't change for anything, but placing them side-by-side and looking for shared commonality drew one conclusion; the best experiences were in the company of others. Of all the fantastic places I'd visited or found myself in as an individual, none I could call highlights.

Chapter 21

Cyberjaya, Malaysia

Cyberjaya is a technology start-up town in Malaysia that attracts foreign companies through a ten year tax break and a simplified working visa process for foreign employees. Situated on the outskirts of Kuala Lumpur's fringe, it started from nothing and several years later still doesn't have amenities such as a supermarket or a cinema. For these one has to travel to nearby Putrajaya, which in terms of wealth (and since this is Malaysia, debt) outclasses Cyberjaya by a margin. Both towns are owned by wealthy benefactors, who as always in Malaysia have significant political connections, and both focus on securing high income by tightly controlling space. In other words, buying land in Cyberjaya is expensive, which in turn makes renting expensive. The usual franchises; Subway, Starbucks, Burger King had moved in, and tower blocks of flats called Condominiums had and were being built to allow a small amount of living space at a premium price. Students were coming from as far as Africa to study at Cyberjaya's private and prestige multimedia university.

My two week trial went as well as I'd hoped for and by the end of it I was offered a position as a Senior Perl Developer. I didn't consider myself experienced to behold the title. The other employees in the company had a significant experience advantage. That didn't mean I couldn't or wouldn't catch up. My wage was pretty basic, good by Malaysian standards but less than I'd have accepted under other circumstances, the main one being if I were in a country like England with a higher cost of living. Who was I to complain, I needed the experience and the money.

Living in Cyberjaya and Malaysia proved much cheaper than Europe. Much, much, cheaper. My rent for a very nice room supplied by the company was 1,000RH which worked out at about £200 a month. I later switched to a room in another condominium at just £100 a month.

To begin with I got on very well with a Scottish lad of similar age called Calum. He'd married and bought a house in Kuala Lumpur and was a professional to understood the issues. I was lucky he was around to begin with as he proved an excellent mentor, and I learned plenty from him. Having suffered several years Calum thoroughly detested the boss and left two month later. I essentially took over his role then began to understand his reasoning.

The technical team were from Iran, India, other parts of South Asia and occasionally America. They were very smart and able, but my bullish attitude to avoid poor decision undertaking began causing friction and some fallout. It wasn't in my nature to carry out a process without thinking it through first. Teaching with this sort of thinking in the U.K would have resulted in a reputation for incompetency. I'd expected so much more from a private company, but the approach here was to fix a problem without looking at the fallout and to 'firefight' issues that cropped up afterwards. Inevitably fixes were being made to fix the fixes and this resulted in several release cycles per day. Subsequently each day brought new problems as code was released without being fully tested. It didn't help that there was no team work and rarely did anyone know what the rest of the staff were doing. We'd hear about the problems from the users. It was quite unprofessional.

Since I wasn't prepared to push out crap code I suffered condescending undertones from some of the staff who wanted a quiet life on what was good pay compared to what they would have been paid back home, and yet everyone appreciated that it was not the way to work, so given that fact, the question was why it has happening. The reason was why Calum and so many had before him had left. The problem was with the boss.

The companies product was a betting platform for binary options (end in favour, not in favour) for forex, shares and other commodities. It was well established with a ten year history and no doubt the boss was around at the right time to begin such a venture, right around the 2000 dot com bubble. The codebase was developed by the boss and his brother and had had multiple revisions, with abortions and half-baked solutions along the way. It was antiquated and without structure, but the boss couldn't let his creation go to the more able and kept a tight lease around its development, as with all other aspects of the company. The CEO literally ran everything. The lease was so tight it acted like a noose. How many employees held a management role at the company? The answer was none.

Despite the companies problems users continued to enter their credit card details and deposit huge sums of money. Occasionally I'd see a single transaction that would have paid for me to travel for five years. I'd completely underestimated the amount of easy money to be made from offering betting services. No wonder banks were rich. For a friend at the company, a Bangladeshi Muslim of similar age called Rizwan, this created a problem. Like me, he'd not realised that it was a betting company he'd be working for which conflicted with his religious beliefs. We discussed this and agreed that everything is a bet one way or the other. Buying shares is a bet on whether they will go up or down and cashing out at the right time. What's an investment if not a bet?

To build on the career change I needed a job that proved opportunities for development and which centred on team work. I decided as soon as I stopped learning at the company I was out. I appreciated the opportunity and I didn't dislike the boss personally, I just couldn't work under his rein.

Three and a half months went by. Bicycle riding was down to a minimum, and that I'd sat on my backside drinking sugary drinks was becoming physically evident. I developed a complex to inspect my stomach in the morning, feeling both contempt and disgust at having lost my riding physic. The lifestyle was just too easy. Burger King became a top favourite, a burger/fries/coke meal costing the equivalent of just £1.50.

About four months into the job, I began a sort of mental upset that began with irregular sleeping and insomnia, but what was happening I couldn't work out. I still thought myself as unstressed with nothing of great importance to worry about..

A week later I could no longer stare at the computer screen - any computer screen. The words seemed to apply pressure to my eyes and if I kept at it my brain felt like it would explode. I had my eyes tested and came back with +0.25 long sighted (reading) glasses, but the strength was minimal and did nothing to alleviate the condition. I thought that was it, finally I was going nuts. Was this it, the burnout, the point where realisation of having hit none of your objectives coupled with a deep and hidden unhappiness came to bare, smacking me in the face like a high speed train?

I tried turning the artificial lights off in the office. I tried switching monitor. I tried taking fifteen minute breaks, sitting outside on a grassed area pressing my eyeballs into the back of my head.

I took medical leave and self prescribed a detox of sunlight (since there was none in the office) and lots of swimming. I contemplated resigning early as I considered the job a factor. To do so meant I'd loose 22% of my pay (which had gone into a pension system I could withdraw only if I'd worked six months). To make this point I'd another ten weeks to go, and two of those would be spent in England when I'd fly back to see family for the first time in fifteen months. I had to figure out how to last eight weeks in the office. But I also had to think long-term.

After the short break my condition had changed little and as I had continued to wear the glasses to no effect I booked an appointment at a private hospital to have my eyes thoroughly checked out. Perhaps my brain was not the issue. Half a day later and the results were in; a slight astigmatism but nothing to be worry about and everything else normal. So it was my brain? The doctor said she had seen this sort of thing before, the tail end effect of a virus, and asked if I'd suffered from anything recently. I told her I hadn't and left the hospital genuinely believing I was going bonkers.

A couple weeks later my surrogate Malaysian family from Alor Star invited me back up for the saturday after the Muslim new year. The entire population seemed to have the same idea and was heading for the island of Lankowi on the same route north. After a nightmarish nine hour bus ride I was thrilled to see the family again and to meet their neighbours and family all of whom were sharing food and warmth via an open door policy. Adam also gave me my first drum lesson. As I watched the video recording of it afterwards I noted how utterly weathered I looked. I left on the sunday bus and endured an even worse eleven hour return trip with all the Malaysians returning to Kuala Lumpur. But it was worth it.

A week later and the now frequent rain brought Mosquitos carrying dengue. Despite my paranoia and sleeping within the tent I'd erected on my bed, I caught it, and was ill for several days. It wasn't as bad as I'd read and on the positive I found by the time it was over my eyes were almost back to normal. Afterwards I flew back to England and spent almost two weeks catching up with friends and family. Being back was almost awkward, a feeling like I didn't belong there. I understood the causality of it all too well.

Attempting to tie loose ends, being back in England permitted me to sort out the house I still owned in Tantobie, Durham. The tenant had left and had wrecked it. My mother went around after he'd left and found the back window had been put through. His dog had been kept under the stairs and it's urine had soaked the floor boards underneath the kitchen tiling. Carpets and sofas had to be thrown. He'd installed a cannabis farm in the loft and had cut out a rafter to get it in. The reason he'd left without a fight was probably due to the amount of debt trailing behind him. Bailiffs turned up and repayment letters came through the letterbox daily. He took nicked my household appliances. I could no longer carry on with the house being a liability and dropped the price back to the amount I'd set when it had initially sold. I also asked the estate agent to try and make contact with the previous buyer to see if he'd still be interested. A week later I had my answer and the house was again sold only this time I'd not be pulling out.

Towards the end of my return home the family got together one evening for a pub meal. This was a first, my parents had never got on since their divorce some fifteen years prior, and my brothers and sister were all leading separate lives. My heading into the sunset had managed to bring everyone together, and I realised how infrequent contact had made the bond between my family stronger. How paradoxical compared to the many close knitted muslim families I'd met along the way.

Back in Cyberjaya, I made final preparations to end my job, collate all my funds and to make ready the bicycle and it's equipment for another trip. My boss offered remote working but the hourly rate on offer was a joke and I declined in belief that better prospects lay ahead. I had not an inkling if I even wanted to travel, but at least I now understood how to avoid the pitfalls.

Although my own interlude was coming to an end, others that I had met along the way were still ploughing through theirs, or had finished entirely. Kevin the Irish cyclist was already in South America, having carried out an insane amount of riding, far more than my own endeavours. I wondered how much he just wanted it to be over. The French couple I met at the Bander Abbas port riding two 125cc Yamaha's from London to Australia in hope of a better life had made it to Sydney, and found there was no work for them there. They returned to the same life they had hoped to escape. The Vespa riding Italian and Canadian couple I met in Pushkar actually turned up at Cyberjaya early on and stayed at my apartment for a couple days. Later they tackled Indonesia, which they loved, and Australia, which they greatly disliked. They shipped the scooter back to Canada, settled back into a daily slog and wondered once again how to break free.

On the 1st of January 2014, after a dismal New Year eve at Cyberjaya's only pub, rubber hit tarmac and I was back on the road; no further forward, no further behind. As Billy Joel's uplifting River of Dreams piped through my headphones and I powered up the hill away from my condominium I knew that the first part of my journey had offered no denouement, neither personal or on paper. It was neither a success or failure, and I considered myself none the happier, only wiser, more secure and further prepared for what lay ahead.

Or so I thought.

Printed in Great Britain
by Amazon.co.uk, Ltd.,
Marston Gate.